For Michael,
   in friendship and many shared
   memories in Oxford

Jens, 1 October 2022

Crisis, Reform and the Way Forward in Greece

This volume discusses different aspects of Greece's political economy during the past decade and reflects on the country's path ahead, examining the major question: did this challenging period succeed in providing a window of opportunity for deeper institutional and societal change? The authors seek to contribute to the discussion of the dynamics of stability and change, of the nexus between external pressure and domestic agency.

Greece offers a most interesting case study, as much in analytical as in empirical terms. Never before did a euro area member require three macro-economic adjustment programmes under stringent policy conditionality and external supervision. This experience shattered past certainties and reshaped the political landscape. A decade later Greece was starting to recover and received international recognition for its reform efforts. However, the COVID-19 pandemic provided an external shock that risks derailing such achievements.

The volume includes chapters by academics and researchers from different professional backgrounds: history, economics, public law, political science, public administration and political economy. Their diverse experience and viewpoints contribute to multidimensional analyses in subject areas such as Greece's constitutional structure, public sector reforms, labour market developments, China's expanding investment footprint and product market reforms.

Calliope Spanou is Professor of Administrative Science and Public Administration at the National and Kapodistrian University of Athens, Greece. From 2011–2015 she was the Greek Ombudsman and she served as Deputy Ombudsman from 2003–2011. She has extensive experience in administrative reform in Greece and in other countries. She holds a PhD (Doctorat d'Etat) in Political Science and Public Administration from the University of Picardie, France.

Europa Perspectives on the EU Single Market

The EU Single Market series, edited by Christian Schweiger, examines the key challenges for and the future perspectives of the European Union Single Market under the fundamentally altered parameters which have emerged in the aftermath of the global financial crisis, the eurozone sovereign debt crisis and the United Kingdom's decision to leave the EU (Brexit). Contributions to the series analyse changes in the Single Market and eurozone governance architecture, in the national varieties of capitalism, as well as the multiple levels of the deepening internal political and economic differentiation, especially potential alterations to the political and economic parameters of the Single Market. The series can comprise authored monographs and jointly edited collections which fall into these categories, but are not expected to be restricted to any of these issues, and volumes may encompass both regional and country-specific studies in the wider context of the subject area.

Christian Schweiger is Visiting Professor at the Chair for Comparative European Governance Systems in the Institute for Political Science at Chemnitz University of Technology in Germany. His research concentrates on the comparative study of political systems, economies and welfare states of the member states of the European Union (particularly the UK, Germany and transformation in the CEE countries), the political economy of the EU Single Market, economic globalisation and transatlantic relations. His most recent publications include the monograph *Exploring the EU's Legitimacy Crisis: The Dark Heart of Europe* (Edward Elgar, 2016) and the jointly edited collections *Core-periphery Relations in the European Union: Power and conflict in a dualist political economy* (Routledge, 2016, with José M. Magone and Brigid Laffan) and *Central and Eastern Europe in the EU: Challenges and Perspectives Under Crisis Conditions* (Routledge 2018, with Anna Visvizi).

Poland in the Single Market
Politics, economics, the euro
Edited by Anna Visvizi, Anna Matysek-Jędrych and Katarzyna Mroczek-Dąbrowska

The Political Economy of the Eurozone in East Central Europe
Why In, Why Out?
Edited by Krisztina Arató, Boglárka Koller and Anita Pelle

Crisis, Reform and the Way Forward in Greece
A Turbulent Decade
Edited by Calliope Spanou

Crisis, Reform and the Way Forward in Greece

A Turbulent Decade

Edited by
Calliope Spanou

Routledge
Taylor & Francis Group

LONDON AND NEW YORK

First published 2022
by Routledge
2 Park Square, Milton Park, Abingdon, Oxon OX14 4RN

and by Routledge
52 Vanderbilt Avenue, New York, NY 10017

Routledge is an imprint of the Taylor & Francis Group, an informa business

British Library Cataloguing in Publication Data
A catalogue record for this book is available from the British Library

Library of Congress Cataloging-in-Publication Data
A catalog record has been requested for this book

ISBN: 978-0-367-19396-6 (hbk)
ISBN: 978-1-032-06355-3 (pbk)
ISBN: 978-0-429-20224-7 (ebk)

DOI: 10.4324/9780429202247

Typeset in Times New Roman
by Taylor & Francis Books

Contents

PART II
Looking ahead: opportunities and challenges   117

Illustrations

Figures

Tables

Contributors

Calliope Spanou is Professor of Administrative Science and Public Administration at the National and Kapodistrian University of Athens, Greece. From 2011–2015 she was the Greek Ombudsman and she served as the Deputy Ombudsman from 2003–2011. She has extensive experience in administrative reform in Greece and in other countries. She holds a PhD (Doctorat d'Etat) in Political Science and Public Administration from the University of Picardie, France. She has been a guest researcher or professor at various academic institutions in Europe, including the Fondation de la Maison des Sciences de l'Homme, Paris, France, and the Robert Schuman Centre for Advanced Studies, European University Institute (EUI), Florence, Italy.

Jens Bastian, PhD (EUI, Florence), is an independent economic analyst. From September 2011 to September 2013 Bastian was appointed by the European Commission as a member of the Task Force for Greece in Athens, Greece. In January 2020 Bastian was appointed Senior Policy Advisor for the Hellenic Foundation for European and Foreign Policy (ELIAMEP) in Athens. His previous professional experience includes working as Lead Economist/Institution Building for the European Agency for Reconstruction, Thessaloniki, Greece, at the Alpha Bank in Athens, as well as holding various academic positions at St Antony's College, Oxford, UK, Nuffield College, Oxford, and the London School of Economics and Political Science (LSE), UK.

Christos A. Ioannou, is an economist (BA, Athens University of Economics and Business, MSc, PhD, LSE), and since 2017 he has been Director for Labour Market and Social Affairs at the Hellenic Federation of Enterprises (SEV). He served as Deputy Greek Ombudsman in charge of social protection, health and welfare from 2013–2017, and as Mediator and Arbitrator at the Organization for Mediation and Arbitration in Greece from 1991–2017. He has also acted as adviser, consultant and director for a variety of national and international private sector and government organizations.

Kostas Kostis studied economics in the Department of Economics at the University of Athens and then economic history in the Ecole des Hautes Etudes en Sciences Sociales in Paris, France. In 1990 he was awarded the Nicolas Svoronos Prize by the Institute of Technological Research. Since 2004 he has been Professor of Economic and Social History in the Department of Economics at the University of Athens, and since 1999 has worked as an adviser to the General Management of Alpha Bank in Athens. From 2006–2009 he was Chair of Modern and Contemporary Greek Studies at the Ecole des Hautes Etudes en Sciences Sociales in Paris.

Manto Lampropoulou, PhD, is an Assistant Professor in the Department of Political Science and Public Administration at the University of Athens and a Research Fellow at the Hellenic Foundation for European and Foreign Policy. She completed her doctoral dissertation and her post-graduate studies at the University of Athens. Her research interests include public administration, public policy and public sector reform.

Michael Mitsopoulos is Director of Business Environment and Regulatory Affairs at the Hellenic Federation of Enterprises (SEV). Previously he worked in the financial sector and as a ministerial adviser. He holds a PhD in Economics from Boston University, USA, has taught at the Athens University of Economics and Business and at the University of Piraeus, Greece, has written books in English and in Greek, and has published articles in the areas of law and economics, education, institutions and growth and taxation.

George Papaconstantinou is Professor of International Political Economy at the School of Transnational Governance of the European University Institute, Florence, Italy. He holds a PhD in Economics from the LSE and his career spans international organizations, politics and academia. He has served as a member of the Greek Parliament, the European Parliament and was Greece's Minister of Finance at the outset of the Greek and eurozone crisis.

Lamprini Rori is an Assistant Professor at the National and Kapodistrian University of Athens. She has previously been a lecturer in Politics at the University of Exeter, UK, a Jean Monnet Fellow at the EUI, a Leventis Fellow in Modern Greek Studies at St Antony's College, Oxford, and a Marie Curie Fellow at Bournemouth University, UK. She holds a PhD in Political Science from Université Paris I, Panthéon-Sorbonne. She was the PI of the Hellenic Observatory LSE grant 'Low-intensity violence in crisis-ridden Greece: Evidence from the radical right and the radical left', an Early Career Fellow at the British School in Athens, a Research Associate at the South East European Studies at Oxford (SEESOX) and Media Officer for the Greek Politics Specialist Group of the UK's Political Studies Association.

Ioannis A. Tassopoulos is Professor of Public Law at the National and Kapodistrian University of Athens (LLB 1986, Athens (Hons); LLM 1987, SJD 1989, Duke Law School). He is the author of five monographs and of many articles in Greek, English and French. His main fields of interest include constitutional law, comparative law and constitutional theory.

Abbreviations

AADE	Independent Authority for Public Revenue
ADMIE	Independent Power Transmission Operator
AIA	Eleftherios Venizelos (Athens International Airport)
AMEL	Attica Metro Operating Company
ANEL	Anexartitoi Ellines (Independent Greeks)
ASEP	Supreme Council for Civil Personnel Selection
CACs	Collective Action Clauses
CASS	Chinese Academy of Social Sciences
CEEG	China Energy Engineering Group
CEXIM	Export-Import Bank of China
COSCO	China Ocean Shipping Company
DEDDIE	Hellenic Electricity Distribution Network Operator
DEI/PPC	Dimosia Epicheirisi Ilektrismou/Public Power Corporation
DEPA	Public Gas Corporation
DESFA	Hellenic Gas Transmission System Operator
DIMAR	Dimokratiki Aristera (Democratic Left)
EAP	Single Payment Authority
EBA	European Banking Authority
EC	European Community
ECB	European Central Bank
ECOFIN	Economic and Financial Affairs Council
EDIS	Public Holdings Company
EDP	Excessive Deficit Procedure
EEC	European Economic Community
EESSTY/ROSCO	Hellenic Company for Rolling Stock Maintenance
EETT/HTPC	Hellenic Telecommunications and Post Commission
EEZ	Exclusive Economic Zone
EFSF	European Financial Support Framework
EGSSE	National General Collective Agreement
EIB	European Investment Bank
ELPE	Hellenic Petroleum
ELSTAT	Hellenic Statistical Authority

ELTA	Hellenic Post
EMU	Economic and Monetary Union
ERDF	European Regional Development Fund
ESAL	Port Planning and Development Commission
ESI	European Skills Index
ESM	European Stability Mechanism
ESF	European Social Fund
ETAD	Public Properties Company
ETHEL	Thermal Bus Company
EYATH	Thessaloniki Water Supply and Sewerage Company
EYDAP	Athens Water Supply and Sewerage Company
FDI	Foreign Direct Investment
GAO	General Accounting Office
GCEP	Government Council for Economic Policy
GDFS	General Directorate/Director of Financial Services
GDP	Gross Domestic Product
GGDE	General Secretariat of Public Revenue
GLF	Greek Loan Facility
HCA	Hellenic Court of Auditors
HCAP	Hellenic Corporation of Assets and Participations
HDB	Hellenic Development Bank
HFC	Hellenic Fiscal Council
HFSF	Hellenic Financial Stability Fund
HRADF/TAIPED	Hellenic Republic Asset Development Fund
HR/M	Human Resources/Management
ICBC	Industrial and Commercial Bank of China
ICRP	Interministerial Committee for Restructuring and Privatization
ILO	International Labour Office
ILPAP	Athens Electric Buses
IMF	International Monetary Fund
ISAP	Athens-Piraeus Electric Railways
MFF	Multiannual Financial Framework
MIP	Macroeconomic Imbalance Procedure
MOU	Memorandum of Understanding
MTFS	Medium-Term Fiscal Framework
NBG	National Bank of Greece
ND	Nea Demokratia (New Democracy)
NGEU	Next Generation EU
NPL	Non-Performing Loan
NPM	New Public Management
OASA	Athens Urban Transport Organization
OECD	Organization for Economic Cooperation and Development
OLP	Piraeus Port Authority

OLTH	Thessaloniki Port Authority
OSE	Hellenic Railways Organisation
OSY	Road Transport Company
OTE/COSMOTE	Hellenic Telecommunications Organization
PAL	Priorities of Adult Learning
PASOK	Panellinio Socialistiko Kinima (Panhellenic Socialist Movement)
PBO	Parliament's State Budget Office
PDMA	Public Debt Management Agency
PEPP	Pandemic Emergency Purchase Programme
PFM	Public Financial Management
PIAAC	Programme for the International Assessment of Adult Competencies
PISA	Programme for International Student Assessment
PPP	Purchasing Power Parity
PSI	Public Sector Involvement
QE	Quantitative Easing
RAE	Regulatory Authority for Energy
RAEM	Regulatory Authority for Passenger Transport
RAL	Regulatory Authority for Ports
RAS	Regulatory Authority for Railways
REER	Relative Effective Exchange Rate
RRF	Recovery and Resilience Fund
SA	Société Anonyme
SEV	Hellenic Federation of Enterprises
SGEI	Services of General Economic Interest
SGP	Stability and Growth Pact
SMP	Securities Market Programme
SOE	State-Owned Enterprise
SSM	Single Supervisory Mechanism
STASY	Urban Rail Transport
SYRIZA	Synaspismos Rizospastikis Aristeras (Coalition of the Radical Left)
TCM	Traditional Chinese Medicine
TIF	Thessaloniki International Fair
TRAM	Athens Tram
ULC	Unit Labour Cost

Introduction

Calliope Spanou

The framework of the volume

The idea for this book was conceived in mid-2018, at the end of the third economic adjustment programme. After eight long years of economic austerity, external surveillance and domestic political polarization, Greece was about to emerge from a protracted crisis as a delayed success story. The country had managed to avert the twin risks of default and 'Grexit' that lurked throughout this period. Parallel to a drastic fiscal consolidation that fuelled strong popular discontent, it had set in motion a series of reforms, most of which were required by the country's international lenders and which were undertaken more or less with domestic determination. Meanwhile, from 2014 onwards, the country was additionally confronted with a migration and refugee crisis that brought to its borders tens of thousands of people fleeing countries such as Syria, Afghanistan and Iraq, thereby deepening its domestic difficulties.

Exiting the adjustment programmes in August 2018 left Greece subject to the 'lighter' but still 'enhanced' surveillance requirements of the European Stability Mechanism (ESM). This meant that it remained under close scrutiny not only with regard to the state of its public finances, with requirements for high primary surpluses, but also the continuation of a prescribed reform agenda.

In 2018–2019 the Greek economy was slowly recovering after a long period of recession. However, many areas remained fragile, e.g. a substantial gap in labour productivity, a low employment rate, particularly among the young, and income inequality above the average for the Organisation for Economic Co-operation and Development (OECD). Despite significant progress in many reform areas, administrative inefficiencies and a heavy regulatory burden hindered domestic and foreign investment and encumbered the business environment, while the fairness of the tax system and the social protection mechanism still needed to be addressed (OECD, 2019: 149–152; OECD, 2020). However, the fragile recovery was confronted by a new external challenge in 2020: the coronavirus (COVID-19) pandemic that hit the Greek economy hard, reversed the recovery (ibid.: 14–19) and required an entirely new set of policy responses.

DOI: 10.4324/9780429202247-1

Why do we now need to discuss the experience of the economic crisis, when new and pressing issues are already knocking on the door? The purpose of this volume is to try and bring this episode to a conclusion, although the repercussions thereof are expected to resonate for a long time. The book starts from past experiences, then looks at the bigger picture during this turbulent decade and reflects on the Greece of tomorrow. To what extent did this challenging period reveal resilience or provide a window of opportunity for deeper change? This volume aspires to contribute to the discussion of the dynamics of stability and change, of external pressure and domestic agency. In this respect, Greece offers a most interesting case study, as much in analytical as in empirical terms.

Up until the sovereign debt crisis, Greece was characterized by high growth rates but remained a relatively closed economy, with low competitiveness and a heavy state presence. In institutional terms, a tendency towards political polarization and a weak and fragmented bureaucracy resulted in erratic and inefficient policies. Although 'stagnation' (Kalyvas et al., 2012) does not seem to be a fully accurate description of the pre-crisis period, the fact remains that the challenges of economic globalization were insufficiently addressed by policymakers in Athens. Despite its many achievements during the pre-crisis decades, the Greek state appeared to be slow and indeed reluctant to reform. Thus, liberalization reforms—mainly of European Union (EU) origin—were slow and met with political and social resistance (Christodoulakis, 2012). Important institutional reforms enacted during the 1990s and early 2000s did not manage to improve administrative performance (Spanou, 2012). The country's poor 'Europeanization' track record belied expectations of EU membership (Featherstone and Papadimitriou, 2012, 2008).

The sovereign debt crisis was linked to this twofold root problem: low economic competitiveness and an overgrown, inefficient state, the second interacting with the first (European Commission, 2010). Moreover, the credibility of the Greek state was badly damaged owing to data misreporting and the revelation of its structural weaknesses, and came close to being assessed—inappropriately—as a 'failing state'. The international media shed a negative light on the country that at times operated as a self-fulfilling prophecy. The situation triggered immediate attention and action, albeit not only domestically. The forced adjustment (Pagoulatos, 2012) that was initiated by the markets and relayed by the three consecutive macro-economic programmes relied on a new type of external constraint represented by the 'policy conditionality' they established. This limited domestic governments' margins for manoeuvre, frequently depriving them of sovereign decision-making in key policy domains (Spanou, 2016).

The Greek political system paid a high price for its past failings. The apparently stable quasi-bipartisan system touched a low point in the 2012 general elections amid vivid popular discontent. Governments that willingly or reluctantly embraced the need for reform quickly exhausted their political capital. New players emerged in the electoral competition, transforming the electoral map and political landscape. Nevertheless, institutions proved resilient to such tectonic changes.

The extent of the problems that came to light underscored the need to reconsider past practices and choices and to find new paths on many fronts. Revisiting one's own recent history under conditions of external surveillance is not an easy task. In this case it fuelled domestic controversies, shattered certainties and created new fault lines in politics, society and the economy.

In such a context, all sides, inside and outside the country, desperately needed a 'crisis-as-opportunity' narrative. This provided the 'positive' twist of a deep crisis, which extended from public finance to all spheres including politics, institutions, the economy and society. The inescapable awareness of past deficiencies could provide the impulse to confront the underlying causes of its failings. A positive narrative could inject some grain of hope: this episode would (or should) represent a critical juncture for a new start.

The consensus was that a new growth model was needed. Investments and exports should contribute a higher share to the gross domestic product (GDP) than the previous focus on domestic consumption fuelled by sovereign debt. To facilitate this transition and improve Greece's economic performance a series of institutional changes would be necessary (Meghir et al., 2017: ix; Bastian, 2015).[1]

Within a short period of time, Greece was required to achieve what had not been accomplished during the previous decades (Katsikas et al., 2018: 17). Deep reforms needed to confront policy legacies and entrenched patterns of interaction between the state, the economy and society. However, such issues cannot be reversed overnight. External pressure was an important factor, but it did not make things any easier. Reforms were seen by many as being imposed from the outside, something that did not help their implementation, let alone their legitimacy (Featherstone, 2015; Katsikas et al., 2018; Spanou, 2020). Greek governments were required to mobilize every bit of political energy to comply with and satisfy the requirements of policy conditionalities, in order not to endanger Greece's economic survival.

The volume of requirements and the immensity of the task have been acknowledged in recent years when Greece's predicament was portrayed with symbolic references to the 'labours of Hercules' or as an endless 'Sisyphean task'. 'Reform capacity' overshadowed other critical aspects, such as the rationale, the sequencing and the appropriateness of reforms as well as the intricacies of the reform environment. Insufficient 'reform ownership' became a standard explanation for the difficulties and limitations of reforms, the complexities of which were largely ignored (Spanou, 2020). The ownership narrative also redirected responsibilities to domestic factors and agency while dispensing international creditors from a critical review of their own reform agenda.

It goes without saying that the need for reform requirements and outcomes is a deeply political assessment. While reform complexities were underestimated or downplayed by the external (troika) actors, domestic governments were confronted with their technical and political implications. Political legitimation is acknowledged as being essential to governments' capacity for technical compliance and implementation (Hardiman et al., 2019). Substantial reforms need to confront policy legacies and require more than external pressure and 'prior action' timetables.

The lack of a critical approach within the pro-reform circles regarding the sequencing of reforms and the effects of their mutual interaction, the need to open at the same time all reform fronts under conditions of drastic fiscal consolidation, and more generally the appropriateness of the agenda in relation to problems and priorities is as striking as the rejection of any change from those who emphatically opposed them. For many decades the experiences of various countries that were forced to implement economic adjustment programmes (mostly under the auspices of the International Monetary Fund) has raised issues of reform appropriateness and strategy (see, for example, Stiglitz, 2000: 572–573; Rodrik, 1990: 943–944). To date, this question has received limited attention in the case of the Greek programmes.[2]

Hence, the most pertinent question is this: was the sovereign debt crisis a critical juncture for Greece? This prompts other questions: did it prove to be the catalyst for a delayed economic and institutional modernization of the country? Did external constraints manage to overcome domestic limitations?

The degree of change that can be observed since 2010 has belied over-pessimistic as well as over-optimistic predictions. A lot has changed, perhaps not always at the pace or the depth required or needed. But it cannot be denied that there was change and that at times this change was painfully real.

The new, restrictive political and economic environment increased the government's responsiveness. The quantity of legislation introduced during this period testifies to the volume of changes implemented, often in a piecemeal manner. In addition to impressive fiscal consolidation, difficult measures were taken in all policy sectors but even more so in those areas that de facto proved to be priorities (such as restructuring of the public sector, the labour market and social security). Despite the occasional setback, the accomplishments are noteworthy when compared with the pre-crisis period.

The image of Greece as slow and reluctant to reform was gradually overturned. The OECD in a series of reports from 2012 to 2015 noted a high degree of reform activity, while underscoring the short-term costs of the reforms and the weight of fiscal consolidation imperatives on structural reform and their distributional effects (OECD, 2015a: 19–20 and 109). For the first time Greece found a place among the 'highly responsive' group of euro area countries in terms of structural reforms (OECD, 2015b).

Closely related to change is the issue of agency. The past decade was typically characterized by the involvement of external actors (most prominently foreign creditors) in political and policy decisions. Many of the reforms were required as part of the policy conditionality of the economic adjustment programmes and were closely monitored by the 'troika' or, as they subsequently came to be labelled, 'the European institutions'. To some extent the latter continue to be present in the framework of the post-programme surveillance requirements and their role is now quasi-institutionalized in the context of Greece's European Semester obligations.

However, reform requirements and the involvement of external actors were not necessarily translated into policy priorities that were critical for the future of Greece. On the one hand, they focused on short-term fiscal results and a mechanistic 'box-ticking'. Indeed, there was no evaluation of the concrete policies implemented or the presentation of a list of goals achieved or that were considered to have been achieved. There are multiple examples. Administrative reforms, despite the extent and ambition thereof, did not always touch upon important underlying deficiencies. Public sector restructuring did not really focus on stimulating competition, while the shift towards an export-led economy was insufficiently reflected in policies to support the reallocation of resources from the non-tradable to the tradable sector (OECD, 2020: 4; Pelagidis and Mitsopoulos, 2016: 155–194).[3] In other words, despite appearances, they were not priorities for the economic adjustment programmes and the monitoring thereof. In many cases, short termism—usually associated with domestic policymaking—characterized the external actors' approach.

On the other hand, the role of domestic actors is often considered as one of permanent opposition to change. Cases of insufficient or superficial implementation are usually put forward in order to explain institutional resistance and policy failings. Thus, it seems that all achievements are attributed to the external actors who exerted pressure and all failings to the domestic actors who opposed them. Such a description of Greece during the past decade could hardly be further from reality.

When the argument of domestic resistance is turned on its head, it emerges that governments also had a critical role in *promoting* change. No doubt such a role has varied depending on the policy sector and the specific period of time. 'Reform fatigue' was acknowledged in 2014 (IMF, 2014: 4 and 23), while the difficulties of enacting drastic fiscal consolidation alongside successive waves of legislative change in a short amount of time constitute legitimate explanatory variables in the political economy of reform.[4]

In essence, what was at stake during this 10-year period, and remains important for the future, was the development of the *domestic capacity* to set goals and to design and implement corresponding policies. This was not the objective of the adjustment programmes and represents an important lesson learned from this experience. Not only does external pressure have limits, but it is hardly ever meant to develop internal capacity for endogenous reforms. This should be the major and overarching objective for the domestic political system. Despite the structural nature of reforms such deeper issues cannot be dealt with by external intervention. They need to be part of a domestic learning process which seems to have started, albeit unevenly, and is at times undermined by political polarization in Greece.

Chapters and authors

The volume provides fruitful insights into the developments leading up to and during the crisis, as well as their implications. With the benefit of the passage of time, it explores how much Greece has achieved in certain critical sectors over the past few years, assesses change with regard to intended outcomes and looks at what kind of prospects this creates for the future.

An overall assessment cannot be fully conclusive at this stage, and, more contributions will be needed before there is a definite answer (if there ever is one). Up until now, the picture seems to have been mixed, not least because of the differences among policy sectors but also the various perspectives taken by the book's authors. The glass may be seen as half full or half empty, something that is reflected in the contributions to this volume. That said, the book tries to draw a critical account of the experience of the crisis and the reform dynamics that were initiated. Furthermore, it draws attention to the challenges that Greece continues to face and address.

The authors represent a valuable mix of academics and researchers from different backgrounds: history, economics, public law, political science, public administration and political economy. Their diverse experience and viewpoints contribute to multidimensional analyses based on a deep understanding of the problems as well as an inner knowledge of the workings of structural reforms. They adopt a variety of standpoints, thus entering into a mutual dialogue and complementing each other in many respects. Some authors have hands-on experience, having been involved in the reform processes or closely monitoring them on the ground. Others use their academic perspective to highlight achievements, drawbacks or contradictions. It is therefore interesting to discover the potential convergence or divergence of their conclusions in terms of assessments, lessons learned and future outlook. It is impossible for such a volume to cover all aspects. The objective is to take stock of developments in selected, critical policy areas and to analyse the deeper issues raised by reforms and their implementation.

The volume is organized in two parts and includes 12 chapters. The first part (Chapters 1–6) looks at the developments leading up to the crisis and the test this represented for the political and institutional system in Greece. Starting from the wider perspective of the sovereign debt crisis, the chapters take the reader through a series of questions and themes. More specifically, the first three chapters set the background for the developments of the previous decade. In Chapter 1, Kostas Kostis provides an overview adopting a historical, cross-temporal approach which allows him to assess the weight of the past on contemporary realities. His starting point is the dramatic changes in the international environment that were wrought by the acceleration of economic globalization during the 1970s. New rules on national economies required deep adjustments in the way the political and economic system operates. He then highlights the Greek economy's inability to adapt to these new circumstances. Avoiding or delaying hard and unpopular decisions, it gradually reached a deadlock, and therefore became extremely vulnerable to external shocks provoked by the international, political and economic environment. Such a failing points to the absence of 'social elites' that, being aware of the challenges, could have taken the initiative and accepted the responsibility to deal with them effectively.

The next two chapters present the developments in Greece and in the EU as a result of the outbreak of the crisis. In Chapter 2, George Papaconstantinou focuses on the *anni horribili* when the consequences of the lack of adjustment became apparent. They were reflected in the triple deficit: a very large fiscal deficit; an equally large external account deficit; and a credibility deficit that was the result of the misreporting of fiscal statistics and the failure to deliver on promises made over the previous years. The three financial assistance packages (2010, 2012 and 2015) were conditional upon a drastic fiscal adjustment and the correction of the country's competitiveness deficit through 'internal devaluation' (domestic adjustments to wages and prices), as well as through a series of structural reforms. Papaconstantinou goes beyond the economic aspects of the adjustment programmes to address the political developments set in motion by the economic and social hardship of austerity, which contributed to the length and severity of the economic crisis in Greece. In comparison to other 'programme countries' (e.g. Cyprus, Ireland and Portugal), problems with implementation and a lack of political and social consensus undermined many of Greece's efforts. Despite such difficulties, the economy slowly started growing again in 2014. Greece did manage to eliminate its fiscal and competitiveness deficits, but at a huge cost to the economy, the labour market and civil society.

In Chapter 3, George Papaconstantinou looks at the action taken to correct the faulty architecture of the eurozone with regard to an asymmetric shock to the common currency. Although its construction faults were ignored for a long time, the Greek sovereign debt crisis contributed to setting in motion not only an emergency response but also broader reform efforts. Papaconstantinou emphasizes that the event that triggered this response left a mark on the fiscal focus of these reforms, while other aspects (such as demands for fiscal union or common Eurobonds) were politically sidelined in Berlin and Brussels. Changes introduced under the 'Six Pack', the 'Fiscal Compact' and the 'Two-Pack' were meant to ensure fiscal discipline, common budget rules and coordination, as well as mutual budgetary surveillance through the European Semester. The new European economic governance rules provided guidance and oversight on the budgeting process before the approval of national parliaments. However, these priorities did not pass the test of an asymmetric shock, which came in the form of the COVID-19 pandemic in 2020. The EU then had to accept further policy innovation in a direction no one could have imagined at the time of the Greek sovereign debt crisis. Once again, change came about as a result of crisis and triggered unprecedented policy responses across Europe.

The next three chapters look at the political and institutional repercussions of the crisis. Lamprini Rori in Chapter 4 considers the 2010s to have been the 'most turbulent decade' since Greece's transition to democracy in 1974. A series of crises have severely challenged its politics, society and the economy. Rori reviews and compares the major crises that beset Greece and still do: the financial crisis; the refugee crisis; the COVID-19 pandemic; and the Turkish hostilities in the Aegean. She then explores their impact on the dominant sociopolitical divisions, the changes in the party system and trends in public opinion regarding satisfaction with governments, social and political trust and expectations for the economy. By developing the argument that crisis management has become the new normality, Rori concludes with an assessment of the resilience of the state machinery and political institutions in Greece.

This argument is taken further in Chapter 5. Ioannis Tassopoulos highlights the considerable resilience of constitutional institutions during these challenging political times. He maintains that the Greek constitutional structure proved flexible enough to accommodate government instability, political polarization and brinkmanship due to its 'extreme simplicity' and what he calls the 'Jacobin element' of Greece's political and constitutional culture. Historical experience of endemic crises and 'national interest' emergencies established the centrality of the prime minister as a result of the need for a clear political responsibility in protecting the strategic and geopolitical interests of the state. The 'geopolitical hard core of the prime minister's powers' entailed wide executive authority and scope for manoeuvre while minimizing the 'checks and balances' (e.g. the absence of a Constitutional Court). Tassopoulos discusses this argument in the context of three problems exacerbated by the Greek crisis: economic decision-making, the challenges presented by the extremist neo-Nazi party Chrysi Avgi (Golden Dawn), and the July 2015 referendum. All three cases were successfully dealt with within the existing arrangements, despite the absence of checks and balances. However, this does not preclude the need for legislative reform to provide certain safeguards. Central among them is elucidating that a referendum on national questions is *advisory* and not obligatory, and hence that it does not dilute the full and integral responsibility of the prime minister and his government for the geopolitical consequences of their eventual decision.

The first part of the volume is concluded with an examination of the effects of the crisis on the image of the EU in Greece. Calliope Spanou in Chapter 6 examines the way the EU is portrayed in the rhetoric of the Greek prime ministers and in the corresponding trends in public opinion during the past decade. Two types of rhetoric are distinguished: one that defended the EU, which was expressed with different emphasis by Prime Ministers George Papandreou and Antonis Samaras; and another developed by Prime Minister Alexis Tsipras, which at times took on strongly anti-EU tonality. However, she emphasizes that even then, some idea of a 'good EU' worth returning to survived and was essentially linked to humanitarian and social values. Parallel developments in public opinion show that the resulting 'soft Euroscepticism' (Verney, 2015) proved difficult to reverse, despite significant improvements in the official discourse on Europe. The slow recovery of the image of the EU in public opinion may be influenced by the new challenges, i.e. combating the COVID-19 pandemic and dealing with security issues in the Eastern Mediterranean.

The second part of the volume (Chapters 7–12) analyses and assesses developments that occurred in certain key areas directly linked to the diagnostics of the sovereign debt crisis, i.e. high debt and deficits as well as low competitiveness. Both were immediately related to the deficiencies of the public sector, which proved inefficient while absorbing a large share of GDP (European Commission, 2010).[5] A series of structural reforms were devised to this effect and were subject to the conditionality of financial assistance. A prominent place among them was occupied by the redefinition of the boundaries between the public and private sectors, administrative reform and the reduction of the administrative burden to improve competitiveness.

The redefinition of boundaries between the public and the private sectors had a clear objective of rolling back the state. Reforms aimed at reducing government intervention in the economy and increasing private sector involvement were accelerated through restructuring and marketization policies (e.g. downsizing, divestment, corporatization, privatization, liberalization). These developments are discussed by Manto Lampropoulou in Chapter 7 with a focus on 'network industries'. Her findings suggest that public sector restructuring has brought about some positive changes in organizational terms; however, the reform design was too heavy and ambitious and aggravated existing problems of fragmentation and co-ordination. Market-oriented reforms were mostly aimed at restructuring for the purposes of privatization rather than for stimulating competition, thus indicating a prioritization of the short-term fiscal impact (privatization proceeds) over long-term goals. Finally, private sector techniques were promoted in the management and governance of state-owned enterprises (SOEs). However, the attempted managerialization did not succeed in completely offsetting government interventions in SOEs, while public service values and the objective of citizen-consumer empowerment constantly remained at the margins of public sector reforms.

Improving administrative capacity would serve all policy fields and related reforms. As such it was placed at the heart of all three adjustment programmes. The administrative reform agenda was extensive but essentially fiscally driven. In Chapter 8, Calliope Spanou explores the question whether underlying causes of administrative deficiencies were effectively addressed. To do so, she compares the significance of reforms undertaken in two core administrative domains: (i) budgeting and fiscal management and (ii) human resources management (HRM). As part of a 'big bang' reform agenda, these were meant to change the structural features of the administrative system regarding the management of economic and human resources. The crisis effectively provided an opportunity to make substantial changes in fiscal management. It proved incapable of bringing about significant results in HRM since it did not challenge the core of pre-existing policy arrangements. Among the factors explaining this inconsistent change, the author highlights the role of domestic actors and the wide margin of discretion they exercised in the area of HRM reforms. By contrast, a learning process took place among actors involved in fiscal management reforms, resulting from past domestic failings, the external surveillance and the new European rules regarding economic governance. She nevertheless observes a slow post-programme learning process in HRM, despite apparent reform reversal by the Nea Demokratia (New Democracy) government after the 2019 elections. Such a learning process is essential for sustainable reform dynamics.

A major challenge highlighted by the adjustment programmes was the shift to an export-led economy. The short-term objective was to deal with the current account deficit. In the medium term this essentially meant to encourage domestic and foreign direct investment, *inter alia*, by reducing state influence on the economy. Both objectives appeared at least as important as the fiscal adjustment. Chapters 9, 10 and 11 analyse developments in these areas from different but complementary perspectives.

Foreign direct investment (FDI) has been a critical component of Greece's economic recovery. Jens Bastian shows in Chapter 9 how FDI in Greece declined in volume and changed in terms of country of origin during most years of the past decade. The crisis years, the imminent risk of euro area exit in 2015 and the contentious politics of debt restructuring have all tended to hinder the process of attracting higher levels of international capital to Greece. Bastian highlights the one notable exception, namely the willingness of China to invest in Greece at a time when other European and/or US companies were treating the country as a toxic investment case. He provides an overview and analysis of the implications of the increasing share and diversity of Chinese investments during the past decade, highlighting the significant growth of China's footprint in Greece since 2009. From its initial investment in the Port of Piraeus Chinese investment has expanded into sectors such as energy, tourism, retail, agriculture and logistics infrastructure. The rising presence of China in Greece may be seen as one of the lasting legacies of the crisis in the years to come. Only belatedly has this expanding Sino-Greek engagement attracted the attention of the EU and the USA.

In Chapter 10, Michael Mitsopoulos focuses on product market reforms which were meant to unleash the growth potential of domestic businesses, improve their international competitiveness and allow them to reap the advantages of participation in the EU Single Market. Greece has clearly lagged behind its European peers in product market regulation reforms. Mitsopoulos critically examines the state of play and the legacy of these reforms and identifies the areas for pressing further action. He concludes that while progress in the area of so-called product market structural reforms has been uneven and slow, a critical body of reforms has been amassed. When compared with reforms documented during other reform episodes, Greece has certainly performed impressively. But given the low starting point, the uncertainty related with the threat of Grexit in 2015 and the recent impact of the COVID-19 pandemic, the market has not yet been able to harvest its full benefits. A final push to complete key reforms may unleash the growth potential of the reform efforts of the past decade, especially if assisted by a retrenchment of the economic impact of the COVID-19 pandemic.

In Chapter 11, Christos Ioannou deals with labour market developments and corresponding reforms and discusses their limitations. He notes that despite three adjustment programmes, Greece is lagging behind EU and euro area averages in term of GDP growth and exhibits persistently higher unemployment rates, both of which are being further adversely impacted by the consequences of the COVID-19 pandemic. For Ioannou, not merely a laggard, Greece is primarily a *diverging* outlier. Structural sources of this divergence are linked to the lack of effective and lasting labour market reforms. While the asymmetrical growth between the non-tradable and tradable sector is at the heart of the crisis of the Greek economy, reallocation of resources from the first to the second sector is slow and insufficient. This is reflected in the divergence in GDP and in the employment rate compared to other euro area countries. Anachronistic labour market regulation and institutions, as well as the lack of a systematic skills formation policy account in large part for the deficits in the Greek labour market.

The last chapter of the volume offers a reflection on future developments in Greece. In Chapter 12, Jens Bastian discusses opportunities and challenges in a post-pandemic Greece. Undoubtedly, the COVID-19 crisis will continue to affect the lives of citizens in years to come. It remains challenging to identify the underlying signs of economic momentum in the country. To what degree things will hold together in 2021 and beyond is anybody's guess. Until a sustainable reopening of economic activity and social life arrives, the resilience of businesses and the patience of private households will be severely tested. Reaching the other side of the bridge will critically depend on a variety of continuous domestic support measures and from different European institutions. Chiefly among the latter are the EU and the European Central Bank. The crisis experience of Greek society during the period 2010–2018 can be an enabling factor in addressing the challenges and opportunities that lie ahead.

A general concluding remark imposes itself. In the contemporary world, challenges are constant and it is important to prepare for the 'black swan' scenario. The most striking feature of the past decade has been the multiplicity of challenges: economic, political, security and now public health. Developments have accelerated to the point that there has barely been time for states and societies to digest current changes and prepare for new challenges. The 'new normal' is the increased volatility of the environment. Within this context Greece is emerging from a decade-long economic crisis during which it was obliged to look into the mirror and assess its performance, mistakes and opportunities. The lessons learned and applied may guide the policy responses during the challenges of the new decade.

Acknowledgements

The writing of this book has greatly benefited from the excellent collaboration with Cathy Hartley, Regional Editor of Routledge, and from the experienced hands of Alison Phillips. Their timely and engaging assistance have made this publication see the light of day.

Notes

1 With notable exceptions regarding the expansion of large corporate and financial institutions into neighbouring countries of south-east Europe, the economy remained consumption- and import-driven. Consumer spending was the biggest contributor to the real economy, reaching up to 70% of the country's GDP before the sovereign debt crisis. However, local businesses needed to import 80% of raw materials and finished products, a level of import dependency which was among the highest within the euro area. See Bastian (2015). The 'government-led growth model' was then put into question by the international markets. Similar problems, albeit not as acute, were faced by other eurozone countries. 'With the inflow of capital into peripheral countries because of EMU, the three future programme countries witnessed significant booms, low unemployment rates and wage increases significantly exceeding productivity developments, especially in the non-traded sector' (Pisani-Ferry et al., 2013: 45). For a wider theoretical interpretation of these developments see the analysis by Streeck (2014).
2 The study by Katsikas et al. (2018) addresses this issue.
3 Economic activity, though shifting gradually to tradable sectors, is still concentrated in traditional and low innovation sectors, thereby contributing to low productivity growth (OECD, 2020: 4).
4 See IMF (2015: 4). The IMF (2014: 23) referred to 'adjustment fatigue' (IMF, 2017; OECD, 2015: 109; ESM, 2017: 60, 72).
5 The size of the government sector grew from 44% of GDP in 2000 to over 50% in 2009.

References

Bastian, J. (2015). Defining a growth strategy for Greece: Wishful thinking or a realistic perspective?, *FES Paper*. October. http://library.fes.de/pdf-files/bueros/athen/11650.pdf.
Christodoulakis, N. (2012). Market reforms in Greece, 1990–2008: External constraints and domestic limitations. In S. Kalyvas, G. Pagoulatos, and H. Tsoukas (Eds.) *From Stagnation to Forced Adjustment: Reforms in Greece 1974–2010* (pp. 91–116). London: Hurst & Co. doi:10.1093/acprof:oso/9780199327829.003.0006.
European Commission (2010). The economic adjustment programme of Greece. *European Economy Occasional Papers*, 61.
European Stability Mechanism (2017). *EFSF/ESM Financial Assistance Evaluation Report*. Brussels: ESM. www.esm.europa.eu/sites/default/files/ti_pubpdf_dw061605 5enn_pdfweb_20170607111409.pdf.

Featherstone, K. (Ed.) (2006). *Politics and Policy in Greece: The Challenge of 'Modernisation'*. London: Routledge.

Featherstone, K. (2015). External conditionality and the debt crisis: The 'Troika' and public administration reform in Greece. *Journal of European Public Policy* 22(3), 295–314. doi:10.1080/13501763.2014.955123.

Featherstone, K., and Papadimitriou, D. (2008). *The Limits of Europeanization: Reform Capacity and Policy Conflict in Greece*. London: Palgrave Macmillan.

Featherstone, K., and Papadimitriou, D. (2012). Assessing reform capacity in Greece: Applying political economy perspectives. In S. Kalyvas, G. Pagoulatos, and H. Tsoukas (Eds.), *From Stagnation to Forced Adjustment: Reforms in Greece 1974–2010* (pp. 31–46). London: Hurst & Co. doi:10.1093/acprof:oso/9780199327829.003.0003.

Hardiman, N., Spanou, C., Araújo, J.F., MacCarthaigh, M. (2019). Tangling with the Troika: 'domestic ownership' as political and administrative engagement in Greece, Ireland, and Portugal, *Public Management Review*, 21(9), 1265–1286. https://doi.org/10.1080/14719037.2019.1618385.

International Monetary Fund (IMF) (2014). *Greece. Fifth review under the extended arrangement under the extended fund facility, and request for waiver of non-observance of performance criterion and rephasing of access*, May 16. IMF Country Report no 14/151. Washington, DC: IMF.

International Monetary Fund (IMF) (2015). *Crisis Program Review*, Policy Papers, November 9. Washington, DC: IMF. www.imf.org/en/Publications/Policy-Papers/Issues/2016/12/31/Crisis-Program-Review-PP5010.

International Monetary Fund (IMF) (2017). *Greece. 2016 Article IV consultation: Press release; Staff report; and Statement by the executive director for Greece*, February. IMF Country Report no 17/40. Washington, DC: IMF. www.imf.org/~/media/Files/Publications/CR/2017/cr1740.ashx.

Kalyvas, S., Pagoulatos, G., and Tsoukas, H. (Eds.) (2012). *From Stagnation to Forced Adjustment: Reforms in Greece 1974–2010*. London: Hurst & Co. doi:10.1093/acprof:oso/9780199327829.001.0001.

Katsikas, D. (Ed.) (2018). *Structural Reforms in Greece during the Crisis*. Athens: ELIAMEP: Crisis Observatory and Bank of Greece (in Greek).

Meghir, C., Pissarides, C.A.Vayanos, D., Vettas, N. (Eds.) (2017). *Beyond Austerity: Reforming the Greek Economy*. Cambridge, MA: The MIT Press.

Organisation for Economic Co-operation and Development (OECD) (2015a). *Economic Policy Reforms 2015: Going for Growth*. Paris: OECD Publishing. http://dx.doi.org/10.1787/growth-2015-en.

Organisation for Economic Co-operation and Development (OECD) (2015b). *Structural Reforms in Europe: Achievements and Homework*. Better Policies Series. Paris: OECD Publishing.

Organisation for Economic Co-operation and Development (OECD) (2019). *Economic Policy Reforms. Going for Growth*. Paris: OECD Publishing. https://doi.org/10.1787/aec5b059-en.

Organisation for Economic Co-operation and Development (OECD) (2020). *Economic Survey of Greece 2020*. Paris: OECD Publishing.

Pagoulatos, G. (2012). The political economy of forced reforms and the 2010 Greek economic adjustment programme. In S. Kalyvas, G. Pagoulatos, and H. Tsoukas (Eds.), *From Stagnation to Forced Adjustment: Reforms in Greece 1974–2010* (pp. 247–274). London: Hurst & Co. doi:10.1093/acprof:oso/9780199327829.003.0013.

Pelagidis, T., and Mitsopoulos, M. (2016). *Who's to Blame for Greece? Austerity in Charge of Saving a Broken Economy.* Basingstoke: Palgrave Macmillan.

Pisani-Ferry, J., Sapir, A., and Wolff, G.B. (2013). *EU-IMF Assistance to Euro-Area Countries: An Early Assessment.* Blueprint Series. Brussels: Bruegel. http://bruegel. org/wp-content/uploads/imported/publications/1869_Blueprint_XIX_-_web__.pdf.

Rodrik, D. (1990). How should structural adjustment programs de designed? *World Development* 18(7), 933–947.

Spanou, C. (2012). The quandary of administrative reform: Institutional and performance modernization. In S. Kalyvas, G. Pagoulatos,, and H. Tsoukas (Eds.), *From Stagnation to Forced Adjustment: Reforms in Greece 1974–2010* (pp. 171–194). London: Hurst & Co. doi:10.1093/acprof:oso/9780199327829.003.0010.

Spanou, C. (2016). Policy conditionality, structural adjustment and the domestic policy system: Conceptual framework and research agenda. Working Paper RSCAS 2016/60. Florence: European University Institute, Robert Schuman Centre for Advanced Studies.

Spanou, C. (2020). External influence on structural reform: Did policy conditionality strengthen reform capacity in Greece? *Public Policy and Administration*, 35(2), 135–157. https://doi.org/10.1177%2F0952076718772008.

Stiglitz, J. (2000). Reflections on the theory and practice of reform. In A. Krueger (Ed.), *Economic Policy Reform* (pp. 453–584). Chicago and London: University of Chicago Press,.

Streeck, W. (2014). *Buying Time: The Delayed Crisis of Democratic Capitalism.* London: Verso.

Verney, S. (2015). Waking the 'sleeping giant' or expressing domestic dissent? Mainstreaming Euroscepticism in crisis-stricken Greece. *International Political Science Review*, 36(3), 279–295. https://doi.org/10.1177%2F0192512115577146.

Part I

Looking back: shattered certainties and resilience

1 The adventure of globalization and the Greek state in the late 20th and early 21st centuries

Kostas Kostis

Introduction

The primary objective of this chapter is to examine contemporary Greek reality from a historical perspective; in other words, to give it a certain temporal depth, something that cross-sectional disciplines, such as economics, sociology or political science, may be unable to do. The main motive behind such an endeavour is none other than the inadequacy of the interpretative approaches regarding the negative developments in Greece during the recent past to get beyond utterly simplistic aphorisms, such as putting the blame exclusively on the development of clientele-like relationships or limiting the scope of inquiry to the shortcomings of the Greek political system or the Greek economy in recent years. In contrast, this contribution offers interpretative angles that do not neglect fundamental aspects of social reality and do not focus solely on fragmented views of society to support political opinions or economic models. This can only be achieved by means of a historical, cross-temporal approach that will assess the weight of the past on contemporary realities.

The deepening of the globalization process

In order to get a good grasp of how Greece arrived at the current situation it is important to go back to the 1970s, when 'everything' changed (Ferguson et al., 2010). The first step in the process of massive change that occurred in that decade was none other than the collapse of the Bretton Woods system, which had ensured the smooth flow of international transactions during a period of rapid global growth in the post-war years. Following this collapse, the world economy turned towards a system of fluctuating exchange rates and, at the same time, increasing and accelerating capital movements.

The second step was taken in 1973 and then again in 1979, when the two major oil crises changed the world economy game: Western countries would no longer have easy access to cheap and unrestricted oil supplies, while deindustrialization would become a key component of their economies. In the meantime, a democratization process, in which Greece, Spain and

DOI: 10.4324/9780429202247-3

Portugal participated, was well under way. This nascent process of democratic globalization accelerated in the coming decades. In 1979, the election of Margaret Thatcher as Britain's Prime Minister formally launched a new regime of capital accumulation known as neoliberalism, which is probably now in its final phase (Kotz, 2015).

Moreover, during the 1970s, there seem to have been many changes in attitudes towards illness and the environment. In 1968, the US Secretary of Health declared that the war on infectious diseases had been won, while a few years later, in 1975, the Dean of the renowned Yale School of Medicine declared that no new communicable diseases were likely to emerge. As it turned out, this prediction reflected nothing more or less than the arrogance with which science and humankind treat nature. Contrary to all predictions up until then, since the 1970s the world has been suffering from a resurgence of infectious diseases and new epidemics and pandemics mainly of viral origin. We have entered the age of emerging epidemics.[1]

Around the same time—and, in fact, partly through—this changing relationship between man and ill health, the impact of human activity on the environment started to become apparent. Ever since, growing environmental sensitivity has coincided with the accelerating degradation of nature.

In other words, while up until the 1970s the world economy was growing in terms of a shallow globalization process that facilitated the rapid development of economies through the adoption of national policies, what followed next was a completely different story. From that decade onwards, the world economy has been based on deep globalization, a development that has been gathering steam at least until 2008. Under these conditions, the room for implementing national policies is rather limited, something that Greece was late to recognize—if it ever did, that is (Kostis, 2019: 431–433).

… And the trajectory of Greece

Politics vs economics

Greece strode into the new era as an undisputed pioneer of what is often referred to as democratic globalization (on democratization waves see Stasavage, 2020: 256–257). One could hardly question the country's achievement on that front, namely the rather smooth transition to democracy and its further strengthening, despite any shortcomings that could be pointed out.[2] The first step in this process was the fall of the dictatorship, followed by the abolition of monarchy by way of the 1974 referendum, and then the legalization of the Communist Party, a third step of highly symbolic significance by Greek standards.

However, regarding the second part of the globalization process, the economic one, Greece did everything possible to avoid the cost of adapting to the new reality. Burying its head in the sand like an ostrich is perhaps the most apt metaphor to illustrate this situation (Kostis, 2019: 431–433).

Whether the actions of those who made these political choices were deliberate or not is a matter of discussion. In the field of economics, it is clear that the initial choices did not consider the facts of a changing world economy. The group of politicians around Prime Minister Constantinos Karamanlis were completely outdated in their economic policy choices or, to put it differently, they were unable to think beyond the economic model they had in mind, which was identical to the one they had adopted during the post-war period and which had completely restructured the Greek economy. Economic choices were also determined by political priorities.

This is also reflected in Karamanlis's decision to get Greece to join the European Economic Community (EEC). In economic terms, this choice may seem fully justified, albeit hasty, given that a country like Greece could not have been left out of a major economic union. However, Karamanlis never raised economic factors to accelerate Greece's accession to the EEC. It is clear from his accession speeches that his main concern was the stabilization of democracy.[3] Sensible as this priority was, it should be recognized as a typical contradiction of Greek politics: an institution of economic integration used for political ends.

Drawing on dependency and centre-periphery theories, Karamanlis's successors, particularly Andreas Papandreou, also perceived that the problems haunting the Greek economy, and Greece in general, were being caused by 'evil foreigners' rather than by the social attitudes that were gradually being established in the country (Kostis, 2013: 302–306 and 435–438).

To Karamanlis, Greece's participation in the EEC also meant a fundamental change of course in the country's foreign policy. The Turkish invasion of Cyprus and the occupation of a large part of its territory by an allied country and member state of the North Atlantic Treaty Organization (NATO) showed that foreign policy orientations needed to be revised. The country's withdrawal, even temporarily, from NATO's military wing—which in retrospect proved to be a false move—called for a counterbalance that only participating in the European integration process could offer. As a result, Greece would cease to consider the threat from the North, i.e. the communist threat, a keystone of its foreign and defence policy, focusing instead on the 'Eastern threat', which would only grow in importance in the coming decades.

Overall, the outcome was rather disappointing. The nation's economic performance steadily deteriorated, business profits shrank (Iordanoglou and Bellas, 2003) and foreign investors saw Greece as an unfit place in which to invest. In different terms, during this period, Greece faced the so-called middle income paradox, a phenomenon that would become fully evident in the 1980s. While the country managed to reach a middle-income level, it was unable to find a way to remain on an upward trend. Although the exhaustion of growth opportunities offered by the relocation of labour from a low-productivity agricultural sector to an urban one—whether related to industrial production, services or even foreign emigration—was not an exclusively

Greek phenomenon, Greece could not find a way to steer the national economy away from its declining course.[4]

At the same time, other countries that up until the early 1970s were in step with Greece, in economic terms at least, managed to break away from outdated models and to adopt advanced technology and high value-added strategies.

Perhaps the most notable example in this category of economies is the Republic of Korea, a country that up until then had followed in the footsteps of Greece in terms of economic development. Likewise, François Mitterrand's socialist France initially experimented with obsolete models, just like Greek socialism, only to soon realize it was leading to a deadlock and rollback. In today's 'new globalization', a preoccupation with strictly introverted policies could not but lead to a deadlock, something that the French socialists, unlike their kindred spirits in Greece, quickly realized.

Greece, therefore, chose to follow a course that, as it turned out, cost it dearly in the long term and was not likely to remain viable over time, unless at great financial cost. These consequences became evident in some extremely critical areas for the functioning of the state and social prosperity.

As a result, in 1974, Greece was still a country with a strong agricultural sector (around 15% of gross domestic product early in the decade), even though after World War II it had undergone a radical transformation towards urbanization based on services and industrial production. Undoubtedly, middle-class groupings had begun to form in the post-war period following the rapid economic growth that inevitably led to the development of the middle class. However, the collapse of the anti-communist state gave those who suffered exclusion and discrimination an opportunity not only to gradually find political and social leverage to ensure social and political integration, but to do so on preferential terms.

In this context, the middle-income classes reached their heyday, which was actually based on three key factors: first, an education system that served as a fundamental mechanism of social advancement; second, a state organization that in various ways (through public deficits in fact) generated income for these groups; and, third, an economy and society that had turned increasingly inwards, hoping in this way to tackle the challenges of the international environment (Doxiadis, 2014). It should also be kept in mind that this period was also marked by the predominance of consumer patterns and lifestyles that challenged the traditional money-saving habits of the Greeks and were further strengthened by the liberalization of the Greek banking system in the late 1980s.[5]

The rise of these middle-class groups was also related to the so-called age of great expectations. Since the restoration of democracy in 1974, pressure for income growth and wealth redistribution became so intense that it was impossible to handle—something that both Karamanlis and Giorgios Rallis were quick to realize. In fact, during the Nea Demokratia (New Democracy; the party founded by Karamanlis) administrations, Greece saw the most significant income redistribution in its history, with absolute poverty falling from 23.5% in 1974 to 8.8% in 1981–82.

However, it was the Panellinio Socialistiko Kinima (PASOK—Panhellenic Socialist Movement) that, in order to strengthen its position and expand its electoral base, took advantage of the low public debt of the early 1980s to boost public sector employment by hiring from the pool of the hitherto marginalized social groups. In defiance of all reason, it used the social security system as a social policy tool. Moreover, transforming the state's interests in favour of the party's interests was taken to the extreme.

The takeover of politics by the state was therefore a fundamental transformation in post-junta Greece, prompted largely by the establishment of constitutional recognition as a necessary prerequisite for political activity. The prominence of political parties soared to great heights especially in the public sector. The rise of PASOK to power led to the assertion of total control over the public sector through the abolition of the position of Ministry General Director, which up until then had been filled by permanent state officials. They were replaced by Special Secretaries, who were non-permanent public servants appointed by the ministers. Incentives were also eliminated to relieve hierarchy congestion and defuse discontent, as more employees could now serve in managerial positions. On the other hand, however, promotions were based on length of time in service and were decided by the civil service council, meaning that, ultimately, they were politically controlled (Sotiropoulos, 2001).

Turning public administration into a political trophy was only one side of the problem. With the ascendancy of PASOK to power, the impressive mobilization that Greece experienced following the collapse of the military regime was channelled not only into an unprecedented mass participation in social organizations but also into the party's efforts to patronize them. A typical example is the trade union movement. Ensuring control over mass mobilizations, exerted up until then by the leadership of the trade union organizations, was replaced by ensuring control over the organizations themselves and by dominating all mass processes. The result was to extend the dominance of political partisanship to the field of trade union processes.

Soon enough these political choices led to corruption and undermined the role that social organizations and the institutional framework were supposed to play in a modern democratic republic such as Greece. In fact, it was a game with no rules and just one goal—to remain in power.

The main loser: the Greek economy

As one can easily imagine, Greece took a course that could only lead to the derailment of its economy. High inflation, reduced competitiveness and fewer investments in an extremely politically polarized climate did not facilitate the search for and the implementation of solutions to the country's various problems. In the early 1990s, it was obvious that Greece was facing a dead end.

Looming bankruptcy was avoided thanks to the resolve of the Bank of Greece. The Konstantinos Mitsotakis administration was the first to try to change the country's ill-fated course, albeit without much success due to the strong opposition it was met with.

Oddly enough, in these totally stagnant conditions, it became clear that the perspective of Economic and Monetary Union (EMU) offered Greece the opportunity to set a national goal, which was adopted by most of the local elites. This consensus facilitated the country's efforts to meet the nominal requirements of the Maastricht Treaty and to eventually join the eurozone in the early 2000s.

However, once this goal had been achieved, Greece refrained from making any attempt to meet the *real* monetary union requirements. It seemed, therefore, that the various professional associations and groups were not willing to sacrifice anything more than what they had already done in support of Greece's accession to EMU, in order to help the country to achieve a real convergence with the other European Union (EU) members. The symbolic banner of this opposition was the abandonment of Minister of Labour and Social Affairs Tassos Giannitsis's reform of the social security system. Strangely enough, the mobilizations against this reform were joined by students, a development that accurately reflects the sentiment of the time and the absurdity of the matter.

The moment of the truth: the 2008 global crisis

In this context, it is no wonder that the 2008 crisis hit the Greek economy very hard, highlighting its extreme weaknesses and lack of competitiveness. Income losses rose to 25%, a figure equivalent to that of the 1912–1922 war period. In fact, the losses in disposable income (i.e. after taking into account the significant tax increases) reached 40%, a stupendous figure for a peacetime economy.

One could argue—and indeed it is very often argued—that the damage was not that severe and that the country has now simply returned to 2000 prosperity levels; in other words, it enjoys a perfectly satisfactory income level. Such an insight is fictitious. The gap between average incomes in Greece and the EU is the same as in 1960, while shortly before the crisis it had reached 85%. Besides, certain countries that used to lag behind Greece in terms of income performance have now almost caught up with it. Stunning examples are Romania and Croatia. Slovenia has already outperformed Greece, while Bulgaria is approaching fast.

In order not to lose further ground to its partners, Greece urgently needs to accelerate its growth rates. If unsuccessful, its position in the eurozone, for which so many sacrifices were made, will be imperilled because it will no longer be realistic.

Based on the current situation and considering the problems caused by the coronavirus (COVID-19) pandemic, Greece will have to go the extra mile to meet the challenges of the times. First of all, it has to sustain high growth rates for an extended period of time. These can only be achieved with massive investments. Let us recall that during the crisis Greece reached a point where depreciation was higher than gross fixed capital investment. In other words, more capital was being burned than made, while at the same time cutbacks in public investments were used to disburse financial benefits in the implementation of pre-election promises.

Now what?

Therefore, investments have become a top priority for the country's future. It is estimated that between €60 billion and €100 billion in investments are needed in order to put Greece on track towards sustainable growth. What kind of investments does the Greek economy need, and where will the financial resources come from?

Evidently, a country that enjoys a certain degree of prosperity cannot be content with *any* kind of investments. In other words, Greece does not need low-tech or low value-added investments —quite the opposite actually. Otherwise, it will be forced to compete with other countries in terms of labour costs—a competitive field in which Greece is clearly at a disadvantage.

Regarding the source of funding, things do not look good there either. Domestic savings are extremely low and are inadequate to finance the investment needs of the economy. Therefore, the country must turn to foreign investors. In fact, this move, despite its disadvantages, is absolutely necessary because there is no alternative means of securing investment funds.

Oddly enough, the Greek state has made foreign investment extremely difficult, no matter how you slice it. The experiences of those who invested in Hellas Gold, the old Athens International Airport and the Piraeus Port Authority (see Chapter 9 in this volume) are not so positive as to attract followers. Solving problems in a timely manner is a significant factor for potential investors. As shown by polls conducted among foreign financiers, the problem for foreign investors primarily stems from inefficiencies in the justice system and only secondarily from high interest rates, bureaucracy and high energy costs (Koch, 2018). Furthermore, the mere fact that Greece has a corporate income tax of 29%, while that of its neighbours is just 10%–15%, suffices to emphasize the negative incentives that foreign ventures have to face when investing in Greece.

It is further questionable whether the education system is in a position to attract and support foreign investments. Not surprisingly, all indications on that front are negative. First of all, secondary education has evolved into a rigid and outdated system that is exclusively focused on preparing students for admission to colleges and universities. As a result, Greek high schools, rather than developing individuals able to meet today's challenges, nurture the kind of person who constantly asks for benefits and favours. In other words, children adopt the value system of a shallow entertainment industry rather than the values of discipline and mental inquisitiveness that empower someone with the ethos of lifelong learning.

Moreover, higher education in Greece seems unable to keep up with the country's needs and requirements (Vettas, 2017). Recently, the president of the Hellenic Federation of Enterprises (SEV) spoke of 60,000 job positions that cannot be filled. Oddly, this is happening in a country with 20% unemployment and double that rate for youth unemployment. It is perhaps characteristic of the situation in Greece that until recently there was a heated debate over the establishment of yet another law school, which is completely unnecessary especially when the disciplines essential to the new economy are still under-represented.

A key issue regarding the relationship between education and the labour market is the mismatch of employee qualifications and those required to adequately fill job positions (see Chapter 11 in this volume). Notably, from 2008 to 2017, the rate of overqualified employment rose by 60.6%. As a result, more than three out of ten highly qualified employees filled job positions with lower qualification requirements. On the one hand, this discrepancy is due to the creation of new job positions mainly in sectors of the economy that are not knowledge-intensive, and, on the other, to the lack of connection between training systems and labour market needs (SEV, 2019).

The structures of the welfare state constitute a further aspect of this problem. They should not burden the economy, but at the same time they should offer at least a minimum guarantee of social justice. Not much needs to be said about social security costs except that they do burden the economy and also discourage business activity. As depressing as these issues may be, when it comes to social justice, things are much worse, thus highlighting the total failure of the post-junta social model.

The Bertelsmann Foundation's EU social justice index[6] weighs six factors: poverty prevention; access to education; access to the labour market; social cohesion and non-discrimination; health; and intergenerational equity. Based on the Bertelsmann index, Greece's performance in 2014 and 2017 was extremely disappointing. In both years, the country ranked dead last among EU members. In certain categories, such as education and life expectancy, Greece posted a decent record but in all other areas it looked terrible. What is even worse is that it showed no signs of improvement over the two most recent years for which index estimates are available. To be precise, there was some improvement but smaller than the EU average. The truth is that Greece continues to languish at the bottom of the rankings, trailing behind countries such as Romania and Bulgaria, which were once regarded as potential economic colonies. What is more, from 2014 to 2017, Greece lost even more ground.

To restore confidence in political institutions, and especially in democracy itself, the country's performance as regards social justice must improve. High levels of poverty, for example, are certainly unlikely to increase public confidence in democratic institutions, while at the same time they leave room for populist politics.

There are significant problems that may well determine the country's future. It is difficult to see how they can be solved in a satisfactory way, so as to avoid negative consequences.

First is social security. Today, a certain balance has been reached on this front, but it does not seem to be long-lasting. With the active workers to insured workers ratio approaching 1:1, the system is still unsustainable and, sooner or later, problems will crop up (Giannitsis, 2016; Tinios, 2010). As estimated by Tassos Giannitsis, 80% of the pre-crisis public debt resulted from financing the pension system. In other words, Greece resorted to public borrowing in order to enjoy a luxurious pension system that was, and still is, way beyond its means. Based on current conditions, it is not unreasonable to argue that this is the most critical issue for the country's economic and political future. Any disruptive change will be a major blow to the middle class and may have serious political repercussions, given that pensioners constitute a huge group of voters who play a key role in determining the outcome of any election.

Specifically, the Greek middle class accounts for 54% of the country's population and has an equally sized disposable income. In 2018, it paid 51% of all income taxes and social security contributions, while utilizing 62% of pension benefits and social transfers. Before the crisis, in 2009, the middle class accounted for 49% of households, held 48% of disposable income, paid 39% of all taxes and contributions, and utilized 54% of pension benefits and social transfers. In other words, during the crisis, the middle class paid 12% more in taxes, while it received an 8% increase in pension benefits and social transfers. The data reflect the economic downturn of the middle class, given that over-taxation and increased retirement benefits inevitably result in diminished economic power. It is argued that the Greek middle class has a feeble, if any, economic potential (SEV, 2020). This development alone suffices to mortgage the future of Greece's economy and society.

The second thorny issue, the demographic problem, is related to the first one. Greece has an increasingly ageing population and this trend is irreversible. Those who claim that immigrants and refugees will boost declining fertility rates are at best naive (Kotzamanis, 2019). This does not mean, however, that Greece could not have reaped a few, perhaps even more than a few benefits, if only its immigration and refugee policies had been smarter.

Future generations of Greeks will include many people who—they or their parents—will not have been born in Greece. As shown by all studies on immigration, this is what will happen, whether some like it or not. It is up to Greece to turn immigration to its advantage and assimilate immigrants economically, politically and socially in an effective way. It is a win-win situation. The only fear is that the lean efforts in this area do not make much sense, typically being driven by short-sighted political choices.

At this point, it should be noted that the country's international relations have taken a rather threatening turn due to a particularly unstable multipolar system, which has reached staggering proportions in the Eastern

Mediterranean. Moreover, de-globalization, a process that has been underway since 2009,[7] is supported by developments in international economic relations and by the strengthening of authoritarian regimes or trends of 'democratic dictatorship'. The situation in the immediate neighbourhood is rather grim, and without getting the economy on its feet it will be difficult for Greece to tackle its problems without cost. Increasing the defence budget is already on the table, and this is only the beginning.

These developments reflect the various aspects of the de-globalization process, a new phase in global relations; it is difficult to know how long it will last and how profound it will be. However, it is obvious that it cannot be ignored.

Based on the above, it seems that a paradigm suggested in another context by Dani Rodrik (2012), a prominent economist and professor at Harvard University, fits the Greek reality.[8] Looking at things from this perspective, it is possible that in the next ten to 20 years, Greece will face a difficult choice with three options, namely growth, globalization as reflected in its participation in the eurozone and democracy.

If this proves to be the case, the country will lose all the gains it has made since 1945, thanks to a great effort to get the country out of poverty and establish a solid democratic state. One should not lose sight of the fact that Greece faced this trilemma in 2015, although at that time there was still room to avoid making a poor, devastating choice.

Dealing with these issues has nothing to do with optimism or pessimism, as so often those who raise them are criticized for holding such attitudes. Any discussion that ignores the facts is pointless. It is also true that these facts do not lead to easy solutions. On the other hand, it must be admitted that it does not help to hide reality in order to reassure citizens. The International Monetary Fund is extremely sceptical about Greece's outlook in the next 20 years, projecting an average growth rate of around 1%. This is far too low to actually help Greece to face the challenges that lie ahead.

Conclusion

In late 2017, Tassos Giannitsis published a newspaper article in which he aptly described the country's current situation and future outlook:

> The heart of the crisis may be economic, but its roots are value, knowledge and culture related, while its handling is political. All of these have to do with the things we know, with our beliefs, assumptions and collective insights, and with the functioning of our society—both as a whole and as composed by social groups at the upper, middle and lower level. This is where the major problem lies: the harsh and widening gap between Greece and the more advanced members of the European Union is a matter of available resources in each country that traditionally play a key role in driving growth and development. Our difference is

not in the challenges we face. Rather, it is in the absence of a critical mass of dynamic people who are concerned about the future of our society and understand the importance of the critical developments taking place in Europe, in Asia, in the world, in the economy, in politics, in the climate agenda, in the relations between societies.

In Greece, a rather complacent country with minimal tolerance for negative criticism and unfavourable predictions, Giannitsis's views were totally disregarded as no one really cared to comment on them. Nonetheless, they strike at the very heart of the basic problem that plagues Greece and prevents it from breaking the gridlock it has found itself in, i.e. the absence of social groups that, being aware of the challenges, could take the initiative and accept the responsibility to effectively deal with them.

This problem, which is by no means an economic one, is most tellingly manifested in the country's political elites. It is a purely political problem, which seems to be reaching its culmination. Greece's political system, the very one that led the country to the catastrophic crisis, seems unable to steer it out of it and put it on a track of real convergence with the other European countries—the only opportunity the country really has to avoid a worse ordeal than the one it has experienced so far. The experiences of 2015 show that when something could have happened, it was the political system that did not let Greece breathe.

Greece's political system has gradually developed into a closed structure mainly focused on reproducing itself and ignoring the impact of its choices on the country. Although this is amply manifested in almost all aspects of daily life, the 2008 constitutional reform alone would suffice to illustrate the point.

The above remarks do not apply to a specific political party—this has to be very clear—but to the political system in general, which, as it is today, is very difficult to transform itself into a reform-friendly entity essential to the country's development and the economy's growth.

This contribution cannot delve into explaining how Greece could get out of the trap it has fallen into. Over the years, the country has evolved into an economy that eats its own flesh, generates no wealth for its people, and destroys existing capital without a care for the future. At the same time, institutions that tolerate rent-seeking mechanisms are still in place and this phenomenon is largely responsible for getting Greece where it is now. The mere fact that the country's social and economic framework has been based on the exploitation and exclusion of the younger generations, while neglecting the economically active population to the benefit of retirees, is enough to highlight the magnitude and complexity of the problem.

However, what this chapter sheds light on is how Greece got into this difficult situation in the first place. Ultimately, in a particularly tough and demanding international environment, it could not rise to the challenge. Furthermore, it convinced itself that it could stay out of trouble by means of tricks and gimmicks. It avoided trying—and to a large extent still does—to pursue the hard and unpopular policies necessary to keep in step with the other eurozone countries. This is why, sooner or later, Greece will have to make difficult decisions at great cost, having in the meantime nurtured an electorate that is incapable of meeting the challenges of the times.

Notes

1 This information is drawn from an unpublished essay by Yannis Tountas entitled Men and viruses (in Greek). I would like to thank the author for giving me access to his work.
2 On the political history of the period and, specifically, on the transition from dictatorship to democracy, see Voulgaris (2013: 80-88). On the issue of building democratic institutions, ibid., 184ff.
3 See 'Announcement of Greece's Request for EEC Membership to the Ambassadors of the Nine Member States to Greece' (in Greek), June 12, 1975, Constantinos Karamanlis Archive, Athens 1997, vol. 8, p. 447.
4 For a discussion on the problems of the 1970s as reflected in the European economy, see Eichengreen (2013: 274–290).
5 On issues related to the middle class see Karzis (2020).
6 Information drawn from the daily newspapers *Ta Nea*, September 15, 2014 and *Kathimerini*, November 19, 2017 (both in Greek).
7 See the remarks made immediately after the outbreak of the crisis by Harold James (2009).
8 In *The Paradox of Globalization*, Rodrik (2012) puts forward a paradigm that applies to the entire global economy, not just a national one, as it is used here.

References

Doxiadis, A. ([2013] 2014). *The Invisible Rupture: Institutions and Attitudes in the Greek Economy*. 2nd edition. Athens: Ikaros (in Greek).

Eichengreen, B. (2013). *The European Economy after 1945*. Athens: Alexandria (in Greek).

Ferguson, N., Maier, C., Manela, E., Sargent, D.J. (2010). *The Shock of the Global: The 1970s in Perspective*. Cambridge, MA: Harvard University Press.

Giannitsis, T. (2016). *Social Security and the Crisis*. Athens: Polis (in Greek).

Giannitsis, T. (2017, December 30). How history slips. *To Vima* (in Greek). www.tovima.gr/2017/12/29/opinions/pws-glistraei-i-istoria/.

Iordanoglou, C.I., and Bellas, C.F. (2003). *The Development of Corporate Capital in Greece: 1963–2000*. Athens: Paratiritis (in Greek).

James, H. (2009). *The Creation and Destruction of Value: The Globalization Cycle*. Cambridge, MA: Harvard University Press.

Karzis, F. (2020). *The Middle Gap: The Heyday and Crisis of the Middle Class in Greece and the World*. Athens: Papadopoulos (in Greek).

Koch, G. (2018, February 2). Why I wouldn't invest in Greece. *Ta Nea* (in Greek). www.tanea.gr/2018/02/02/economy/giati-den-tha-ependya-stin-ellada/.

Kostis, K. (2013). *Business and the State in Greece: The Story of Aluminum of Greece SA*. Athens: Polis (in Greek).

Kostis, K. (2019). *The Wealth of Greece: The Greek Economy from the Balkan Wars to the Present Day*. Athens: Patakis (in Greek).

Kotz, D.M. (2015). *The Rise and Fall of Neoliberal Capitalism*. Cambridge, MA: Harvard University Press.

Kotzamanis, V. (2019). Can non-natives solve Greece's low fertility problem? *Demo News Journal*, 36 (in Greek). www.e-demography.gr.

Rodrik, D. (2012). *The Paradox of Globalization: Democracy and the Future of the World Economy*. Athens: Kritiki (in Greek).

SEV (2019, February 28). One in three Greeks has an underqualified job! Special Report: Qualification mismatch, Hellenic Federation of Enterprises (SEV). *Economy and Business. Bulletin for the Greek Economy* (in Greek). www.sev.org.gr/.

SEV (2020, March 9). Aiming for the dynamic development of the middle class. Hellenic Federation of Enterprises (SEV). *Economy and Business. Bulletin for the Greek Economy*, 179 (in Greek). www.sev.org.gr/.

Sotiropoulos, D.A. (2001). *The Top Level of Political Clientelism: Organization, Staffing and Politicization of the Higher Ranks of Central Administration in Greece, 1974–2000*. Athens: Potamos (in Greek).

Stasavage, D. (2020). *The Decline and Rise of Democracy. A Global History from Antiquity to Today*. Princeton, NJ and Oxford: Princeton University Press.

Tinios, P. (2010). *Social Security: A Reading Method*. Athens: Kritiki (in Greek).

Vettas, N. (2017). Education and the Greek economy. In C. Meghir, C.A. Pissarides, D. Vayanos, N. Vettas (Eds.), *Beyond Austerity: Reforming the Greek Economy* (pp. 309–358). Cambridge, MA: The MIT Press.

Voulgaris, Y. (2013). *Post-junta Greece, 1974–2009*. Augmented and revised edition. Athens: Polis (in Greek).

2 Anni horribili

The years that changed Greece

George Papaconstantinou

Introduction

Greece's economic troubles were not a one-off accident occurring at a specific point of time at the end of the first decade of the euro. They were a culmination of mismanagement over decades; the result of a self-serving political system that nurtured an economy with characteristics badly misaligned with the requirements of a common currency zone; and a society dominated by special interests, dependent on receiving the spoils awarded by the political system and rewarding it with allegiance.

The period leading up to the adoption of the common currency in 2001 was a rare one when policymakers pursued policies aimed at Greece's convergence with its European partners. However, this was mostly limited to satisfying the nominal convergence criteria required by the Maastricht Treaty; real convergence of the economy's structures, behavioural norms and institutions was limited. Once the adoption process of the euro was complete, policymakers (in Greece as in the rest of the EU) and markets mistook the new currency zone as a risk-free environment which facilitated borrowing and postponed the necessary adjustments.

In the eurozone, Greece grew strongly; however, this growth was fuelled by foreign borrowing and was directed at imports. Internal and external imbalances widened, and despite robust growth, public debt remained close to the level of the country's gross domestic product (GDP) (Meghir et al., 2017). By the time the US-originating financial crisis had crossed the Atlantic and impacted Europe, Greece was the most vulnerable country in the eurozone. In the dramatic decade that followed, the common currency and its foundations were severely tested, and Greece's economy, society and politics underwent a shock and a painful transformation.

This chapter recounts the narrative of this period. It takes the reader through the economics and politics that led to the revelation of the country's true fiscal situation and the period leading up to the first bailout in 2010. This was followed by the second support package in 2012, with its associated debt restructuring in 2013. The chapter then examines the evolution of the economy and society which led to the political upheaval in 2015, the

DOI: 10.4324/9780429202247-4

referendum in the middle of that year, and the ensuing third support package, up to its conclusion in 2018.

The 2009 fiscal revelation and its aftermath[1]

A few days after the October 2009 national elections in Greece, it was revealed that the public deficit for that year was projected to be more than double the 6% of GDP officially reported to Eurostat by the outgoing government a few days before the election.[2] This revelation of a dramatic fiscal situation set in motion a chain of events that culminated in 2010 in the first recorded bailout of a eurozone country as Greece gradually lost access to international markets.

Having reported the higher fiscal figures to the Eurogroup and Eurostat, in November the newly elected government submitted a budget for 2010 aimed at reducing the deficit by almost 4 percentage points of GDP. Credit rating agencies reacted to the fiscal data announcements with a series of downgrades, signifying that it had now become riskier to buy or hold Greek government bonds. By year-end, the spread on ten-year government securities (the difference in risk between investing in a ten-year Greek bond and a similar German government bond) had edged up to between 200 and 250 basis points.

Markets and credit rating agencies had under-priced Greek risk in the belief that in the eurozone, all member states faced a similar level of risk. They were now repricing Greek sovereign risk, in a broader environment of generally rising deficits and debts in all the eurozone countries. Of all the countries, however, Greece represented the weakest link. It was facing a triple deficit: a very large fiscal deficit; an equally large external account deficit; and a credibility deficit, due to misreporting of its fiscal statistics and lack of delivery on promises made over the years. As a result, it was facing a rapidly closing window for its funding needs.

The Hellenic Republic continued funding itself in international markets during late 2009–2010 at increasingly higher rates, as concerns gradually shifted from short-term liquidity to longer-term solvency issues.[3] As a response, the government adopted additional deficit-reducing measures and a three-year plan to bring the deficit below 3% of GDP by 2012; at the same time it attempted to convince its EU partners that what was effectively required was a 'financial backstop' to act as a guarantee of no default for Greece against speculative behaviour pushing borrowing costs to unsustainable levels.

In early 2010, the economic environment was deteriorating rapidly, with gradually rising spreads, a damning report on Greek statistics (European Commission, 2010a), and the announcement by the European Central Bank that Greece would not receive special ECB treatment in terms of easier rules for banks posting collateral to borrow from the Eurosystem. ECB work exploring the legal and logistical issues of a country withdrawing from the

EU (European Central Bank, 2009) added to adverse market sentiment, while despite Greece's fiscal efforts, concerns about its fiscal position were compounded by questions about the economic and political risks inherent in a massive fiscal correction (Standard and Poor's, 2009).

Based on the 'no bailout' provision of the EU Treaty stipulating that EU members could not assume the debts of a member state in trouble but also fearful of domestic political fallout, the Eurogroup during this period refused to countenance setting up a support mechanism for Greece. However, the realization that despite Greek fiscal efforts markets required an EU-wide response led the Eurogroup and the European Council over the first months of 2010 to arrive gradually at decisions necessary for the setting up of a *sui generis* support mechanism for Greece.

While Greece adopted additional fiscal measures in March 2010, the Council on March 25 agreed in principle on a support scheme of voluntary coordinated bilateral loans by eurozone members to Greece. This would be financing of last resort (*ultima ratio*), at punitive interest rates ('interest rates will be non-concessional'), while 'disbursement would be decided subject to strong conditionality'. On the insistence of Germany, the International Monetary Fund (IMF) would also participate both in funding any loan arrangement as well as by taking part in the design of the attached policy conditionality and in overseeing its implementation (Euro Summit, 2010a).

European leaders had created in principle a support mechanism for Greece, hoping that it would act as a deterrent but that it would not actually have to be used. Markets, on the other hand, considered its use inescapable; this was reflected in further rating downgrades and the sharp rise in Greek bond yields during April. Liquidity trickled to a stop, despite the ECB decision to continue extending credit to Greek banks, effectively overruling the rating downgrades which made Greek collateral unacceptable. Meanwhile, Greek banks were losing about 2% of deposits every month since the beginning of the year (Bank of Greece, 2014).

Against this background, the announcement by Eurostat on April 22 revising upwards yet again the 2009 Greek fiscal deficit convinced both the Greek government and its eurozone creditors that recourse to the support mechanism was now urgently required.[4] With spreads having broken the 600-point barrier (meaning that the country would be borrowing at close to 10%), the Greek government requested the activation of the support mechanism.

The first bailout

Eurozone member states and the IMF agreed that a 'troika' of the Commission, the ECB and the IMF would negotiate the loan agreement and the accompanying conditionality with the Greek government, for final unanimous approval by the Eurogroup. During the negotiations, among the creditors, the European side had to balance the need for a credible path of fiscal consolidation against the desire of member states to limit their funding of Greece. The IMF, on the other hand, found itself in a previously untried 'troika' arrangement.[5] In this context, it was asked to design a programme for a country facing a combination of internal and external imbalances, without two crucial policy levers—debt restructuring and currency depreciation—to correct balance of payment problems. The latter was impossible in a currency union, while the former was in 2010 ruled out explicitly by the EU and vehemently opposed by the ECB.

On the debtor side, the Greek government was facing its own constraints. For the price of avoiding immediate bankruptcy, it was called upon to immediately take further austerity measures, in addition to those already adopted, while also committing to a multi-year drastic fiscal consolidation which would certainly deepen the recession the economy had entered in 2008. In the process, it would need to effectively surrender control over much of its economic policy to creditors, while fully absorbing the political cost for addressing a problem not of its own making, as opposition parties would not support the assistance programme.

The conditionality for the EU/IMF financial support was embedded in a Memorandum of Understanding (MOU) agreed between the Greek government and its creditors, following the EU decision in May 2010 (Euro Summit, 2010b). It represented a policy blueprint for the following three years, complete with timetables, specific costed measures, with a monitoring mechanism to ensure that commitments were kept (European Commission, 2010b; IMF, 2010). As could be expected, the MOU commitments reflected the imbalance of power between creditors and debtor (Ardagna and Caselli, 2014; Lim et al., 2019).

Greece was required to undertake an unprecedented fiscal effort to reduce the deficit by 10 percentage points and to bring it below 3% of GDP by the end of 2014. In addition, it signed up to reforms in the public sector, the labour market and the business environment to make the economy more competitive. The core of the conditionality involved fiscal retrenchment, with the fiscal path constrained by the loan envelope creditors were willing to commit to. Allowing for a more gradual deficit reduction would have made sense but would have meant a higher debt burden (as cumulative deficits add to the debt), and therefore necessitate more money from the EU and the IMF.

Hence the need for €30 billion of deficit-reducing measures in the MOU, adding up to 13% of GDP during the 2010–14 period, in addition to the 5% in fiscal measures adopted before the bailout.[6] Of the total 18 percentage points, almost half (7.5 percentage points in old and new measures) was scheduled for 2010. In terms of the policy mix, the emphasis was on expenditure cuts (two-thirds vs one-third from revenue increases).[7] The former included drastic cuts in public salaries and (both public and private) pensions; the latter included value-added tax (VAT) increases (with a 23% top rate), excise and real estate taxes, and a levy on profitable firms.

The counterpart to this policy conditionality was a €110 billion loan (€80 in bilateral loans from the eurozone and €30 from the IMF), paid in instalments, upon successful completion of specific measures, to cover financing needs for the first two years of the programme and part of the third, when Greece was assumed to partly regain market access. The loans would have a maturity of three years and carry a variable interest rate around 5% (lower for the IMF loans). It was understood at the time that lending terms were punitive and the repayment period short; however, they were dictated by political reality in lending countries, and the modalities were subsequently improved. The first disbursement to Greece (€20 billion, of which €14.5 was the first tranche of eurozone aid, and the rest by the IMF) took place on May 18, just in time for a €8.9 billion bond maturing the next day to be repaid, thereby avoiding technical default.

The programme logic entailed Greece addressing its fiscal deficit through a 'front-loaded' fiscal adjustment and its competitiveness deficit through 'internal devaluation' (adjustments to wages and prices). It was understood that this would inevitably lead to a recession; however, it was assumed that the elimination of the twin deficits (and the credibility deficit) would quickly restore confidence and boost investment, thereby acting as a counterweight to recessionary pressures, and in the process help Greece to return to markets by 2012.

There are a number of reasons why these expectations were not realized, and actually necessitated recourse to a second bailout in 2012. Some were internal: despite early successes, analysts and the market came to believe either that the government was not fully committed to the reform effort, or that it would not be able to carry it out due to social and political pressures. In addition, the final revision of the 2009 fiscal accounts by Eurostat in October 2010 added an additional 1.8 percentage points to the starting point of the fiscal effort, complicating it further and casting doubt on credibility.

The most important factor, however, related to continuing concerns regarding the sustainability of Greek debt. The first bailout explicitly excluded debt restructuring; however, concerns that in its absence the programme was not viable were voiced early on and became pronounced once the recession turned out to be deeper than expected, thus worsening the debt-to-GDP ratio (Wyplosz and Sgherri, 2011).[8] The denomination risk loomed large in market analysis.

In this environment, a decision made in Deauville, France, in October 2010 became the turning point which convinced markets and policymakers that a return to market financing was impossible in the timetable foreseen by the programme. In the context of a limited EU treaty change that would, as of 2013, turn the temporary bailout fund into a permanent mechanism, it was agreed that financial support would in certain cases require the participation of private investors in the eventual bailout, taking losses through a 'haircut'.

The decision effectively implied that private bondholders of Greek debt (as well as of debt in other periphery countries) were facing a high probability of future losses in their holdings. The European banks took the announcement to imply the prospect of losing money on the Greek bonds they had decided—in a gentleman's agreement with governments—to retain a few months earlier, during the May bailout. This immediately drove up borrowing costs, reversing the positive assessment that markets had held of the Greek programme up until then, and the decline in Greek spreads which could be observed since the beginning of the programme was reversed.[9]

Debt restructuring and the second bailout

The Deauville decision sealed the fate of the first Greek bailout just as that was delivering tangible benefits. In 2010 Greece recorded the biggest public deficit reduction by a eurozone country: more than five percentage points of GDP in one year. Adjusted for the cycle, the correction was equivalent to cutting the deficit from 10% of GDP in 2009 to 1.5% in 2010. To this were added reforms such as an independent statistical authority; changes in the pensions system; liberalization of professions; and simplified procedures to establish a business. But this was against a worse than expected recession, continuing deposit outflows in Greek banks, and rating agencies treating Greek bonds as junk. In this environment, the planned 2012 return to the markets became an untenable prospect.

By early 2011, eurozone countries were coming to the realization that Greece would need a second support package and, more importantly, that it would need to be accompanied by significant debt relief. What was until that point explicitly ruled out, had after Deauville become inevitable. With continued credit rating downgrades and speculation about an imminent debt restructuring, by April Greek spreads had hit the 1,000 mark (10% above German rates) and seemed unstoppable. Meanwhile, after Ireland's support package in November 2010, Portugal followed suit in June 2011, with Spain and Italy also experiencing market pressure.

Against these developments, and under the influence of the shifting German position and IMF support, the July Euro summit approved a second support package for Greece (initially €109 billion, raised to €130 billion in October) accompanied by private sector debt reprofiling with bondholders accepting net present value losses, and a debt buy-back. They also agreed on further lowering of support loan interest rates, and longer maturities for official debt (15–30 years). To stave off contagion, the European Financial Stability Facility/European Stability Mechanism (EFSF/ESM) was also made more flexible, and was now allowed to act on a precautionary basis, intervene in secondary markets and lend money to governments so that they can recapitalize banks (European Stability Mechanism, 2019).

However, the July summit decisions did not prove sufficient to resolve Greece's problems with markets, nor stem the broader tide touching all European vulnerable sovereigns. By the time the Euro summit convened in October, it was clear that the July decisions had to be revisited. Helped by the latest IMF debt sustainability analysis, which was arguing for a 'deeper PSI', the Greek government asked for a decision that would involve a large nominal reduction in Greece's privately held debt. As leaders were discussing options, in a basement room of the building, a negotiating team was facing off with representatives of the banks which were major holders of Greek debt. The agreement eventually reached invited 'Greece, private investors and all parties concerned to develop a voluntary bond exchange with a nominal discount of 50% on notional Greek debt held by private investors' (Euro Summit, 2011).

This decision on the first-ever nominal haircut for the debt of a eurozone country was a remarkable volte-face compared with the refusal to countenance any debt restructuring at the beginning of the crisis. It was the final recognition that debt sustainability in Greece could not be achieved by very high primary surpluses and privatizations. It was also the end point of a discussion that went through all the possible options of debt management, from asking banks to maintain exposure to Greek bonds by rolling them over at maturity, to coordinated rollover of maturing debt, to finally the upfront exchange of existing debt with new bonds.

The debt exchange offer was launched in February 2012, after the Greek government passed a law introducing 'retroactive collective action clauses' on 90% of the outstanding bonds which under Greek law were effectively ensuring that bondholders' qualified majority decisions would bind all bondholders. Bonds held by the ECB and the central banks were explicitly excluded from the debt exchange offer. Over €200 billion worth of bonds were offered in the largest 'voluntary' sovereign debt haircut in history. Bondholders received new bonds with a face value equal to 31.5% of the amount exchanged, as well as EFSF notes maturing within two years for 15% of the face value of the debt exchanged, and an additional 1% in GDP-linked securities if growth exceeded specified targets. This meant a total of 47.5% of the original value or a 52.5% nominal haircut (almost 80% in net present value terms).

Earlier concerns about a systemic risk from a debt restructuring did not materialize. After having shed Greek debt early in the crisis, few foreign banks' holdings of Greek government bonds were worth even 10% of their capital. In addition, by buying credit default swaps most banks had shifted risk elsewhere—on to insurers, who were not as important to the financial system as a whole. The 'selective default' credit rating announced at the time by rating agencies was soon removed and there was no triggering of default clauses elsewhere in the system. However, Greek banks were still heavily loaded with Greek government bonds, and the new bailout had to include €40 billion earmarked for recapitalizing them. This money increased the debt; it meant that the net haircut was not as large as the initial numbers suggested.

Politics trumps economics

In economic terms, the 2012–2013 debt restructuring was the culmination of the 'enforced' policy choices prompted by the revelation of the large fiscal deficit in 2009, which led to the liquidity-centred first bailout in 2010 and eventually the second one in 2012 that addressed the underlying solvency problem through the debt restructuring exercise. Nevertheless, the narrative of this period cannot be complete without an understanding of the political events which the 2009 revelation set in motion. These shed light on the dynamics of the crisis, and to a large extent explain both its length and severity, as well as the special case of Greece compared to other 'bailout countries' such as Ireland, Portugal or Cyprus (Hardouvelis and Gkionis, 2016).

Faced with a much worse situation than it had ever imagined, the first crisis government of PASOK under George Papandreou which took upon itself the 2010 decisions came up against some of its own pre-election rhetoric and alienated a large part of its core constituency and of the voting public. The austerity of the first bailout, despite representing the counterpart to the loans and as such the only hope for avoiding outright bankruptcy, was voted down not only by parties on the left but also by the conservative opposition which was largely responsible for the fiscal derailment of the years before 2009.

The economic and social hardship of austerity inevitably eroded the government's popularity, especially in an environment where opposition parties were claiming that painless solutions involving no economic sacrifices were at hand. The opposition in parliament was matched by a surge in a 'Can't Pay, Won't Pay' movement on the streets. This climaxed in late 2011, even as the government had secured a second support package and debt relief in the October Europe summit. Faced with protests verging on insurrection, Papandreou announced a referendum on the decision reached in Brussels, hoping to secure a mandate to continue. He backtracked a few days later, after European leaders—fearful that the referendum would destabilize financial markets—objected to its terms and instead asked him to make it about Greece's position in the eurozone. Instead, he resigned and gave way to a 'transition' government.

That government headed by the technocrat ex-ECB Vice President Loukas Papademos was tasked with finalizing the debt restructuring exercise. It resigned once the public sector involvement (PSI) was complete and its few months in office represented the first exercise in coalition politics during the crisis. It also set the stage for a coalition government led by Nea Demokratia (ND—New Democracy) after the May 2012 election failed to produce a governing majority. Following a repeat June election, a three-party government was formed, and ND leader Antonis Samaras as prime minister continued to implement the bailout-imposed policies he had denounced while in opposition. The new government faced its own problems: the 2013–2016 medium-term fiscal plan barely passed in parliament, while disagreements on debt sustainability and the 4.5% primary surplus target delayed the disbursement of loan tranches. Nevertheless, in late 2012 the Eurogroup agreed to further reduce interest rates on official loans, defer interest payments by ten years and extend debt maturities by 15 years.

However, the political climate continued to deteriorate, in part due to the success in bringing the fiscal deficit under control via the successive austerity measures in place since 2010. By the end of 2013, Greece had attained a small primary surplus, having started with a primary deficit of over 10% in 2009. After six years of recession, and a cumulative loss of more than a quarter of the nation's output since 2008, GDP expanded slightly in 2014. In the banks, deposits stabilized; Greek banks also started to regain access to the international interbank market. As a sign of the turnaround, in 2014 the Greek sovereign was back in international markets, issuing a five-year bond, three years behind the schedule set in the 2010 bailout.

Nevertheless, politics trumped economics. Following its defeat in the June 2014 elections to the European Parliament, the Samaras government tried to regain popular trust by abandoning some of the reforms and arguing for a 'clean exit' from the second bailout which was coming to its end. This alienated Greece's creditors and financial markets but did not manage to stem the tide of the Synaspismos Rizospastikis Aristeras (SYRIZA—Coalition of the Radical Left). Since narrowly losing in the May 2012 elections, SYRIZA had made consistent gains in the polls. In the snap elections called in January 2015, it finished first and formed an unlikely coalition government with the extreme right anti-bailout Anexartitoi Ellines (ANEL—Independent Greeks) party.

The referendum and the third bailout

The SYRIZA victory in January 2015 represented a remarkable upset in Greek politics. The parties which had dominated the political scene since the restoration of democracy in 1974 were either humbled or destroyed. Frustrated with the economic and social hardship as well as by the humiliation of the bailout years, the Greek people elected to power a populist party with no previous experience in government or in the political and the institutional mechanics of the European decision-making process, whose core election promise was to 'end austerity'.

In this vein, the new SYRIZA-ANEL government proceeded to renegotiate with the EU and the IMF the existing bailout agreements. Although their two main tenets—that Greece needed debt relief and less austerity—were accepted by most analysts, investors and even policymakers, the attempt at renegotiation ran into trouble. The new government felt its mandate entitled it to make drastic and immediate changes to the existing agreements; Greece's official creditors, on the other hand, were unwilling to give concessions to a government which rejected the bailout arrangement and whose programme promised to restore wages to pre-crisis levels, opposed product and labour market reforms, and vowed to block privatizations.

The six-month dramatic stand-off was marked by personality clashes, and by extensions to the existing bailout during which the government was asked to propose alternative measures to the ones it was rejecting but which would still bind Greece to the fiscal targets set and the aims of the structural reforms envisaged in the programme (Dijsselbloem, 2018; Varvitsioti and Dendrinou, 2019). Meanwhile, during this period, the ECB decided that it would no longer accept Greek government bonds as collateral for Greek banks and pushed all Eurosystem lending onto the more expensive Emergency Liquidity Assistance (ELA) mechanism.

As the small primary surplus which existed at the end of 2014 evaporated in the first months of 2015, the state stopped providing suppliers with sufficient cash to enable them to cover wages and pensions. While the problem with cash reserves became more acute, at the end of June, following intensive discussions on a new programme with the EU which seemed to be close to reaching an agreement, the Greek government abruptly pulled out of the negotiations and Prime Minister Alexis Tsipras announced a referendum. He asked the Greek people to decide one week later on the latest EU proposal and urged for a 'no' vote.

Immediately after the referendum announcement, the government was forced to put in place capital controls for fear of a bank run, while the ECB 'froze' the ELA provided to Greek banks at its current level. In a week of chaos and with looming shortages in basic necessities, in a highly polarized campaign, the referendum produced a clear 'no' majority exceeding 60%. At that point, however, faced with the imminent exit of Greece from the eurozone, Tsipras signalled to the EU his willingness to compromise. In the week that followed, the Greek government sent proposals for a new adjustment programme involving significant additional fiscal measures, in excess of those proposed by the creditors before he called the referendum.

In order to avoid the country's collapse, a large cross-party majority in the Greek parliament backed the proposals made by the government to the EU, which formed the basis for the third bailout agreed by EU leaders in a tense all-nighter a few days later. The meeting's outcome was highly uncertain, as the discussion took place against the background of a proposal tabled by the German Ministry of Finance for Greece to temporarily leave the eurozone. The terms for the new €84 billion loan finally agreed at that July meeting were harsh; they included transferring €50 billion of Greek assets to a privatization fund whose proceeds would mostly pay down debt. And in order for the first loan tranche to be disbursed, a host of fiscal measures ('prior actions') first needed to be supported by the Greek parliament and implemented immediately.

On the back of the third bailout which effectively annulled the result of the referendum, Alexis Tsipras went to the polls; despite a third of his members of parliament quitting the party in protest, he was returned to power to continue governing in a coalition with the right-wing ANEL party. Over the next four years and against all odds, he became the first crisis prime minister to serve out a full term. During his tenure, he faithfully implemented the bailout policies he had campaigned against, while maintaining a left-wing anti-bailout narrative that was completely antithetical to the very policies he was pursuing.

By the time Greece exited its third bailout in August 2018, the government was running a significant primary surplus (in excess of the 3.5% of GDP target set in the programme), mostly based on higher taxes and a shrinking public investment budget. The economy was growing again, albeit below expectations; this lacklustre performance was at least partly due to the fact that while achieving fiscal targets, progress on structural reforms was uneven, with both the EU institutions and foreign investors unconvinced of government commitments to changes to make the economy more competitive and raise its long-term potential growth rate.

A tale of three bailouts

Ten years and three bailouts later, it is clear that Greece represents a special case among the eurozone countries which, in the aftermath of the 2007–2009 global financial crisis, had to rely on financial assistance from the EU and the IMF. It was unique in many respects: it triggered the changes in the EU institutional infrastructure required to assist countries in trouble; its problems were more deep-seated and multidimensional than those of others; and it was the only country to require a total of three support packages (plus a debt restructuring). This concluding section briefly compares the characteristics of the three 2010, 2012 and 2015 bailout programmes.

The design of the 2010 support package for Greece was the direct result of political realities at the time; the relatively short fiscal path to bring the deficit below 3% of GDP and regain market confidence was dictated by the level of financial support that creditors were willing to commit to, itself reflecting political attitudes against bailouts in creditor countries. The absence of a debt restructuring component in the package followed from the same logic (debt relief should only be given to countries which 'deserve' it), to which should be added the reluctance to impose losses on European banks holding Greek debt (Blustein, 2015).

The 2012 support package effectively recognized the failure of the first package to create conditions that would restore market financing to Greece and through the adoption of the PSI pointed to the high debt burden as the key factor. To these one should add internal implementation problems (a 'lack of ownership') as well as broader eurozone systemic issues which impacted Greece. In terms of design, the second support mechanism was similar to the first, with fiscal, structural and financial policies. In terms of the fiscal mix, the balance moved more towards revenues, with possibly a larger negative impact on output. There was also more attention to structural reforms in product and labour markets, and more policy detail prescribed, reflecting implementation failures in the first 2010 support framework.

Both the May 2010 €110 billion bailout and the March 2012 €130 billion one have been criticized for inflicting too much austerity and getting the depth of the recession wrong (see Figure 2.1). Underestimating 'fiscal multipliers'—which show the impact of a contractionary fiscal policy on recession was considered an important part (Christodoulakis, 2013). Yet the large multipliers can be explained more by the uncertainty in the external environment and political uncertainty in Greece than by programme design or implementation flaws.[10]

It is undoubtedly true that the austerity that was imposed deepened the recession. Deficit reduction is by nature recessionary; it subtracts public resources and private purchasing power from the economy. But the recession had already started in 2008 and worsened in 2009 (the economy had contracted by more than 4% that year); the record fiscal deficit had not helped to prevent it. The logic of the programmes was that the recessionary impact would be partly offset by increased investment from a more sustainable fiscal situation and growth-inducing reforms. The reasoning was not wrong, but it took much longer than expected. The fiscal front-loading was dictated by lenders' willingness to fill the 'financing gap'. Stretching fiscal adjustment over more years would have been the right thing to do but it meant that creditors would have to agree to a larger financing envelope in 2010.[11]

Both programmes—and especially the first—did succeed in drastically reducing the deficit, but also in completing important reforms and stabilizing the banks. Within three years, most of the competitiveness lost during the 2001–2009 period had been recouped. Greece was named the fastest reforming OECD economy, though with still much to do (OECD, 2016). At the same time, the economic and social cost was severe, in terms of record-high unemployment and increased poverty and inequality (Giannitsis and Zografakis, 2015).

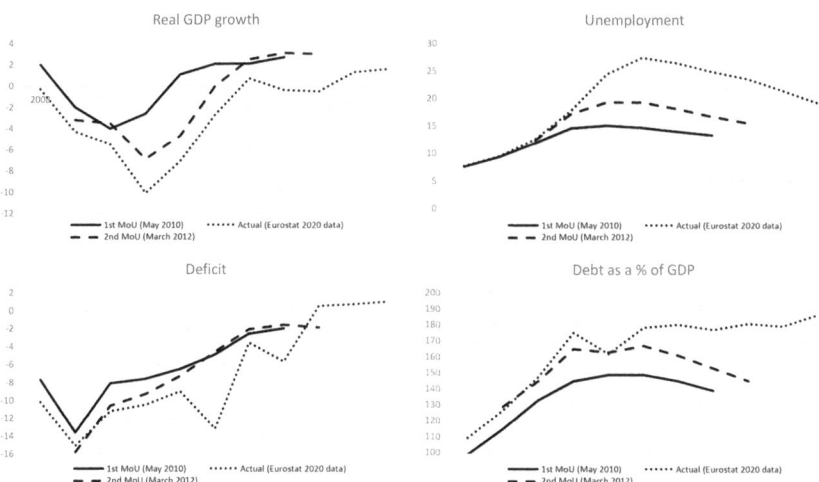

Figure 2.1 Getting it wrong: macroeconomic projections and realizations
Source: European Commission (2010b, 2012), Eurostat data.

In addition to the fiscal path, there are a number of valid criticisms that can be levied at the design of the support programmes: there should have been greater focus on structural reforms from the beginning; product market reforms should have taken precedence over those in the labour market (see Chapters 10 and 11 in this volume); the gradual shift of the burden of fiscal consolidation towards tax increases as opposed to expenditure cuts should have been prevented; and it should have been recognized that it is difficult to implement extensive structural reforms alongside tough austerity.

Certain initial design problems such as high interest rates and short repayment periods were corrected, starting in 2011. In effect, it can be argued that successive revisions and additional support became necessary due less to design faults and more because of external factors such as the Deauville decision and the delays in addressing debt sustainability. And a large part of the problem can be traced to the fact that both programmes were implemented in conditions of extreme international volatility, dominated by expectations of a 'Grexit' and currency redenomination.

Implementation problems and a lack of political and social consensus in Greece also did much to undermine efforts. Unlike in other countries where governments in bailout agreements enjoyed opposition support, the government in the initial 2010 bailout shouldered alone responsibilities that were not of its own making, with intense opposition from right and left. It took two years and two elections for some sort of broader consensus to start emerging.

The third bailout, signed in August 2015, was not different in design to its predecessors.[12] In exchange for ESM financial assistance of up to €86 billion over a four-year period with €25 billion set aside for the recapitalization of banks, it included extensive fiscal measures, targeted a lower medium-term primary surplus of 3.5% of GDP, and complemented this with product, labour and financial market reforms (European Commission, 2017).[13] What differentiates it is that it was in large part avoidable. After five years of severe economic and social pain, the economy was growing again, with the state spending less than it collected in taxes, excluding interest payments. After growing in 2014 for the first time in six years, GDP was projected to grow by close to 3% in 2015. Instead, it contracted in both 2015 and 2016.

A final remark concerns the financial system. Unlike in other eurozone countries in crisis such as Ireland and Spain, banks were not at the root of Greece's economic problems (Pisani-Ferry, 2014). They were, however, heavily impacted because uncertainty prompted high deposit outflows and due to their high exposure to Greek government bonds. Following delays in addressing the problem in the first support framework, a more radical policy response became necessary as the PSI effectively wiped out banking capital. This involved consolidation and recapitalization with private capital participation. Through consolidation, a fragmented banking sector became one of the most concentrated, with four banks accounting for over 90% of the market. Recapitalization proved more difficult and required three rounds from 2013 onwards, with doubts still lingering over capital adequacy, especially in view of the legacy of the high ratio of non-performing loans.

The past decade has transformed Greece. When the crisis hit, the country was living on borrowed time, with an economy operating beyond its means, weak institutions and a self-serving political system. It has been a forced transformation; the fiscal and competitiveness deficits have disappeared, but at a huge cost to the economy and society. However, attitudes and institutions have lagged behind this transformation. Greece has yet to face up to why it found itself in a deep economic and social crisis, often preferring to look for easy answers as well as foreign culprits. While it is undeniable that grave mistakes were made by Greece's European partners in handling the crisis and in imposing a larger than necessary economic and social cost, the roots of the problems facing the country were domestic.

Notes

1 The account of this period relies extensively on Papaconstantinou (2016).

2 In the words of the Governor of the Bank of Greece who made the announcement: 'What I can say on the basis of cash data for the first three-quarters of the year is that unfortunately the deficit is already 10% of GDP. Given its dynamic and what can be done in the next few months, I would venture with a large degree of certainty that the deficit—unfortunately—will touch or even surpass 12%.' See Papaconstantinou (2016).

3 In early November 2009, the Hellenic Republic issued a 15-year bond for €7 billion, at a 5.3% rate; and in late January 2010 a five-year bond for €8 billion, at a rate of 6.2%. The last long-term issues before the May bailout were in early March: a ten-year bond for €5 billion, at a rate of 6.3%; and in early April, a seven-year syndicated bond issue for €5 billion, with a 310 spread, and a rate just below 6%. See bond historical data at pdma.gr.

4 The successive revisions to the Greek deficit data show a disturbing picture. The budget tabled by the New Democracy government in December 2008 aimed for a 2009 fiscal deficit equal to 2% of GDP. In March 2009, the Greek Stability and Growth Programme sent to the European Commission had already revised the 2009 deficit to 3.4% of GDP. On October 2, 2009, just a few days before the national election, the outgoing government submitted Excessive Deficit Procedure tables to Eurostat with a fiscal deficit for 2009 revised to 6% of GDP. Having examined the national accounts and based also on Bank of Greece data, the new Panellinio Socialistiko Kinima (PASOK—Panhellenic Socialist Movement) government which assumed power after the October election, tabled in November 2009 the 2010 budget with a significantly revised fiscal deficit for 2009 of 12.7% of GDP. In April 2010, following an in-depth review of Greek fiscal data, Eurostat revised the 2009 fiscal deficit to 13.6%, and in October 2010 revised it further to 15.4%. The latest Eurostat tables from 2020 give a final 2009 fiscal deficit for Greece of 15.1% of GDP.

5 In order to lend to a country, IMF statutes required that country to be able to declare its debt sustainable 'with a high probability' at the end of the programme. Given that lending to Greece was exceptionally large (€30 billion or 30 times Greece's IMF quota), that the 2009 debt-to-GDP ratio was 130%, and that debt restructuring was not foreseen as part of the programme, the IMF board amended the statutes, allowing the Fund to lend when 'there is a high risk of international systemic spill-overs'. For a discussion, see Henning (2016).

6 In any fiscal adjustment effort, the measures adopted exceed the targeted nominal deficit reduction, as the contraction of the economy necessitates additional adjustment to attain the original deficit target.

7 Despite this *ex ante* expenditures-revenues split, a number of authors have argued that the programme places an excessive reliance on revenue increases and the associated recessionary impact. See Visvizi (2012).

8 The ECB and all Eurozone countries were explicitly ruling out debt restructuring at the time of the first Greek bailout in 2010. Nevertheless, the IMF hinted at some sort of debt reprofiling in its May 2010 report: 'there may be scope for bolstering this [market access] by seeking coordinated voluntary rollover understandings among creditor groups'. See IMF (2010).

9 Most commentators would agree that by effectively pre-announcing that in future sovereign bailouts would require losses to be imposed on private creditors, the 'Deauville decision' drove spreads higher, forcing the hand of Portugal and Ireland. This is not a consensus view, however. For a more sceptical viewpoint, see Mody (2014).

10 In fact, if fiscal multipliers had been correctly assessed initially, and given the reluctance to increase the money available to Greece, it is likely that even more fiscal measures would have been sought to compensate for the impact of the recession.

11 For a critical assessment of the Greek support programmes from participating institutions, see Independent Evaluation Office of the IMF (2016) and European Stability Mechanism (2020).

12 For an *ex post* assessment of the ESM programme conducted by an independent evaluator for the ESM board, see European Stability Mechanism (2020).

13 Overall, under the three programmes disbursements to Greece totalled €288,7 billion. The breakdown is as follows: under the first Greek Loan Facility programme €73 billion was disbursed (€52.9 billion from Eurozone countries and €20.1 billion from the IMF), out of a total official lending envelope of €110 billion; under the second (EFSF) programme €153.8 billion was disbursed (€141,8 billion from Eurozone countries and €12 billion from the IMF); and under the third (ESM) programme €61.9 billion was disbursed (all from Eurozone countries), out of a total official lending envelope of €86 billion.

References

Ardagna, S., and Caselli, G. (2014). The political economy of the Greek debt crisis: A tale of two bailouts. *American Economic Journal: Macroeconomics*, 6(4), 291–323. doi:10.2307/43189946.

Bank of Greece (2014). *The Chronicle of the Great Crisis: The Bank of Greece 2008–2013.* Athens: Bank of Greece. www.bankofgreece.gr/BogEkdoseis/The%20Chronicle%20Of%20The%20Great%20Crisis.pdf.

Blustein, P. (2015). *Laid Low: The IMF, the Eurozone and the First Rescue of Greece.* CIGI Papers, No. 61, April. www.cigionline.org/sites/default/files/cigi_paper_no.61web.pdf.

Christodoulakis, N. (2013). From Grexit to growth: On fiscal multipliers and how to end recession in Greece. *National Institute Economic Review*, 224(1), 66–75. www.oeetak.gr/downloads/articles/christodoulakis.pdf.

Dijsselbloem, J. (2018). *The Euro Crisis: The Inside Story.* Amsterdam: Prometheus.

European Central Bank (2009). *Withdrawal and Expulsion from the EU and the EMU: Some Reflections.* Legal Working Paper Series, no. 10, December. Frankfurt: ECB.

European Commission (2010a). *Eurostat Report on Greek Government Deficit and Debt Statistics (January)*. Brussels: European Commission. http://ec.europa.eu/ eurostat/documents/4187653/6404656/COM_2010_report_greek/c8523cfa-d3c1–495 4–8ea1–64bb11e59b3a.

European Commission (2010b). The Economic Adjustment Programme of Greece. *European Economy Occasional Papers*, no. 61. http://ec.europa.eu/economy_fina nce/publications/occasional_paper/2010/pdf/ocp61_en.pdf.

European Commission (2012). The Second Economic Adjustment Programme of Greece. *European Economy Occasional Papers*, no. 94.https://ec.europa.eu/econom y_finance/publications/occasional_paper/2012/pdf/ocp94_en.pdf.

European Commission (2017). *The ESM Stability Support Programme for Greece, First and Second Reviews July 2017*. Background Report. European Commission DG ECFIN, Institutional Paper 064, November. www.esm.europa.eu/sites/default/ files/2017_11_13_ec_background_report_on_esm_programme_for_greece.pdf.

European Stability Mechanism (2019). *Safeguarding the Euro in Times of Crisis: The Inside Story of the ESM*. Luxembourg: European Stability Mechanism.

European Stability Mechanism (2020). *Lessons from Financial Assistance to Greece: Independent Evaluation Report*. Luxembourg: European Stability Mechanism.

Euro Summit (2010a). *Statement by the Heads of State and Government of the Euro Area*, March 25.www.consilium.europa.eu/media/21429/20100325-statement-of-th e-heads-of-state-or-government-of-the-euro-area-en.pdf.

Euro Summit (2010b). *Statement of the Heads of State or Government of the Euro Area*, May 7.www.consilium.europa.eu/media/21430/20100507-statement-of-the-heads-of-state-or-government-of-the-euro-area-en.pdf.

Euro Summit (2011). *Euro Summit Statement*, October 26. www.consilium.europa.eu/ uedocs/cms_data/docs/pressdata/en/ec/125644.pdf.

Giannitsis, T., and Zografakis, S. (2015). *Greece: Solidarity and Adjustment in Times of Crisis*. Düsseldorf: Macroeconomic Policy Institute. www.boeckler.de/pdf/p_im k_study_38_2015.pdf.

Hardouvelis, G., and Gkionis, I. (2016). A decade long economic crisis: Cyprus versus Greece. *Cyprus Economic Policy Review* 10, 3–40, 1450–1461. www.ucy.ac. cy/erc/documents/Hardouvelis_Gkonis_3-40.pdf.

Henning, R. (2016). *Tangled Governance: International Regime Complexity, the Troika, and the Euro Crisis*. Oxford: Oxford University Press.

Independent Evaluation Office of the IMF (2016). *The IMF and the Crises in Greece, Ireland, and Portugal: An Evaluation by the Independent Evaluation Office*. Washington, DC: IMF. www.ieo-imf.org/ieo/files/completedevaluations/EAC%20-% 20Full%20Report.pdf.

International Monetary Fund (IMF) (2010). *Greece: Staff Report on Request for Stand-By Arrangement*. Washington, DC: IMF. www.imf.org/external/pubs/ft/scr/ 2010/cr10110.pdf.

Lim, D., Moutselos, M., and McKenna, M. (2019). Puzzled out? The unsurprising outcomes of the Greek bailout negotiations. *Journal of European Public Policy*, 26 (3), 325–343. https://doi.org/10.1080/13501763.2018.1450890.

Meghir, C., Pissarides, C.A.Vayanos, D., Vettas, N. (Eds.) (2017). *Beyond Austerity: Reforming the Greek Economy*. Cambridge, MA: MIT Press.

Mody, A. (2014). *The Ghost of Deauville*. CEPR/VoxEU. https://voxeu.org/article/ ghost-deauville.

Organisation for Economic Co-operation and Development (OECD) (2016). *OECD Economic Surveys, Greece.* March. Paris: OECD. www.oecd.org/eco/surveys/GRC% 202016%20Overview%20EN.pdf.

Papaconstantinou, G. (2016). *Game Over: The Inside Story of the Greek Crisis.* Athens: Papadopoulos.

Pisani-Ferry, J. (2014). *The Euro Crisis and its Aftermath.* Oxford: Oxford University Press.

Standard and Poor's (2009). *Greece Long-Term Sovereign Rating Lowered to 'BBB+'. On Obstacles to Fiscal Consolidation; Ratings Remain on Watch Neg. Global Credit Portal – Ratings Direct,* December 16.

Varvitsioti, E., and Dendrinou, E. (2019). *The Last Bluff.* Athens: Papadopoulos.

Visvizi, A. (2012). The crisis in Greece and the EU-IMF rescue package: Determinants and pitfalls. *Acta Oeconomica,* March. www.researchgate.net/publication/ 264627939_The_crisis_in_Greece_and_the_EU-IMF_rescue_package_Determinant s_and_pitfalls.

Wyplosz, C., and Sgherri, S. (2011). *The IMF's Role in Greece in the Context of the 2010 Stand-By Arrangement.* Independent Evaluation Office of the IMF Background Paper BP/16–02/11. www.imf.org/ieo/files/completedevaluations/EAC__BP_ 16-02_11__The_IMFs_Role_in_Greece_in_the_Context_of_the_2010_SBA.PDF.

3 The years that changed the EU

The Greek crisis and euro area reform

George Papaconstantinou

Introduction

The Greek crisis acted as a wake-up call for the eurozone. Following the revelation of the real state of the country's fiscal accounts and its progressive loss of access to international markets, the countries of the common currency area quickly came to a number of realizations. The first was that risk in the euro area was not symmetric; it was possible for a euro area member to be subject to an asymmetric shock, with the potential of being forced to default on its debt obligations, something which represented a unique situation for a eurozone member. The second was that the common currency area lacked the tools to handle this situation—in fact, in the process of its creation such situations had been effectively ruled out; hence policy tools had to be improvised and created from scratch.

Following these immediate realizations came a more fundamental one: that the design faults of the eurozone, known since its creation, could no longer be ignored. The Greek crisis had exposed the weaknesses of the eurozone construction which were not addressed in the heady first decade of the euro. Doing so required a concerted and determined effort to reform and reframe the institutional architecture of the common currency area, over and beyond the immediate support measures for Greece. This implied the completion of EMU by addressing particularly the policies and tools required for a true fiscal union, and equally importantly the creation of the the banking and capital markets union which had hitherto been ignored.

This chapter examines the reform effort undertaken (and still under way) in the eurozone and the EU as a whole as a direct result of the Greek sovereign debt crisis. It will argue that while the roots of the eurozone crisis can be traced back to the 2007–2008 US subprime crisis, Greece acted as trigger for both the short-term 'firefighting' response as well as the medium-term attempts to revisit the institutional architecture of the euro. At the same time, as the core reason for the Greek crisis was fiscal profligacy, this influenced the direction and scope of the broader reform efforts, which as a result became one-sided and overly focused on fiscal balances, leaving out important reforms required for the proper functioning of the euro area.[1]

DOI: 10.4324/9780429202247-5

Before the Greek storm

Given the design faults of its construction, a crisis in the eurozone was, with hindsight, an accident waiting to happen. While that accident is often thought to have originated in Greece in early 2010, the problem had already manifested itself in a different guise in a number of eurozone countries, including some of Europe's 'virtuous' northern nations. What is more, the roots of the crisis can be found not in Europe, but in the financial and economic problems caused by the housing bubble and toxic debts of the subprime mortgage market in the United States.

A lack of robust regulatory oversight in the US banking system resulted in extensive financial engineering and contributed to the creation of a housing bubble. Housing prices rose sharply as borrowers took advantage of low interest rates and easy lending conditions. Meanwhile, lenders masked the riskiness of their loan portfolios by issuing mortgage-backed securities and by 'packaging' risky loans into synthetic financial assets such as collateralized debt obligations, which were then rated highly by credit rating agencies. These higher levels of subprime lending, together with speculation on residential housing, drove prices higher and increased the indebtedness of households.[2]

When in 2007 the bubble burst and housing prices collapsed, borrowers with variable rate mortgages found themselves with negative equity, unable to refinance their loans and meet obligations. Mass foreclosures ensued, coupled with a sharp decline in the value of securities backed by housing loan portfolios held by financial institutions, followed by the collapse and takeover of Bear Sterns in March 2008, the takeover of mortgage corporations Freddie Mac and Fannie May, the bailout of insurance giant AIG and eventually Lehman Brothers filing for bankruptcy in September 2008. By that time, credit had seized, household spending and business investment had plunged, and the US economy had gone into a recession. International financial markets responded by tightening credit globally and the US recession spread.

While the US administration was undertaking a massive bailout of its remaining banks, injecting almost US $1 trillion into the economy, Europe was struggling to cope with its own problems. When the US subprime mortgage crisis hit, the European banking sector was characterized by some of the same weaknesses as those in the United States: insufficient capital and liquidity, and a weak regulatory and supervisory environment. In many respects, this was the result of a number of years during which, in Europe just as in the United States, a benign attitude to the self-correcting power of markets had taken hold and dominated economic thinking as well as associated policy responses.

European banks were hence vulnerable to the US-originated crisis because of their exposure to toxic US banking products but also because of their weaknesses, which included excessive reliance on short-term loans from international markets. As the crisis enveloped the United States, it quickly crossed the Atlantic and banks in a number of major European countries succumbed to difficulties. The first manifestation of the problem was a lack of faith: banks could no longer ascertain the financial health of their counterparts, so they stopped lending to each other, and the interbank market froze. As a result, in mid-2007, tensions emerged in the European financial markets, but they were initially thought to be simply a liquidity shock.

It was in fact much more than that: the problems in the interbank market also laid bare the weaknesses of an incomplete European banking system. In an increasingly integrated European financial market, regulation and oversight continued to be at the national level. Lacking a supranational entity that could guarantee the health of banks exposed to one another on a European and global scale (or take appropriate measures where this was not the case), banks retreated from the market and liquidity dried up. The situation deteriorated despite the efforts of the European Central Bank (ECB) to counteract the rapidly worsening liquidity conditions in the interbank markets by introducing long-term refinancing operations for commercial banks.[3]

By the time Lehman Brothers collapsed in the United States in September 2008, liquidity concerns had already mutated into concerns about the solvency of major European banks. One after the other, European governments were forced to provide assistance to their exposed financial institutions in order to contain the systemic risk by putting in place massive bank bailouts. In October 2008, the United Kingdom announced a bailout package for its banks totalling £500 billion. It included short-term loans, funds for recapitalization as well as guarantees to facilitate interbank lending.[4]

Soon afterwards, eurozone countries had to follow suit. Their response was similar to that in the UK, with bank bailouts taking place on a massive scale. By 2009, they totalled around 8% of gross domestic product (GDP) in Germany, 5% in France and 12% in the Netherlands.[5] This first wave of bailouts in 'core' eurozone countries was subsequently followed by a second one in peripheral member states. Spain and Ireland were particularly affected, where the banking sectors were overexposed to a collapsing real estate market. In Ireland, this was despite the attempt to change expectations by offering a blanket guarantee of all deposits in Irish financial institutions.[6]

There was one big difference between the first wave of bank bailouts in eurozone countries such as Germany and France and those in Ireland or Spain. In the former case, the governments putting the assistance packages in place had a robust fiscal situation, and as a result the bailouts did not greatly affect sovereign borrowing costs. In the latter case, however, given governments' weak fiscal positions, markets quickly responded by widening the spread on sovereign bonds (the difference between a country's borrowing costs and those of Germany, reflecting the risk premium of lending to a particular country): the 'doom-loop' between banks and sovereigns was thereby quickly established.[7]

Bringing out the firefighters

Ireland in 2008 with its banking problems came close to lighting the touch-paper. However, it was the revelations of Greece's true fiscal deficit in late 2009 that lit the fuse for the eurozone crisis, souring market sentiment towards sovereign debt in general.[8] In 2008, public deficit positions had worsened throughout the eurozone as counter-cyclical expenditures increased and revenues collapsed in the recession. In 2009, the crisis exposed weaker EU economies to much higher deficits, and at the same time higher borrowing costs. In that single year, the public deficit in the euro area widened by four percentage points and the gross public debt by ten percentage points of GDP.[9]

In this deteriorating fiscal environment, the chain of events set in motion following the election of the new Greek government in October 2009 would impact on financial and economic conditions in Europe and the world, and force the EU to confront and eventually attempt to repair some of the design flaws in its institutional architecture. It would also greatly impact the direction of EMU reform, with the strong emphasis on austerity measures, and a delayed acceptance of the origination of problems in the banking sector.

Chapter 2 in this volume discussed in detail the characteristics of the main eurozone response to the Greek crisis: the creation of the Greek Loan Facility (GLF) as a support mechanism for Greece in 2010 together with the associated policy conditions. It was the first of its kind, an ad hoc construction initially expected to be confined to one specific country only. Instead, as a number of eurozone countries ended up requiring financial support, it evolved into a stand-alone mechanism with permanent characteristics; its further evolution is a large part of the debate on the future of the euro area taking place today.

Indeed, once EU leaders realized that bailing out Greece was not enough to stem the crisis, the idiosyncratic intergovernmental loan arrangement for Greece was supplemented by a more general financial support instrument. Barely a week after the GLF was agreed, the creation of the European Financial Support Framework (EFSF) was billed as 'a European stabilization mechanism to preserve financial stability in Europe' (Euro Summit, 2010). Technically, it would take the form of a special purpose vehicle backed by a joint guarantee by eurozone governments allowing it to raise €440 billion of market funds. To this would be added €60 billion of an existing mechanism administered by the European Commission. Following decisions taken by the IMF, this total of €500 billion would be supplemented by an additional €250 billion of its resources, making a grand total of €750 billion, a sizeable 8% of the euro area's GDP.

The creation of the EFSF was an important milestone in the eurozone crisis, and not only because it marked the first time that a general-purpose financial backstop was created for sovereigns. It was also the first step to revisiting the institutional architecture of the eurozone since its inception.

Governments were finally evolving and adapting to the new situation. At the same time, and perhaps more crucially in terms of the final impact on the markets, the ECB had organized its own response: to activate 'exceptional measures'—secondary market sovereign debt purchases through the Securities Market Programme (SMP).[10] It was the beginning of a clear shift in the policy of the Eurozone's central bank, and one that would evolve further in response to the crisis in the coming months and years.[11]

A turning point

The onset of the crisis found the Eurozone lacking the tools and even the understanding needed to address the problem of an asymmetric shock to the common currency area and the impact of one Eurozone member defaulting on its debts. After initial denial and months of inaction there came ad hoc solutions steeped in the rhetoric of moral hazard; eventually, the response shifted from firefighting to creating new tools and an attempt to design a new architecture for the Eurozone.

This involved introducing a more robust framework for crisis management and support, gingerly moving towards the creation of a genuine 'fiscal union' by deepening policy coordination, as well as strengthening institutions for more effective governance. At the same time, it was eventually recognized that in most countries the origin of the crisis was not in the fiscal stance *per se* but lay instead in the banking sector, whose liabilities ended up on public balance sheets as governments bailed out the banks or guaranteed their deposits. This eventually led to an attempt at breaking the banking/sovereign feedback loop and to significant but as yet incomplete moves towards creating a banking union in Europe.[12]

In this sequence of events, the singular moment which marks the inflection point in the Eurozone crisis is in late July 2012 when the new ECB president made it clear that the Eurozone's central bank would use 'within its mandate' all the instruments at its disposal to preserve the integrity of the common currency area (Draghi, 2012). Mario Draghi's 'whatever it takes' remark succeeded where many previous attempts at staving the crisis had failed previously; they set off a global market rally and sent the spreads on government bonds tumbling. Despite further road bumps at a later date, such as the 2013 Cyprus bailout episode[13] and the 2015 Greek referendum, the Draghi pronouncement is the point when the eurozone turned a corner.

The Draghi pronouncement was successful not only because it committed the ECB firepower, but also because it came at the end of a long period in which eurozone countries had gradually proved they had more than just political will; they had also had put in place economic tools to mitigate market concerns about the integrity of the eurozone. It came after the bailouts of Greece, Portugal and Ireland, and the agreements to lend money to Spain and Cyprus, as well as after the creation of the EFSF and its successor permanent European Stability Mechanism (ESM).

Crucially, Draghi's remark also came after the decision by European leaders in June 2012 to try to break the vicious circle between banks and governments. They decided to move ahead with the unification of the European banking sector under a single supervisory body (the Single Supervisory Mechanism or SSM) and to give the new ESM the power to recapitalize banks directly (Euro Summit, 2012). Taken together, these initiatives showed the markets that they should not underestimate the political capital invested in the euro.

By the end of 2012, European leaders could claim that the worse of the crisis was behind them. The year-end summit approved a blueprint for future changes prepared by Council President Herman van Rompuy. It addressed both the fiscal and banking aspects of the crisis: it included steps for stronger fiscal governance, as well as for unifying the European banking system through common supervision, harmonized bank resolution and national deposit guarantee frameworks (European Council, 2012).

A new policy toolbox

However, the discussion on the reform of the eurozone institutional architecture had actually already begun in 2010, once the crisis became apparent, before the May 2010 Greek bailout. A Task Force was created under Council President van Rompuy, composed of ECOFIN ministers of finance; it addressed a broad set of issues (mainly the fiscal stance, but also the banking system, structural policy, and governance issues) and submitted a report to the European Council in October 2010 (Task Force to the European Council, 2010).

The 2010 van Rompuy report shows clearly how the initial reading of the roots of the crisis was focused on a failure of fiscal discipline. Indeed, it was in that area where most subsequent initiatives were concentrated, starting with the main thrust of the 'Six Pack' set of legislative measures in 2011 (applicable to all 27 member states but with specific rules for eurozone countries). Of the six measures, four were aimed at reinforcing the Stability and Growth Pact or SGP (both the preventive and the corrective part of the Pact—the Excessive Deficit Procedure or EDP).[14]

The Six Pack was followed by two other initiatives: the 'Fiscal Compact' and the 'Two-Pack'. The former is part of the 2012 intergovernmental Treaty on Stability, Coordination and Governance. Its main provisions are related to fiscal discipline, including a limit on cyclically adjusted deficits, and giving budget rules 'binding force and permanent character, preferably constitutional'—in other words it introduced constitutional debt brakes.[15] The Two-Pack notably introduced the 'European semester', requiring member states to submit draft budgets to the Commission in the context of an annual cycle of coordination and surveillance and to take any guidance into account before budgets are adopted by national parliaments.[16]

Given that the prevailing narrative of the eurozone crisis was one of irresponsible countries flouting the SGP provisions on fiscal balances and ending up requiring financial assistance, it is not surprising that most reform energy was aimed at reinforcing the Pact itself. The experience had indeed shown that neither the rules nor the enforcement mechanisms had managed to prevent large fiscal imbalances. They produced too little debt reduction in the first decade of the euro and too much fiscal austerity during the crisis. The response was therefore in two directions: tinkering with the rules, and reinforcing the mechanisms for compliance.

The changes instituted did not touch the main headline figures which form the bedrock of the SGP: the 3% deficit-to-GDP ratio and the 60% debt-to-GDP ratio remained the basis for assessing fiscal positions. However, in light of the high debt-to-GDP ratios across the EU, greater focus was put on debt, with an attempt to make the 60% limit operational and the progressive institution of a 'debt brake' at the national level.[17] Member states exceeding the limit were now required to reduce their debt-to-GDP ratio by at least one-20th (5%) a year on average over three years.[18] In terms of the deficit, the new rules attempted a more nuanced reading of the 3% limit, complementing it with the requirement that countries limit structural deficits (i.e. adjusting for the economic cycle) to 0.5% of GDP (or 1% for those whose debt-to-GDP ratio is well below 60%).

This more nuanced approach moved the debate between the Commission and EU member states to the calculation of potential GDP and of structural deficits. This proved to be problematic in practice, as it related effectively to variables that cannot be directly observed and are sensitive to the underlying assumptions. At the same time, the new rules in principle allowed for more flexibility during a crisis. In the event of a significant deterioration in the economy of a member state, more time was allowed to bring a budget deficit below the limit. This was a direct result of the focus on the underlying budgetary position over the medium term and was contingent on the member state making efforts to address its structural problems.[19]

Improving the enforcement of the SGP was the second dimension of the reforms. This involved changes to both the preventive and the corrective 'arms' of the Pact. In terms of the former, the institution of the European semester process provided the overall framework for better prevention and early warning on fiscal slippage; on the corrective side, the usual EDP for countries breaching the deficit or debt criteria now became characterized by swifter sanctions and greater (though not full) automaticity. Decisions on sanctions were now taken by reverse qualified majority voting, making it harder to block them.

At the same time, while most of the emphasis of the reforms was on preventing or redressing an unfavourable fiscal situation, some of the measures introduced were rooted in the understanding that broader macroeconomic and structural policies were equally important in triggering the economic and financial crisis. In this vein, the Macroeconomic Imbalance Procedure (MIP) process in the Six Pack with the submission by countries' of annual Reform Programmes was aimed at monitoring broader economic policies that could detect at an earlier stage problems such as those leading to a banking crisis or a collapse in competitiveness.

While the MIP was crafted so as to mirror the preventive and corrective aspects of the SGP, it soon became clear that it fell far short of attaining the same level of importance in monitoring and compliance. This was for two reasons. The obvious one was the fact that excessive deficits or debts tend to be more closely correlated with adverse market outcomes, presenting a more immediate danger to overall systemic stability. Macroeconomic imbalances on the other hand, while equally important, seem less 'urgent' in nature.

However, the second reason may be even more salient: at the heart of the debate on dealing with macroeconomic imbalances one can find widely differing policy positions on deficits and surpluses in the external account of countries. On this issue, EU member states were and remain deeply divided: while in principle there should be in a common currency area a symmetric concern about excessive surpluses *and* excessive external deficits, this is not the case. In practice, attention focuses almost exclusively on large and persistent deficits; generally the large surpluses of countries such as Germany are discussed but rarely addressed.

Governance reform

In addition to the need for new policy tools, the crisis demonstrated that the governance of the eurozone itself required an overhaul; the innumerable summits called in Brussels to urgently address problems likely to threaten the very integrity of the common currency attested to that. In this direction, the 2013 Treaty on Stability, Coordination and Governance formalized regular Euro summits, composed of eurozone heads of state and of government, with their preparation and follow-up entrusted to the Eurogroup. That group has evolved from an unofficial gathering of eurozone ministers of finance to become semi-formalized since the 2009 Lisbon Treaty; given its crucial role in decision-making and its extensive powers, it has attracted criticism over the opacity of its decision-making, its lack of accountability and limited democratic oversight.[20]

The formalities regarding summit meetings created some structure and gave eurozone matters a more solid institutional footing. But the single most important new policy direction for the eurozone since the advent of the crisis related to substance, not to process: the creation of support mechanisms for countries in distress. Following the idiosyncratic GLF created in 2010 and the EFSF created almost simultaneously as a temporary mechanism to assist other eurozone countries in a similar situation, it became clear that a permanent financial backstop would be necessary.

The creation of the ESM in 2012 was anchored in the need to safeguard the financial stability of the euro area as a whole and of its members, and its role is to provide financial assistance to those euro area countries experiencing or threatened by severe financing problems. Such financial assistance came with strict conditionality through the agreement of a Memorandum of Understanding setting out the macroeconomic, financial and structural polices necessary for the recipient country to return to market financing.

The ESM was set up as an intergovernmental organization by a dedicated treaty, with capital from eurozone countries but raising the necessary funds for its operations in international financial markets (European Stability Mechanism, 2019).[21] Its lending toolkit had a number of elements: loans in the context of a macroeconomic adjustment programme; loans for indirect bank recapitalization; primary and secondary market purchases of government bonds; a precautionary credit line; and funds for the direct recapitalization of institutions. Of these, only the first two have been used to date, with a total disbursement over €250 billion: programme loans in Greece, Portugal, Ireland and Cyprus; and loans for indirect bank recapitalization in Spain.[22]

The ESM is an important part of the current debate about the future of the eurozone. While its positive role in helping to defuse the crisis is widely acknowledged, there are distinctly different views on its evolution, role and responsibilities, including in relation to other EU institutions such as the European Commission. This is not a technical debate; it is a deeply political one. It reflects the chasm which exists within the eurozone and the EU more broadly on different visions about the eurozone and the institutional architecture necessary to support it.

The fractures of the crisis

The euro project was supposed to seal the common economic destiny of Europe. Rather than bringing countries closer together, however, the opposite happened. Since the introduction of the euro, we have witnessed a divergent evolution of eurozone economies: while GDP per capita has increased since 2000 in the eurozone as a whole, this has been far from uniform. Broadly speaking, countries in the north have fared better than those in the south, as have the new EU entrants after 2013, which were in a catch-up process. In Greece and Italy, real GDP per capita was the same or even slightly lower in 2018 than in 2000 (Figure 3.1). This divergence strained relations and fuelled distrust and resentment, at a time when decision-making shifted from the European Commission to the leaders of the EU's stronger countries.

A north–south economic gap has long been present in the EU; successive waves of accession countries expanded their geographical boundaries but also brought in increasingly divergent economic models and levels of development. However, the eurozone crisis made these internal divisions more evident by reopening the economic gap, as an external shock to a monetary union which pushes countries into recession opens disparities in growth and unemployment that become embedded in an environment of a single currency (Smart, 2017). Furthermore, this period created an important new division in Europe which did not explicitly exist until then and which has defined it since: that between creditor and debtor states.[23]

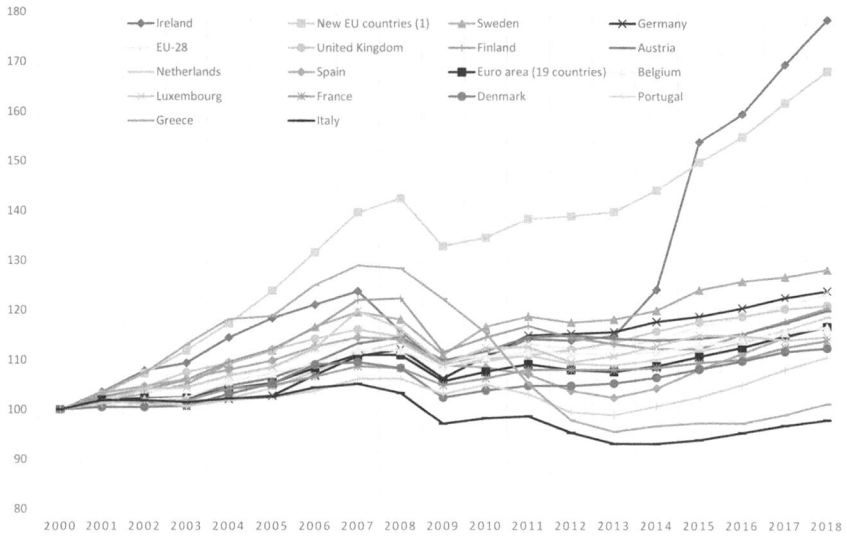

Figure 3.1 Evolution of real GDP per capita in EU countries*
Notes: *Real GDP per capita calculated as chain-linked volumes (2010).
(1) All 12 new EU countries which joined after 2013.
Index: 2000 = 100.
Source: Eurostat.

As a result, the weight of the EU's economically successful countries in decision-making during the crisis became more important than ever. This related to creating a support mechanism, the timing and terms involved, the follow-up decision to create the ESM as a permanent support mechanism, as well as issues such as when and how to address Greece's debt sustainability by imposing large losses on private bondholders. The decisions taken have also often yielded unintended consequences, as with the October 2010 Deauville agreement that private investors must contribute to future bailouts (discussed in the previous chapter). While this paved the way for the permanent rescue mechanism from 2013, the pre-announcement that bondholders could end up taking losses drove up borrowing costs and reversed markets' positive assessment of the Greek programme, arguably tipping Ireland and Portugal also into rescue mechanisms.

Undoubtedly, the tone was set in the eurozone's strongest economy—Germany. Its policy stance before and during the crisis can be attributed to the country's narrowly defined interest as a capital surplus country and traced to its experience with hyperinflation during the Weimar Republic period. However, it also related to the characteristics of the ordoliberal approach which has dominated German economic thinking (Dulien and Guérot, 2012). This approach favours rules-based stability and considers correcting fiscal imbalances a priority. It thus considered the debt crisis in the eurozone periphery as the result of overspending by irresponsible governments. Rescue packages were seen at best as a necessary evil; financial support should therefore be on punitive terms to make recourse to such non-market financing unattractive.

The problem with this approach was twofold. First, during the crisis it became the dominant economic policy beyond the weaker peripheral countries, and forced a fiscal contraction for the entire eurozone, even in countries which had some fiscal space and could act as a counterweight to the necessary consolidation in crisis countries. At the same time, it influenced decisively the design and implementation of financial support programmes, often imposing unnecessarily harsh austerity or lending terms, with a significant economic, social and political fallout.

The dominant division between creditors and debtors may have been unavoidable in the crisis circumstances but proved to be politically toxic. The crisis enabled populist voices in the north to rail against bailing out weaker countries, with similar voices in the south protesting against the way stronger countries seemed bent on imposing their will. In creditor countries, the bailouts were seen as both unnecessary and a betrayal of the conditions for agreeing to swap their national currency for the euro; in turn, this pushed governments in these countries to insist on punitive conditions for both the loans and the attached conditionality which were far removed from any economic logic. In debtor countries, the harsh conditions accompanying the official loans bred resentment and anger. What should have been seen as an act of (flawed) solidarity and even enlightened self-interest to make the common currency work, was instead interpreted as an imposition by external powers.

Adhering to the European project undeniably entails the voluntary surrender of some part of national sovereignty, but during the crisis the debtors saw this as a naked attempt by creditors to impose their control. And just as politicians in the north failed to explain that their countries had been major beneficiaries of the euro, politicians in debtor countries failed to tell the truth about the painful domestic adjustments required for the common currency to be able to function. The crisis therefore clearly demonstrated that traditional European appeals to solidarity were no longer enough, even though a clear understanding of the mutual interests being served by a single European currency was more essential than ever.

The evolving policy agenda

Despite dire predictions about the impending collapse of the eurozone, the common currency area survived the worst of the crisis—albeit at a high economic and political cost. Partly due to the policy initiatives formulated during the crisis, but also in part because of a realization of the difficulties of any member leaving the euro, few analysts continue to predict today that the euro is doomed.[24] At the same time, even the euro's strongest proponents recognize that the crisis exposed some of the 'original sins' of the eurozone's construction. And while there has been an energetic attempt to start rebuilding the EMU architecture, the work is by no means concluded.

A few years after the worst of the sovereign crisis was over, and in light of the reform progress already made, the debate seemed to eventually settle around a limited number of specific but also difficult to resolve policy issues, believed to represent the core in any attempt to reform EMU.[25] They included creating appropriate common budgetary instruments such as a macro-economic stabilization function to better deal with country-specific shocks;[26] a related central fiscal capacity that would equip the euro area with a proper fiscal policy; a joint financial instrument to reduce risk at the level of the euro area (the European Safe Asset);[27] a mechanism for restructuring unsustainable sovereign debt in eurozone countries; reforming/streamlining fiscal rules beyond the changes already undertaken;[28] and increasing banking system resilience and stability through common deposit insurance (the European Deposit Insurance Scheme).

Not all of these proposals were deemed equally important or urgent; what seemed necessary was an agreement on a minimal agenda that would not deliver an ideal EMU but would at least produce a viable EMU (Papaconstantinou and Pisani-Ferry, 2019). Such an agenda would include a focus on competitiveness and structural reform, using the EU budget to this end, combined with clever financial engineering (such as the Juncker plan); finishing the last mile in completing the banking union with the adoption of the European Deposit Insurance Scheme (EDIS), concentration charges and an integrated resolution mechanism; and a reform to simplify the SGP that lengthened the leash for member states, and with a quid pro quo of more responsibility in the case debt proved unsustainable (but no procedural or arithmetic automaticity).[29] To this should be added a broader growth agenda centred around the transition to a green economy, a prerequisite for higher sustainable growth rates in the future.

The COVID-19 pandemic that broke out in 2020 significantly changed the terms of this debate. At the level of EU member states, there was an unprecedented fiscal response in both size and swiftness, as governments attempted to cushion the economic costs of the pandemic and sustain the recovery, in the process significantly increasing deficits and debts, but also breaking all the taboos of economic orthodoxy in hitherto 'virtuous' countries. This response was facilitated by a relaxation of EU rules on fiscal deficits and state aid as well as by a voluntaristic engagement of the ECB, whose open-ended use of purchases of sovereign obligations ensured both liquidity in markets and low borrowing costs for governments.

At the level of the EU as a whole, we have also witnessed a significant departure from past practice. The external and symmetric nature of the crisis made it harder for a 'moral hazard' narrative to take hold; this in turn made it possible for the EU to confront head-on the need for assistance to countries that were particularly hard hit given their prior vulnerability to high debt levels. It led to the July 2020 Council decision launching the Next Generation EU initiative, involving the Commission borrowing in markets on behalf of EU member states, backed by new 'own resources', and distributing part of these funds as outright transfers rather than loans. While this was 'an exceptional response to temporary but extreme circumstances' (European Council, 2020), at the same time it did create a new environment for the appropriate policy tools to be able to complete EMU and help it to better address economic shocks.

Conclusion

In the crisis years, sometimes prompted directly by the Greek crisis, in other instances responding to the broader systemic weaknesses which the eurozone sovereign debt crisis made plain, policymakers embarked on a sustained effort to reform the policy tools and more broadly the institutional architecture of the EU and its common currency area. The reform attempt was aimed at strengthening its resilience as well as creating mechanisms to minimize the cost of another asymmetric shock, while addressing well-known but neglected weaknesses such as the absence of a banking and capital markets union.

In this reform effort, there was one central element which bridged technical solutions with political outcomes: the European institutions and their evolution; more broadly, the governance of the European project. The crisis exacerbated the long-existing tension in EU policymaking between the national and the supranational. To overcome existing institutional arrangements such as the 'no bailout rule', which seemed to stand in the way of saving the common currency, states sidelined the Community method in favour of a new intergovernmentalism. This may have worked as a method for defusing the crisis, but in the longer term it undermined the legitimacy of the EU project.

In the years following the sovereign debt crisis, it became evident that a new institutional balance was required between member states on the one hand and the European collective on the other. This could involve specific new institutions, legislative changes, new budgetary and other policy instruments or governance changes. A number of specific proposals were made in this context; however, underlying these lay a more general issue: the need to recalibrate the roles and relationships between the key EU institutions—the Council, the Commission, the Parliament, as well as the Eurogroup and, most importantly, the ECB. Movement in this direction has until recently seemed difficult. However, the 'policy innovation' that has characterized the response to the COVID-19 pandemic may provide some hope for progress. Perhaps the COVID-19 crisis will end up completing the reform effort that started as a result of the sovereign debt crisis.

Notes

1 The chapter draws extensively on Papaconstantinou (2020).
2 There are numerous references to the US financial crisis. Some of the most acclaimed include Sorkin (2009), the interview-based classic; Geithner (2014),

giving the view from one of the main government participants; and Sinn (2010) from a critical academic viewpoint.

3 A brief account is given in Praet (2012).

4 Statement of the UK Chancellor Alastair Darling (October 8, 2008) on financial stability and the measures announced by the UK government: https://web.archive. org/web/20081011062730/http://www.hm-treasury.gov.uk/statement_chx_081008.htm.

5 As quoted in Draghi (2018). See also Stolz and Wedow (2010).

6 For a blow-by-blow account of the events surrounding the Irish deposit guarantee, see Cardiff (2016).

7 On the relationship between banks and sovereigns, see Mody and Sandri (2012).

8 An interesting counterfactual relates to how the eurozone crisis would have played out if Ireland rather than Greece had been the first to fall, thus exposing the weaknesses of EU banking systems and their regulatory oversight.

9 For the eurozone as a whole, Eurostat data (as reported in 2019) show that the government fiscal deficit widened from 0.7% of GDP in 2007 to 2.2% in 2008 and to 6.2% of GDP in 2009. Gross government debt jumped from 65% of GDP in 2007 to 68.7% in 2008 and to 79.2% of GDP in 2009.

10 The institutional mechanics at play are interesting here; to guard its independence, and ensure that the countries will assume their responsibility for creating a financial backstop, the ECB's decision to buy bonds in the secondary market was taken simultaneously to the Economic and Financial Affairs Council (ECOFIN) decision to create the EFSF; when asked during the ECOFIN session, ECB officials actually refused to confirm their plans to EU ministers. See Papaconstantinou (2016).

11 The ECB decision was backed by a large majority of the board, but was not unanimous. The criticism was blunted by the conditions attached to the May 9, 2012 decision (the creation of the financial backstop by ECOFIN) and the fact that the intervention was 'sterilized' by operations to reabsorb the liquidity injected by buying bonds, and therefore did not represent monetary easing.

12 For a discussion of the importance of identifying the causes of the eurozone crisis, see Pisani-Ferry (2011) and Jones (2015).

13 For a discussion of the Cypriot case, see Demitriades (2017).

14 See   www.consilium.europa.eu/uedocs/cms_data/docs/pressdata/en/ecofin/119888. pdf for a summary of the March, 15 2011 Council decision on the Six Pack.

15 The treaty can be found at http://europa.eu/rapid/press-release_DOC-12-2_en.htm. The initial plan was to amend existing treaties but this was blocked by the UK which wanted to exempt the City of London from future EU financial regula-tions; hence the solution for a separate treaty. The stand-alone treaty was even-tually signed by all EU member states except the UK, the Czech Republic and Croatia.

16 See http://ec.europa.eu/economy_finance/publications/occasional_paper/2013/pdf/ ocp147_en.pdf for the decisions relating to the Two-Pack.

17 The importance of debt issues following the crisis is also exemplified by the fact that following the adoption of the Fiscal Compact, and in order to better coor-dinate the planning of national debt issuance, each EU member state is required to submit its public debt issuance plans in advance to the European Commission and Council.

18 As an illustration, with a debt-to-GDP ratio of 120%, the average annual reduc-tion must be one-20th of the difference from the 60% benchmark, i.e. 3 percentage points of GDP. In practice, the calculation is more complex as interim values during every three-year period also impacts the final debt reduction requirement.

19 The 2015 Commission Communication issuing guidance to encourage structural reforms and investment and use the new flexibility under the SGP can be found at http://europa.eu/rapid/press-release_IP-15-3220_en.htm.

20 The issue of transparency in the Eurogroup has been addressed by the European Ombudsman. See www.ombudsman.europa.eu/en/case/en/48285.
21 The text of the Treaty establishing the European Stability Mechanism can be found at www.esm.europa.eu/sites/default/files/20150203_-_esm_treaty_-_en.pdf.
22 This €250 billion figure includes EFSF loans. While the ESM is the successor to the EFSF, the EFSF continues to exist as a separate legal entity alongside the ESM (with which it shares staff and resources) but does not make any new loans.
23 It could be argued that the differing contributions to the EU budget and the fact that some EU countries were net recipients means that the creditor/debtor distinction was not new. But those were processes embedded into EU rules and not politically visible to the public; post-2010, however, 'bailout loans' became the focus of public debate.
24 Even convinced critics of the eurozone and its policies, who believe that the process is faulty by design, could never have succeeded, and is to blame for all of Europe's troubles, become more circumspect when it comes to its dismantling. Two examples are Stigliz (2016) and Mody (2018).
25 The paper by German and French economists ('7+7') which has in many ways shaped the recent debate is Bénassy-Quéré et al. (2018); a review of the debate is in Pisani-Ferry (2018). See also Buti et al. (2017).
26 A discussion can be found in Koester and Sonderman (2018); objections to the approach are in Heijdra et al. (2018).
27 The discussion on a European Safe Asset is summarized in Claeys (2018).
28 See Darvas et al. (2018) and Feld (2018).
29 A similar approach which discusses the minimal conditions for EMU reform in the absence of further political integration is Eichengreen and Wyploz (2016).

References

Bénassy-Quéré, A.et al. (2018). *Reconciling Risk Sharing with Market Discipline: A Constructive Approach to Euro Area Reform.* CEPR Policy Insight No 91. https://cepr.org/active/publications/policy_insights/viewpi.php?pino=91.

Buti, M., Deroose, S., Leandro, J., Giudice, G. (2017). *Completing EMU.* https://voxeu.org/article/completing-emu.

Cardiff, K. (2016). *Recap: Inside Ireland's Financial Crisis.* Dublin: Liffey Press.

Claeys, G. (2018). *Make Euro-Area Sovereign Bonds Safe Again.* VoxEu.org. https://voxeu.org/article/make-euro-area-sovereign-bonds-safe-again.

Darvas, Z., Martin, P., and Ragot, X. (2018). *The Economic Case for an Expenditure Rule in Europe.* https://voxeu.org/article/economic-case-expenditure-rule-europe#:~:text=Proposals%20for%20reforming%20the%20euro,framework%20has%20not%20worked%20well.

Demetriades, P. (2017). *A Diary of the Euro Crisis in Cyprus: Lessons for Bank Recovery and Resolution.* London: Palgrave Macmillan.

Draghi, M. (2012). Speech at the Global Investment Conference in London, July 26. www.ecb.europa.eu/press/key/date/2012/html/sp120726.en.html.

Draghi, M. (2018). *Risk-reducing and Risk-sharing in our Monetary Union*, Speech at the European University Institute, Florence. www.ecb.europa.eu/press/key/date/2018/html/ecb.sp180511.en.html#1.

Dulien, S., and Guérot, U. (2012). *The Long Shadow of Ordoliberalism: Germany's Approach to the Euro Crisis.* European Council of Foreign Relations Policy Brief. www.ecfr.eu/publications/summary/the_long_shadow_of_ordoliberalism_germanys_approach_to_the_euro_crisis.

Eichengreen, B., and Wyploz, C. (2016). *Minimal Conditions for the Survival of the Euro.* https://voxeu.org/article/minimal-conditions-survival-euro.

European Council (2012). *Towards a Genuine Economic and Monetary Union.* Report by President of the European Council Herman Van Rompuy, June 26, Brussels. www.consilium.europa.eu/media/33785/131201.pdf.

European Council (2020). *Special Meeting of the European Council (17–21 July 2020): Conclusions.* www.consilium.europa.eu/media/45109/210720-euco-final-con clusions-en.pdf.

European Stability Mechanism (2019). *Safeguarding the Euro in Times of Crisis: The Inside Story of the ESM.* Luxembourg: ESM.

Euro Summit (2010). *Statement of the Heads of State or Government of the Euro Area,* May 7. www.consilium.europa.eu/media/21430/20100507-statement-of-the-heads-of-state-or-government-of-the-euro-area-en.pdf.

Euro Summit (2012) *Euro Summit Statement,* June 29. www.consilium.europa.eu/m edia/21400/20120629-euro-area-summit-statement-en.pdf.

Feld, L., Schmidt, C., Schnabel, I., Wieland, V. (2018). *Refocusing the European Fiscal Framework.* https://voxeu.org/article/refocusing-european-fiscal-framework.

Geithner, T. (2014). *Stress Test: Reflections on Financial Crises.* London: Random House.

Heijdra, M., Aarden, T., Hanson, J., van Dijk, T. (2018). *A More Stable EMU Does Not Require a Central Fiscal Capacity.* https://voxeu.org/article/more-stable-em u-does-not-require-central-fiscal-capacity.

Jones, E. (2015). The forgotten Financial Union. In M. Matthijs, and M. Blyth (Eds.), *The Future of the Euro* (Chapter 3). Oxford: Oxford University Press. https://oxford.universitypressscholarship.com/view/10.1093/acprof:oso/9780190233235.001 .0001/acprof-9780190233235-chapter-3.

Koester, G., and Sondermann, D. (2018). *A Euro Area Macroeconomic Stabilisation Function: Assessing Options in View of their Redistribution and Stabilisation Properties.* European Central Bank Occasional Paper series No. 216. www.ecb.europa. eu/pub/pdf/scpops/ecb.op216.en.pdf.

Mody, A. (2018). *The Eurotragedy: A Drama in Nine Acts.* Oxford: Oxford University Press.

Mody, A., and Sandri, D. (2012). The eurozone crisis: How banks and sovereigns came to be joined at the hip. *Economic Policy*, 27(70), 199–230. https://dx.doi.org/ 10.1111/j.1468-0327.2012.00281.x.

Papaconstantinou, G. (2016). *Game Over: The Inside Story of the Greek Crisis.* Athens: Papadopoulos.

Papaconstantinou, G. (2020). *Whatever It Takes: The Battle for Post-Crisis Europe.* New York: Agenda Publishing.

Papaconstantinou, G., and Pisani-Ferry, J. (2019). *A Big Leap Forward: Institutions and Policies for a Viable Euro Area.* Paper presented at the conference 'Where is Europe Going?' organized by the Caloust Gulbenkian Foundation, Lisbon,March 22. https://content.gulbenkian.pt/wp-content/uploads/2019/03/21165801/Policy-pap ers_EN_Para-onde-vai-a-Europa_web.pdf.

Pisani-Ferry, J. (2011). *The Euro Crisis and its Aftermath.* Oxford: Oxford University Press.

Pisani-Ferry, J. (2018). Euro area reform: An anatomy of the debate. *CEPR Policy Insight* No. 95, October.

Praet, P. (2012). *The Role of the Central Bank and Euro Area Governments in Times of Crisis.* Speech at the German Federal Ministry of Finance, Berlin. www.ecb.europa. eu/press/key/date/2012/html/sp120419.en.html.

Sapir, A., and Schoenmaker, D. (2017). *We Need a European Monetary Fund, but How Should It Work?*, Brussels: Bruegel. http://bruegel.org/2017/05/we-need-a-european-monetary-fund-but-how-should-it-work/.

Sinn, H.-W. (2010). *Casino Capitalism*. Oxford: Oxford University Press.

Smart, C. (2017). *The Financial Education of the Eurozone*. M-RCBG Associate Working Paper Series No. 69, Harvard Kennedy School. www.hks.harvard.edu/sites/default/files/centers/mrcbg/files/Smart_final_69.pdf.

Sorkin, A. (2009). *Too Big to Fail*. London: Penguin.

Stigliz, J. (2016). *The Euro: How a Common Currency Threatens the Future of Europe*. New York: Norton.

Stolz, S., and Wedow, M. (2010). *Extraordinary Measures in Extraordinary Times: Public Measures in Support of the Financial Sector in the EU and the US*. Deutsche Bundesbank Discussion Paper Series 1: Economic Studies No. 13/2010. www.econstor.eu/bitstream/10419/37071/1/631858768.pdf.

Task Force to the European Council (2010). *Strengthening Economic Governance in the EU*. Final Report to the European Council. October 21. Brussels: European Council. www.consilium.europa.eu/uedocs/cms_data/docs/pressdata/en/ec/117236.pdf.

4 From 'black sheep of the eurozone' to 'European shield'

Ten years of crisis politics in Greece

Lamprini Rori

Introduction

If crises constitute opportunities for change, the 2010s were the years which could have transformed Greece. Having to deal with a debt crisis which soon became financial, several episodes of a refugee crisis, a pandemic and an enduring crisis in foreign policy, the perfect storm in which the country found itself often felt like a multifaceted experiment in seeking to assess its strengths, weaknesses and limits. The turbulent 2010s altered the social status and the living standards of a large part of the population; the sociocultural fabric of the society; and the size and configuration of the Greek economy. This roller-coaster decade attracted international attention, which at times presented the country as an exotic experience of decay (Panagiotopoulos and Sotiropoulos, 2020), as a project of modernization of broader historical and global significance justifying intervention (Kalyvas, 2020), as the 'black sheep' of the European family or as a heroic partner protecting EU borders. All these dynamics have profoundly challenged and affected politics and institutions.

Long-lasting features of the political system have hindered crisis politics. Marked by a tradition of a strong but distrusted state, low social capital and political trust (Sotiropoulos, 2020), Greece entered the crisis era with a section of its electorate already feeling alienated from, unrepresented by and disappointed in the political system. Alongside family and the Orthodox Church, political parties have been the strongest institutions. Despite their weak democratic internal functioning, political parties in the Third Republic have progressively colonized the state and suffocated civil society. Aided by an electoral law that is seemingly proportional but in reality favours the leading party, as well as by a clientelist public administration (Spanou, 2020), the two main protagonists of the post-1974 era, the Panellinio Socialistiko Kinima (PASOK—Panhellenic Socialist Movement) and Nea Demokratia (ND—New Democracy), have easily maintained their alternation in power, by offering state spoils in exchange for votes. Nonetheless, the favouritism and corruption of the parties as well as the changing aspirations of the electorate have weakened party identifications, creating a breeding ground for the

DOI: 10.4324/9780429202247-6

critical stance and the volatility that would erupt alongside the forthcoming crises. Polarization has been a quasi-constant characteristic. With the exception of the 1996–2004 swing to the centre under Konstantinos Simitis' leadership, the party system has always been subject to tension and polarization. The polarized pluralism of the 1970s was followed by a polarized two-party system in the 1980s. In that sense, polarization under crises figured as an inherent mode of doing politics in Greece (Tsirbas, 2020), even if it added tensions to the political process and harvested negative political outcomes.

The aforementioned chronic deficiencies of the political system accelerated political change in the decade under study. The chapter aims to present and discuss the crises that took place from 2010 to 2020, by linking them to changes in electoral competition and the party system, as well as trends in public opinion. We proceed with the chapter in four stages. First, we present the major crises that erupted from 2010, by describing their highlights and major characteristics. Second, we compare them by attempting to identify the similarities and differences between them. The next two sections look at the effects of this decade of crises on politics and state-society relations. We discuss the dominant sociopolitical divisions of the period under study and overview the changes in the party system. Finally, we look at the trends in public opinion regarding satisfaction with governments, social and political trust and expectations for the economy. We conclude by commenting on the performance of institutions during this turbulent decade.

Ten years of crises: the sequence

Four different types of crises have challenged politics and institutions since 2010. This section looks at the main characteristics of each crisis, assesses the government's management thereof and compares the similarities and differences in their nature and blueprint.

The financial crises

In 2010 Greece made global headlines due to its incapacity to meet its loan repayments related to the public debt, which subsequently evolved into an extended financial crisis. The risk of defaulting and exiting the eurozone led to a series of bailout agreements between the country and the 'troika',[1] acute austerity measures and a severe contraction of the economy, by as much as 27% of gross domestic product (GDP). Three economic adjustment programmes, three parliamentary elections and four prime ministers later, the country exited the strict monitoring of the bailout framework in August 2018, having secured low debt repayments until 2030, without, however, being exempted from its fiscal constraints to maintain primary government surpluses equivalent to 3.5% of GDP until 2023 and 2.2% until 2060. The economy had been expanding since 2017 at an average of almost 2%

annually. Greece introduced structural reforms, improved price competitiveness via labour and product market reforms, boosted exports, reduced unemployment, buttressed consumption, rebuilt its fiscal credibility and successfully returned to the international bond markets, with rating agencies having raised its sovereign rating.

The political change subsequent to the 2019 parliamentary election was associated with positive indicators on the economic front, revitalizing hopes for the country's economic recovery: market capitalization rose by 47% in 2019; tourism was booming; consumption picked up; pro-business labour bills and taxation measures were voted in; capital controls were lifted in September 2019; and significant foreign investments were secured.

The outbreak of the coronavirus (COVID-19) pandemic in early 2020 derailed any projection for the national economies and the eurozone as a whole. Despite its asymmetric impact on member states drawing on discrepancies in debt levels and the capacity of countries' health systems, the pandemic posed an existential threat to the EU, forcing contingent changes in economic governance. The need for an increase in governmental public spending was initially backed by EU institutions through the adoption of a Temporary Framework that boosted states' flexibility in supporting the economy and businesses[2] and then by relaxing the fiscal rules of the Stability and Growth Pact.[3] The European Central Bank (ECB), the European Council and the European Investment Bank (EIB) introduced programmes and funds that were tailored to tackle the financial and economic implications of COVID-19.[4] Following the game-changing Franco-German proposal to distribute grants to member states in need in May, on July 21, 2020, the European Council agreed to a EU recovery fund of €750 billion branded NextGenerationEU (NGEU) in order to support member states affected by the COVID-19 pandemic to be distributed during 2021–2023, as well as a €1,074 billion budget of the EU budget (the Multiannual Financial Framework) for the period 2021–2027.[5] It was the first time that the EU decided to engage in fiscal stimulus, allocating €390 billion from the NGEU directly to member states in forms of grants via the Recovery and Resilience Facility (RRF). Drawing on the lessons of the eurozone crisis management that limited assistance to member states in the form of bailouts, this was a historic decision that changed economic governance in the EU (Ladi and Tsarouchas, 2020).

The financial implications related to COVID-19 abruptly disrupted economic recovery, with Greece facing possibly the severest disruption in the eurozone. Uncertainty, travel and social distancing restrictions had a negative effect on production, employment and tourism, exacerbating long-standing labour market challenges. The government responded swiftly in order to bolster liquidity and incomes, strengthen the health system and restart closed sectors. Important regulations were introduced such as measures to support household income and corporate liquidity, the freezing of corporate tax, insurance and debt obligations, providing income support for freelancers and scientists, subsidies for the unemployed and job retention schemes, the reduction of value-added tax on goods and services affected by the pandemic, and low-cost loans for businesses and professionals.[6] The cost of the pandemic in the state budget rose to €26 billion in 2020, whereas GDP contracted by 10.5%, with the state disbursing €18 billion in direct payments in order to mitigate losses related to the economic lockdown (see Chapter 12 in this volume).

Nonetheless, Greece benefited significantly from the EU's economic response to the pandemic. For the first time since the outbreak of the financial crisis, eligibility requirements were lifted, and the country participated with its government securities in the ECB's assets purchase programmes like any other EU country, helping to hold down the risk premium on Greek debt below the mid-2019 levels. Flexibility in the application of EU rules on public finances and fiscal policies deactivated the term regarding primary surpluses, which had trapped the Greek economy for over a decade. Greece was allocated €32 billion from the RRF, of which €18 billion was to be disbursed in the form of grants and the remainder as loans. Additionally, it was to receive €26.5 billion from the next EU budget. Policies on how to distribute the relevant funds followed recommendations drafted by an expert committee chaired by Christopher Pissarides, the co-recipient of the 2010 Nobel Prize for Economic Sciences. The transformation of Pissarides' proposals into actual governmental policies constituted the first economic programme with domestic ownership since the beginning of the financial crisis.

The global pandemic

When the first COVID-19 case was confirmed on February 26, 2020, Greece cancelled all carnival celebrations and imposed regional restriction measures.[7] On March 23, it tightened the restrictions by imposing a national lockdown, during which citizens were placed under curfew with exceptions for daily exercise, grocery shopping and essential trips, for which they had to inform the state. Measures were progressively lifted from May 4 onwards. Practically banned until June, tourism was then unconditionally reinstated. Despite strong advertising investment and being more accommodating than other countries in terms of quarantining tourists on arrival at their destination, tourism did not pay off as expected, hardly reaching 25% of the 2019 levels.

The prompt and decisive governmental response to the outbreak of the pandemic minimized deaths, enhanced its popularity and earned citizens' trust and obedience. By institutionalizing official information campaigns led by experts and by addressing direct messages from the prime minister to the citizens, the government boosted its leadership credentials. The Greek success story made headlines in the international media. Nonetheless, the positive outcome of the first wave made both the citizens and the state complacent, whereas the economic derailment sustained economic activity despite significant increases in the levels of infection.

The second wave of the pandemic hit the country hard, especially northern Greece, with regional hospitals being unable to provide care to an ever increasing number of patients.[8] When cases spiked in late 2020, a second nationwide lockdown was implemented in November, albeit with looser restrictions. Schools remained closed for over two months and switched to distance learning. Amid a gloomy context of rising deaths, the commencement of the vaccination programme at the end of the year fuelled hopes. Despite a highly organized operation, applying strictly defined order criteria, the limited number of vaccines supplied by the EU resulted in a slow pace of vaccination. A rising number of cases and deaths led to a third national lockdown in February 2021. Cumulative fatigue, reluctance to make stark choices between the need to ease the pressures on the national health system and on economic activity, created repeated inconsistency in governmental messages, fuelling disobedience and anti-vaccination movements.

Public and social life abruptly had to follow new norms. Hence, the pandemic resulted in policymaking and fast-track lawmaking in extraordinary conditions for numerous aspects of public life. School and workplace closures, a ban on public events and gatherings, stay-at-home restrictions, the wearing of face masks, testing and contact tracing, international and domestic travel regulations, income support measures, debt or contract relief, vaccination policy, public information campaigns all challenged governmental reflexes and public administration. They did accelerate reforms in a number of sectors, such as the digitization of public services, online education and distance learning, parental leave for employees working from home while caring for their children, and new norms and practices in tourism. Possibly the biggest opportunity for reform was that applicable to the health system, but it was missed. Only limited supplies were made available for intensive care units. While generous private donors and EU funds boosted resources, no systematic reform plan was put in place for staffing, equipment and infrastructure.

All in all, management of the pandemic varied over time and sector. Despite limited human and material resources and lack of preparation, state capacity performed beyond initial expectations. Nonetheless, the duration of the virus—which at February 2021 had caused 179,802 cases and 6,297 deaths[9]—stretched the system to its limits and led to the introduction of radical measures which did not prevent short- and medium-term damage to several economic sectors. Despite and because of its duration, magnitude and impact on the economy, labour, human psychology and social relations, the global pandemic was a critical juncture for a series of immediate changes in governance both at the supranational and the national level. The EU avoided the mistakes made during the sovereign debt crisis of 2010–2012, when countries of the south in need of support had to implement acute austerity measures in return for bailouts. The pandemic accelerated integration at the EU level, creating a series of economic governance tools which permitted liquidity in the bonds market and financial assistance to states. At the same time, the pandemic led to state interventionism and the imposition of certain measures such as increased government spending and welfare supply; by accelerating reforms in a number of areas; and by ordering restrictions to human rights and monitoring their implementation.

The refugee crisis

Increased migration flows from Turkey were one of the biggest challenges that the Greek state had to face during the decade, with 911,471 refugees and migrants entering the country in 2015 alone. The government led by Synaspismos Rizospastikis Aristeras (SYRIZA—Coalition of the Radical Left) and Anexartitoi Ellines (ANEL—Independent Greeks) initially facilitated transit of migrants from the east of the country to the northern borders. Increasing numbers of refugees arriving from Turkey and other EU member states' lack of solidarity and reluctance to host them, as well as the closure of the Balkan corridor, escalated to a critical situation, with the Greek prime minister appealing to the values held dear by European member states in order to attract assistance from the EU. The government supported and implemented the EU-Turkey agreement in March 2016,[10] the idea behind which was to discourage the arrival of migrants. People arriving in Greece by sea could be returned to Turkey, even if they were entitled to international protection as refugees. In return, Turkey would receive financial support and institutional rewards. As a result, refugee flows were reduced considerably.

The deal stopped the flows, but trapped refugees in the Greek islands. It sped up asylum procedures of detaining refugees in poor conditions in camps in the Eastern Mediterranean islands, despite criticism by national and international human rights organizations and institutions about inadequate resources and the lack of infrastructure in health and education. In 2017, national and international human rights organizations also raised allegations of *refoulement* of Turkish asylum seekers operated by Greek authorities, about which UNHCR and the Council of Europe expressed concerns. By the end of 2019, there were more than 36,000 people in the hotspots on the islands of the Aegean, built to host a maximum of 5,400 persons and only for short lengths of time[11], despite over 20,000 transfers to the mainland.[12] This made conditions in these hotspots untenable[13] and exacerbated tensions among the islands' populations, often culminating in violence (Georgiadou and Rori, 2019).

The change in government in mid-2019 marked a shift in external perception of the management of the refugee crisis, with the Ministry of Migration being initially merged with the Ministry for Citizens' Protection. This move was interpreted by human rights activists as a choice for securitization over the immigration and refugee agenda. A significant increase in the number of arrivals from 50,508 in 2018 to 74,613 in 2019 precipitated governmental decisions[14] to decongest camps on the Aegean islands by transferring immigrants and refugees to the mainland as well as plans to set up closed pre-departure centres for those who were to be deported or sent back to their country of origin. The government blamed Turkey's unwillingness to abide by the agreement and EU partners' intransigence to end voluntary burden-sharing within the Union. Efforts to persuade the municipal and regional representatives to assume internal burden-sharing proved ineffective, with reactionary local societies on the mainland denying the mitigation, at times escalating to violent, xenophobic attacks in Northern Greece and the Eastern Aegean Islands. A backload of 79,900 applications for asylum demands led to delays, ineffective examination of cases and attribution of status to applicants not satisfying the conditions.[15]

The situation deteriorated further in March 2020, when Turkey encouraged tens of thousands of migrants to cross the Greek land border, while at the same time publicly declaring that it would no longer take measures in order to prevent migrants from trying to reach Europe, in an effort to renegotiate a series of issues, such as ensuring European support for its actions in Syria, renegotiating the landmark 2016 migration agreement between the EU and Turkey, and progress in visa facilitation procedures. Over the course of 15 days, some 60,000 migrants were prevented from entering Greece via the north-eastern customs passage of Kastanies. As tensions continued to escalate, police forces implemented deterrence and prevention measures along the border, while the government stopped accepting asylum applications for a month and condemned Turkey's provocative stance in the EU, which progressively aligned with Greece by making supportive declarations, as well as despatching senior EU representatives to pay visits at the border. The more EU partners witnessed state capacity in securing the borders, the more their stance changed on the matter, shifting to public recognition of Greece as a decisive actor rather than Turkey, as was the case in 2016. The president of the European Commission identified the EU with the Greek border, claimed that Greece was providing a European shield to immigration flows, offered manpower, resources and infrastructure.[16] However, several reports accused the Greek authorities and/or FRONTEX of carrying out the pushback of migrants in the Aegean Sea.[17]

Another critical episode took place in early September 2020, when refugees and migrants were forced to abandon the camp of Moria in the island of Lesbos, after a fire broke out and destroyed the site. Initially constructed to shelter 3,000 people, the camp was overcrowded with 12,000 people living in and around it, in abysmal conditions of hygiene and safety, due both to mismanagement and to policies of deterrence adopted by the EU. Triggered by insiders aiming to motivate EU in order to 'decongest' the camp and lift detainment measures justified by the outbreak of the COVID-19 pandemic, refugees and migrants were subsequently forced to camp for days on the road leading to the island's capital in primitive humanitarian conditions, carrying personal belongings and supporting their family members. Given such pressures, ten EU countries mobilized in order to receive unaccompanied children and EU officials accelerated discussions on the new migration pact and the building of a new reception and identification centre. A temporary camp was quickly constructed by the national authorities assisted by UNHCR in the island and an operation of persuasion was successfully put in place, in order to relocate the migrants. However, efforts to decongest the islands were hindered by local populations and authorities amid rising anti-immigrant sentiment on the mainland. A joint EU and International Organization for Migration programme funding two-months of accommodation for recognized refugees after leaving the islands was implemented towards this aim, whereas the new EU migration plan proposed at the end of September targeted increased protection of external borders with active support for frontline coastal nations, speeding up return of rejected asylum seekers and stepping up pressure on other countries to take back their citizens.

Even though the aforementioned episodes did not improve the status and living conditions of refugees, crises in both Evros and Lesbos did secure a positive reaction for the government domestically. In terms of crisis management, the state machinery responded effectively and a valuable experience was gained. In terms of political capital, Greece gained credibility and leverage in dealing with migration and protecting the external borders of the EU. In terms of communication, the country was framed as a strong partner, supported by the senior officials of the EU politically, financially and operationally. Both crises created a momentum which altered the negative image that was portrayed of Greece in the European media during the financial crisis. However, Greek anti-migration policies have been the object of harsh criticism from the media and non-governmental organizations internationally.

Greek-Turkish relations

The power vacuum created in the Eastern Mediterranean by the US withdrawal from the Middle East, the discovery of allegedly considerable gasfields in the Eastern Mediterranean, as well as Turkey's backsliding to authoritarianism and nationalism are the origins of the most recent crisis between Greece and Turkey (Pagoulatos and Sokou, 2021). Greek-Turkish relations have remained fragile since 2016, as challenges to the territorial status quo established by international treaties that formed a part of Recep Tayyip Erdoğan's revisionist foreign policy were carried out aggressively both in his statements and in his actions.

The demand of the Turkish authorities to extradite eight Turkish officers, who landed in Greece in the aftermath of the 2016 coup in Turkey, seeking political asylum, raised tensions between the two countries.[18] Turkish revisionism over the Lausanne Treaty perpetuated these tensions, with declarations by the Turkish president in 2016 and during his official visit to Greece in December 2017 evoking the Turkish speaking minority of Thrace. Bilateral disputes over the delineation of territorial waters, the continental shelf, the Flight Information Region and the sovereignty of some islets were ongoing, as the Turkish authoritarian turn went hand in hand with increased provocations. In 2017 and 2018, Turkey purchased oil and gas extraction vessels and carried out surveys and drilling in a legally demarcated exclusive economic zone (EEZ) of the Republic of Cyprus, in some cases on the basis of licenses issued by the so-called internationally unrecognized 'Republic of Northern Cyprus'. In November 2019, it concluded an illegal EEZ delimitation agreement with the internationally recognized government of civil war-torn Libya, through which the larger Greek islands such as Crete, Rhodes, Kassos and Karpathos were deprived of the right to EEZs, thereby violating the relevant provisions of the international law of the sea. Turkey's strategy of escalation proceeded in full development: one month after the crisis over refugee flows in Evros, it commenced a series of seismic surveys in the Eastern Mediterranean in April; in July and August it converted the historic, orthodox monuments of Hagia Sofia and Chora Church into mosques; and it increased the number of illegal flights over large Greek islands in the Aegean. Greece condemned officially the agreement with Libya and reacted by signing a maritime delimitation agreement first with Italy in June, then with Egypt in August 2020. It also reached an agreement with Albania to seek a solution on the delimitation of their maritime zones before the International Court of Justice in The Hague, Netherlands. Between July and November 2020, the Turkish authorities put out ten naval alerts (Navtex) to Greece that its *Oruc Reis* research vessel, escorted by Turkish warships, was to carry out a seismic drilling survey in a non-delimited maritime zone claimed by Greece. Tensions escalated further when Greek and Turkish ships were involved in an accidental collision in August. In September, the Turkish authorities fully supported the 'Mavi Vatan' ('Blue Homeland') nationalist, revisionist doctrine repeating the need for revision of the Lausanne Treaty.

Greece reacted both militarily and politically. It asked the EU Council of Ministers for Foreign Affairs to meet in order to addressing these acts of Turkish aggression. The EU authorities, although initially reluctant to impose sanctions on Turkey, expressed solidarity towards Greece, while condemning Turkish violations against Cyprus's sovereignty. Greece also sought and obtained support from the United States. US Secretary of State Mike Pompeo urged Turkey to refrain from taking any illegal actions, while French President Macron declared that Turkey was no longer deemed a partner in the region. Along with Cyprus, Greece called for an embargo on arms sales to Turkey. Whereas Germany rejected the proposal, the European Council decided to take soft measures against Turkey which were lifted in March 2021. Relations with Israel and the United Arab Emirates were also strengthened. International pressure led to the de-escalation of the long-standing crisis in the Eastern Mediterranean in October with Turkey refraining from carrying out seismic research in the Eastern Mediterranean and both countries agreeing to revitalize exploratory talks for the delimitation of maritime zones.

Even though several crises between the two countries have occurred since the 1974 Turkish invasion of Cyprus (Rori, 2005), the most recent one was the longest, lasting almost one year. It profoundly challenged the NATO leadership, which initially undermined its seriousness, but finally activated a deconfliction mechanism between the two parties. Greece used diplomatic and military means, succeeding promptly in different fields. It concluded agreements for its maritime zones with important regional players such as Egypt. Diplomatic pressure resulted in manifest support from strong allies. Despite the fact that dialogue between the two countries might not culminate in arbitration via international organizations, it served to deter the clash and de-escalate the conflict.

Comparing the crises

The four crises have in common the amplified role played by the EU, which testifies to the dependence of modern states on extended resources at the supranational level. The considerable complexity and frequency of crises in the current context of economic, geopolitical and climate risks not only call for international and regional alliances, but demand ever-increasing mechanisms, procedures and fields of cooperation. Despite divergences and antagonisms between partners and institutions, the EU has evolved considerably as a result of those crises.

The first difference pertains to the nature of the four crises—financial, borders, sanitary and foreign policy—suggesting different policy strategies, expertise and resources in the management of these. Constrained by poor infrastructure, limited resources and ineffective institutions, the executive power and the state machinery have been confronted with economic, security, public health and military demands for investment in human and material capital, in circumstances of pressure, fear and uncertainty.

The way in which the financial crises differ from the subsequent crises has to do with the dominant perceptions of the causes and the framing of pertinent policies related to each crisis. The causes of the financial crises were mainly perceived as endogenous: chronic structural deficiencies of the Greek economy, as well as political inefficacy to succeed fiscal consolidation, were all domestic fallacies which led to the country seeking financial assistance from external sources, which came with conditionality on the terms of the bailout agreements. On the contrary, the causes of the refugee crisis, the pandemic and the escalation of Greek–Turkish hostilities were deemed and framed as exogenous: the increased refugee and migrant flows since 2016 are related to wars and political instability in Syria, Afghanistan and several African countries; the COVID-19 virus that emerged in China diffused worldwide and entered Greece; the crisis in the Greek–Turkish relations, albeit not new, is currently being provoked by Turkey's generally belligerent stance in the Eastern Mediterranean under Erdoğan's leadership.

The management of those crises, furthermore, implies differences in the origin of parameters that governments needed to take into account: during the financial and the refugee crises governments had to abide with external constraints, mainly EU norms and policies. On the contrary, during the pandemic and the dispute with Turkey, the government went native. Domestic pressures weighed more in their handling, as divisions regarding national security and fissures between obedient and not obedient to the restrictions imposed due to the pandemic produce rifts which cut across the electorate.

A fourth difference involves dominant perceptions on the role of the state. Whereas the bailout agreements primed the reduction of the size and the role of the state in a series of economic and administrative activities, the refugee crisis, the pandemic and the foreign policy crises bring back into play the value of state interventionism. Intricately linked with security, the three subsequent crises imply the notion of a strong state demanding high technocratic skills for the management of complicated issues. The role of experts has been exalted especially with respect to public health issues. Digital qualifications and reform are also at the core of needs linked to the pandemic. It remains to be seen whether the prolonged needs and long-term changes that those crises bring to the labour market and the social fabric will be sufficient to incentivize highly skilled technocrats to work in the public sector.

The quality of leadership affects and is also affected by the management of those crises. Whereas the pandemic—at least in its first phase—and the Greek–Turkish conflict have rallied public opinion around the government, the financial and the refugee crises have divided the electorate at large, triggering electoral shifts and changes in the party system.

Sociopolitical divisions and party system changes

Greece experienced profound sociopolitical divisions and subsequent changes in its party system during the 2010s. The bailout agreements and the austerity which followed them placed positioning over the bailouts at the top of issues dividing parties and the electorate until the mid-2010s (Rori and Marantzidis, 2012). A toxic ambiance of ideological polarization and unprecedented levels of fragmentation raised fears over the evolution of the party system towards a version of polarized multipartyism resembling to the Weimar Republic, especially since radical and extremist parties of the far right and the far left constituted relevant choices for a growing part of the electorate in the polls (Dinas, 2020).

Through a series of critical elections (Moschonas, 2015), a profound realignment marked by two parliamentary elections in May and June 2012 established a centrifugal competition which brought to the centre of a fragmented political arena radical parties such as SYRIZA and splinter parties like ANEL and Dimokratiki Aristera (DIMAR—Democratic Left), as well as erstwhile marginal actors like the neo-Nazi Chrysi Avgi (Golden Dawn) (Dinas and Rori, 2013). The moderate multi-partyism that emerged from the June 2012 election sealed the end of the two-party system as known since 1981, where the executive power was shared in alteration between PASOK and ND, and established a new one, extending the range of political supply from the communist left to the extremist right. Abandoned first by a series of members of parliament who resigned, were dismissed or migrated to other parties, the erstwhile powerful PASOK progressively electorally evaporated, punished by its voters, a large number of whom opted for a more radical choice on the left, offered by SYRIZA. Even though the polarization and fragmentation did not hamper democratic stability in the end, rage and despair fuelled numerous protests, whereas political violence marred several social movements and public demonstrations (Georgiadou and Rori, 2019).

The government which emerged from the transition towards the new party system was the first in European politics to escape from this pattern of coalitions between expected allies according to conventional left-right spatial competition. Formed by the populist, radical left SYRIZA (Stavrakakis and Katsambekis, 2014; Pappas, 2014) and the populist, radical right ANEL (Georgiadou, 2019), this coalition was the most resilient governmental alliance throughout the ten-year crisis, lasting four and a half years. The 2019 parliamentary election was the first national election since the country exited the bailout programmes in August 2018, bringing back into play the left-right positioning of voters. ND's landslide victory, with 38.85% of the vote, led to a comfortable parliamentary majority and, hence, to the first single-party government since 2012. Alongside SYRIZA's electoral resilience, which won 31.53% of the vote, the emerging two-party system marked the return of the party system to a new normality (Rori, 2020).

The erstwhile radicalization of the electorate, which was marked by a majority of voters placing themselves on the left and the centre-left from 2011 until 2016, faded away, increasingly balancing voters' self-placement on the two sides of the axis (Figure 4.1). The similar levels of voters being self-placed around the left and the right since 2016, as well as the slight rise of centrist voters since 2019, testify the return towards a centripetal electoral

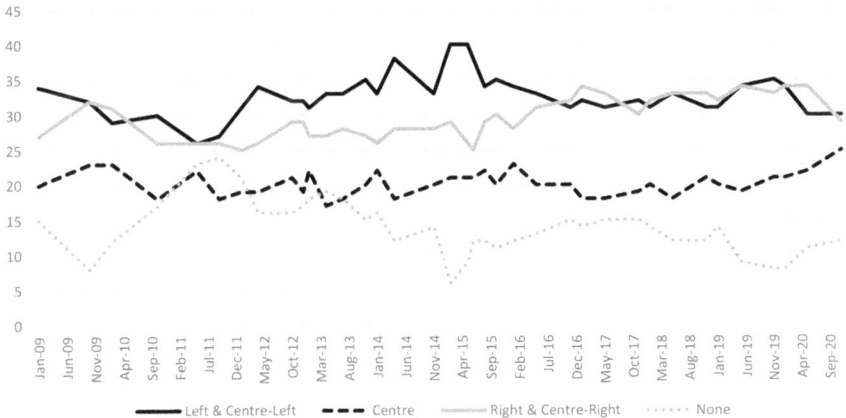

Figure 4.1 Left-right self-placement, 2009–2020.
Source: Metron Analysis. www.metronanalysis.gr.

competition (Figure 4.1). Whether citizens self-recognized as centrists will lean towards the centre-right or the centre-left will depend on the result of the next parliamentary election.

Satisfaction, trust and expectations in public opinion

Survey data pertaining to governmental satisfaction show that even though newly elected governments are positively assessed, their popularity is abruptly reduced when they deal with crises. The financial crisis has inflicted the highest cost on governments, with PASOK abruptly losing support among public opinion after the signature of the first bailout agreement in April 2010 and minimizing it among extended anti-austerity indignation and protest in mid-2011 (Figure 4.2). The most popular government of the decade has been the coalition government of SYRIZA-ANEL, after a historic victory for the radical left in January 2015, with a record level of satisfaction reaching 76% (Figure 4.2). That said, the admiration was only temporary. As soon as the compromise to the third bailout agreement was a *fait accompli* in the summer of 2015 and after a referendum that pointed towards the opposite direction, public opinion reflected high levels of dissatisfaction, even if voters gave the government a second chance in the subsequent snap parliamentary election of September 2015 (Rori, 2016). The ND government elected in July 2019 has enjoyed the longest period of positive evaluations in the turbulent decade under study, despite having to manage three crises in a row, if not because of the management of those crises.

Being traditionally considered as a country with an underdeveloped civil society (Sotiropoulos, 2017), strong party clientelism, low interpersonal trust, as well as low trust in institutions (Ervasti et al., 2019), Greece was expected to lose further levels of trust during a decade of insecurity, fear, losses and grievances. Indicators pertaining to social and political trust mostly confirm

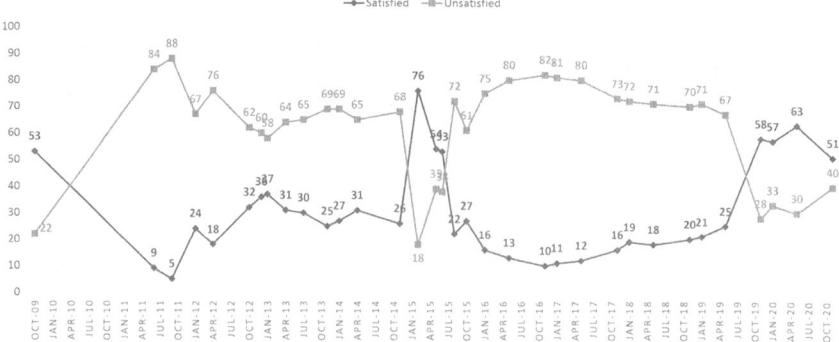

Figure 4.2 Government satisfaction, 2009–2020 (%).
Source: Metron Analysis. www.metronanalysis.gr.

those trends. In Figure 4.3, social trust is assessed by asking to what extent one can trust other people, whereas political trust is assessed by asking for trust in the parliament. Both variables are measured on a scale from 0 to 10; values marked refer to the mean. The means of both measures are low, with interpersonal trust being systematically higher than political trust, albeit only slightly. Both kinds of trust have risen from 2012 to 2020, with political trust having done so more than social trust. Although the victory of SYRIZA fuelled political trust in February 2015, it was not sufficient to reverse the chronic tendency of poor records (Theocharis and van Deth, 2015). It soon evaporated and remained stable until May 2019, when emerging political change created hopes which were manifest in the increase in political trust. The evolution of social and political trust in the decade under study does not leave much room for optimism. Citizens remain sceptical and reluctant to trust. Nonetheless, fluctuations ex ante political changes testify that voters are not a priori cynical, disenchanted or apolitical, but rather they invest hopes and political expectations, which are soon refuted, however.

Expectations for the economy (Figure 4.4) remain generally negative in the period under study, with the exception of two positive fluctuations: first, few months preceding and succeeding the victory of SYRIZA in January 2015; second, from the victory of ND in July 2019 until the outbreak of the COVID-19 pandemic in Greece in early 2020. Expectations about the evolution of the economy in November 2020 reached the same plummeting levels scored in July 2013, reflecting citizens' despair about the future of the economy and possibly latent personal economic grievances.

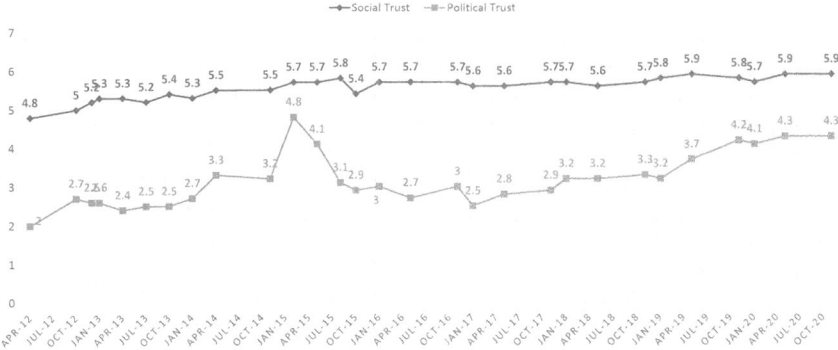

Figure 4.3 Social and political trust, 2012–2020 (average)
Source: Metron Analysis. www.metronanalysis.gr.

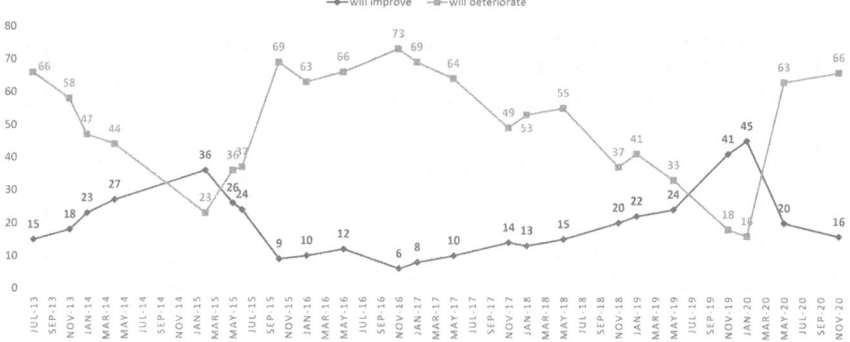

Figure 4.4 Expectations for the economy, 2013–2020 (%)
Source: Metron Analysis. www.metronanalysis.gr.

Conclusion

Undoubtedly and fairly, the 2010s will be remembered as a gloomy decade in Greek political history. A sequence of unpredictable blows starting with the debt crisis and ending with a global pandemic, have made the juncture of the crisis 'the new normality'. Without adhering to a generalized 'crisology' as a frame of analysis and interpretation, the abrupt character, the scale and variety of short-term problems created, as well as the magnitude of long-term effects induced by the four aforementioned crises, permit us to make the case for such an argument. Impositions from a rapidly changing financial, geopolitical, environmental, international system advocate the inflation of risks and challenges.

Each of those crises will have their own impact on politics, institutions, the society and the electorate, the assessment of which it is too early to make. This chapter has attempted to review and compare the main characteristics of these extraordinary episodes in the history of Greece, which have caused significant disruptions. Economic reforms and changes in voting intentions subsequent to the first crisis have been prominent, even if the party system seems to have stabilized towards a new, asymmetrical two-party system. In party politics, polarization seems to remain the prevalent operational logic (Tsirbas, 2020), despite fluctuations depending on the agenda. Inasmuch as the debt crisis had a profound effect upon the economy and the party system, it did not provoke 'a lasting change or a shift of paradigm' in public administration (Spanou, 2020). It remains to be seen whether continuity over change will prevail in the blueprint of the pandemic, which has been a catalyst for the acceleration of small, albeit numerous changes in governance and policies. Nonetheless and despite chronic deficiencies, lagging behind in terms of modernization and Europeanization, the state machinery and institutions have manifested remarkable resilience in the light of the cumulative challenges posed by austerity, refugee flows, COVID-19 and the Greek–Turkish frictions. Despite structural problems and institutional failures, Greece remains low in the global rankings of fragility,[19] enjoying stability and state capacity in a number of performance indicators, as well as an improving trend since 2017 for the first time since 2006. A series of qualitative indicators pertaining to institutions and the electorate, such as the electoral evaporation and the judicial verdict against the neo-Nazi 'criminal' organization Golden Dawn, as well as centripetal voting tendencies, might point towards a social inclination favouring reforms in public administration and the shape of the state.

Notes

1 The initial scheme of the European Commission, the ECB and the IMF was reinforced by the European Stability Mechanism since the Third Adjustment Programme.
2 European Commission, 'State aid: Commission adopts Temporary Framework to enable Member States to further support the economy in the COVID-19 outbreak', March 19, 2020. https://ec.europa.eu/commission/presscorner/detail/en/IP_20_496.
3 European Council, Statement of EU ministers of finance on the Stability and Growth Pact in light of the COVID-19 crisis, March 23, 2020. www.consilium.europa.eu/en/press/press-releases/2020/03/23/statement-of-eu-ministers-of-finance-on-the-stability-and-growth-pact-in-light-of-the-covid-19-crisis/.
4 In order to counter the rise in public debt, corollary to the suspension of state aid rules and the increase in public spending, the ECB decided on a Pandemic Emergency Purchase Programme (PEEP) of €750 billion, reinforced by €600 billion in June 2020 and by another €500 billion in December 2020, totalling €1,850 billion (for the PEPP, see www.ecb.europa.eu/mopo/implement/pepp/html/index.en.html). The Council established SURE, a temporary recovery fund of €100 billion giving loans to self-employed people and to employers for job retention schemes and three immediate instruments of €540 billion for member states, businesses, jobs and workers in April 2020 (For SURE, see www.consilium.europa.eu/en/policies/coronavirus/timeline/). One month later, €200 billion were allocated by the EIB to firms affected by the crisis (for the EIB funding, see www.eib.org/en/about/initiatives/covid-19-response/index.htm).
5 European Commission, 'EU budget 2021: A kick-start of the European recovery', December 18, 2020. https://ec.europa.eu/commission/presscorner/detail/en/IP_20_2489.
6 All the COVID-19 related legislation can be found on the relative website of the Greek government. https://covid19.gov.gr/category/oikonomia-ergasia/?fbclid=IwAR0Vt4UB5VNo4BPU8tTnGJndgC0s1kIZjhYr1Am8U20tagkxEvTJ52NQ3p8.
7 Early in March the government decided to enforce workplace and school closures. In mid-March, it restricted public gatherings, closed educational, cultural and religious institutions, ordered the closure of hotels, shops, restaurants and all retail businesses other than supermarkets and pharmacies, banned the arrival of non-EU residents and travel to and from European countries, with the exception of expatriates.
8 The country was divided in risk zones and measures were imposed locally, according to the level of risk. Deficient, untrained and understaffed regional medical institutions soon reached their limits and patients with confirmed cases of COVID-19 had to be distributed to hospitals throughout the country.
9 Source: World of Meters, Greece, February 2, 2021. www.worldometers.info/coronavirus/country/greece/?fbclid=IwAR20hdzg-9KGcl9G24I_fbfBPDABlebeAmwNfwSQrJJHZH-c9T9WLJGS8x0.

10 European Council, EU-Turkey Statement, March 18, 2016. www.consilium. europa.eu/en/press/press-releases/2016/03/18/eu-turkey-statement/.

11 UNHCR, Greece: Fact Sheet, December 1–31, 2019. https://data2.unhcr.org/en/ documents/download/73592.

12 European Commission, Communication from the Commission to the European Parliament, the European Council and the Council. Progress report on the Implementation of the European Agenda on Migration. Brussels, October 16, 2019. https://ec.europa.eu/home-affairs/sites/homeaffairs/files/what-we-do/policies/ european-agenda-migration/20191016_com-2019-481-report_en.pdf.

13 Human Rights Watch, Greece Needs to Face Reality About Asylum Seekers, October 4, 2019. www.hrw.org/news/2019/10/04/greece-needs-face-reality-about-a sylum-seekers.

14 Unrestricted access of foreigners to the public health system via a social security number was cancelled, granting health care access to immigrants with documents and access to the job market six months after entering the country to those whose asylum application had not already been rejected. Legislation to tighten up the asylum process was passed in October 2019, cutting options for appeal and facil-itating the deportation of failed asylum seekers. The composition of second-instance committees for rejected applications was altered, definitions on the vulnerability of applicants was revised and the target for the time needed for final decision per case was set at three months instead of two years. Recruitment of 370 employees in the asylum service did little to alter the regime. The magnitude of the issue, the workload and the urgent demand in resources and policies led the government to revise its strategy by separating the police from the asylum services and reinstituting the Ministry of Immigration and Asylum in February 2020.

15 For instance, Georgia and Albania were included in the list, whereas in reality they were safe countries with respect to the refugee status.

16 European Commission, Remarks by President von der Leyen at the joint press con-ference with Kyriakos Mitsotakis, Prime Minister of Greece, Andrej Plenković, Prime Minister of Croatia, President Sassoli and President Michel, Kastanies, March 3, 2020. https://ec.europa.eu/commission/presscorner/detail/en/statement_20_380.

17 Human Rights Watch, 'Greece: Investigative pushbacks, collective expulsions', June 2020. www.hrw.org/news/2020/07/16/greece-investigate-pushbacks-collecti ve-expulsions; IOM, 'IOM alarmed over reports of pushbacks from Greece at EU border with Turkey', June 2020. https://greece.iom.int/en/news/iom-alarmed-o ver-reports-pushbacks-greece-eu-border-turkey.

18 Even though the government allegedly initially assured Erdoğan that the extradi-tion would be fast-tracked, the Greek Supreme Court rejected the request, amid fervent awareness and support raised by the Greek civil society, thereby priming human rights. Anger from the Turkish side made the Greek government request the cancellation of asylum status, which was rejected by the Court.

19 Greece is ranked 127th out of 178 countries in the Fund for Peace's Fragile States Index (2020).

References

Dinas, E. (2020). The electoral system. In K. Featherstone, and D.A. Sotiropoulos (Eds.), *The Oxford Handbook of Modern Greek Politics* (pp. 203–218). Oxford: Oxford University Press. doi:10.1093/oxfordhb/9780198825104.013.13.

Dinas, E., and Rori, L. (2013). The 2012 Greek parliamentary elections: Fear and loathing in the polls. *West European Politics*, 36(1), 270–282. https://doi.org/10. 1080/01402382.2013.742762.

Ervasti, H., Kouvo, A., and Venetoklis, T. (2019). Social and institutional trust in times of crisis: Greece, 2002–2011. *Social Indicators Research*, 141(3), 1207–1231. https://doi.org/10.1007/s11205-018-1862-y.

Georgiadou, V. (2019). *The Far Right in Greece, 1965–2018*. Athens: Kastaniotis (in Greek).

Georgiadou, V., and Rori, L. (2019). Low-intensity violence in crisis-ridden Greece: Evidence from the far right and the far left, Policy Brief, LSE Hellenic Observatory Research Programme. www.lse.ac.uk/Hellenic-Observatory/Research/Projects-2018/ Low-intensity-violence-in-crisis-ridden-Greece-Evidence-from-the-radical-right-and -the-radical-left.

Kalyvas, S. (2020). The developmental trajectory of the Greek state. In K. Featherstone, and D.A. Sotiropoulos (Eds.), *The Oxford Handbook of Modern Greek Politics* (pp. 23–37). Oxford: Oxford University Press. doi:10.1093/oxfordhb/ 9780198825104.013.2.

Ladi, S., and Tsarouhas, D. (2020). EU economic governance and Covid-19: Policy learning and windows of opportunity. *Journal of European Integration*, 42(8), 1041–1056. https://doi.org/10.1080/07036337.2020.1852231.

Moschonas, G. (2015). Critical elections and the interpretation of elections of September 2015. *Syghrona Themata*, 37(130–131), 26–28 (in Greek). www.synchrona themata.gr/krisimes-ekloges-ke-i-erminia-ton-eklogon-tou-septemvriou-2015-1/.

Pagoulatos, G., and Sokou, K. (2021). US-Greece relations in the Biden era: Why the road to rebuilding the transatlantic alliance runs through Athens. *Atlantic Council*, February 19. www.atlanticcouncil.org/blogs/new-atlanticist/us-greece-relations-in-the-bi den-era-why-the-road-to-rebuilding-the-transatlantic-alliance-runs-through-athens/.

Panagiotopoulos, P., and Sotiropoulos, D.P. (2020). *Political and Cultural Aspects of Greek Exoticism*. Basingstoke: Palgrave Macmillan. https://doi.org/10.1007/978-3-030-19864-0.

Pappas, T. (2014). *Populism and Crisis-Politics in Greece*. Basingstoke: Palgrave Macmillan.

Rori, L. (2005). Crises et conflits dans les relations gréco-turques des années 1974–2000: l'attitude des socialistes grecs. *Cahiers de la Méditerranée*, 71(2), 49–61.

Rori, L. (2016). The 2015 Greek parliamentary elections: From great expectations to no expectations. *West European Politics*, 39(6), 1323–1343. https://doi.org/10.1080/ 01402382.2016.1171577.

Rori, L. (2020). The 2019 Greek parliamentary elections: Retour à la normale . *West European Politics*, 43(4), 1023–1037. https://doi.org/10.1080/01402382.2019. 1696608.

Rori, L., and Marantzidis, N. (2012). Sinistra e destra in Grecia dal XX al XXI secolo. *Memoria e Ricerca*, 41, 69–83.

Sotiropoulos, D.A. (2017) *The Greek Civil Society and the Financial Crisis*. Athens: Potamos (in Greek).

Sotiropoulos, D.A. (2020) State-society relations in Greece. In K. Featherstone, and D.A. Sotiropoulos (Eds.), *The Oxford Handbook of Modern Greek Politics* (pp. 38–54). Oxford: Oxford University Press. doi:10.1093/oxfordhb/ 9780198825104.013.3.

Spanou, C. (2020). Public administration. In K. Featherstone, and D.A. Sotiropoulos (Eds.), *The Oxford Handbook of Modern Greek Politics* (pp. 170–186). Oxford: Oxford University Press. doi:10.1093/oxfordhb/9780198825104.013.11.

Stavrakakis, Y., and Katsambekis, G. (2014). Left-wing populism in the European periphery: The case of SYRIZA. *Journal of Political Ideologies*, 19(2), 119–142. https://doi.org/10.1080/13569317.2014.909266.

Theocharis, Y., and van Deth, J.W. (2015). A modern tragedy? Institutional causes and democratic consequences of the Greek crisis. *Representation*, 51(1), 63–79. https://doi.org/10.1080/00344893.2015.1011464.

Tsirbas, Y. (2020). The party system. In K. Featherstone, and D.A. Sotiropoulos (Eds.), *The Oxford Handbook of Modern Greek Politics* (pp. 219–238). Oxford: Oxford University Press. doi:10.1093/oxfordhb/9780198825104.013.14.

5 Prime minister and state strategy

On the risks and value of simplicity, in response to endemic crisis

Ioannis A. Tassopoulos

Introduction

The financial crisis, or Greek crisis, of 2009/2010 hit the Greek political system in an explosive way. But during the crisis, the country's constitutional institutions showed considerable resilience. Through a series of appeals to the popular vote, they eventually led to the restoration of political balance and stability, culminating a decade later in the formation of a one-party government led by Nea Demokratia (ND—New Democracy) in 2019. To understand this course of events, a crucial factor is the extreme simplicity of the Greek constitutional structure: there is a unicameral Vouli (parliament); an electoral system that until recently has facilitated stable governments; an all-powerful prime minister and no constitutional court. It is posited that this simplicity developed partly as an institutional response to the need for a clear, legitimate and politically responsible answer to the constantly recurring priority of protecting the strategic interests of the state, which in Greece usually fall under the rubric of 'national issues'.

The point is that crisis is endemic to Greece (Tassopoulos, 2020: 84–97). The economic crisis was rapidly succeeded by the refugee crisis which, besides the humanitarian aspect, developed features of a hybrid conflict over control of the borders; then came the coronavirus (COVID-19) pandemic; followed by the stand-off with Turkey over the exclusive economic zone, which brought the two countries to the brink of war and triggered a new arms race (Dertilis, 2009: 70; Nikolaidou, 2016: 18–27) in Greece. The refugee crisis and the migrant movement in the Aegean and Eastern Mediterranean have a strong geopolitical dimension; the latter stretching to the limits an economy that had already suffered from the blows of COVID-19.

Greece's institutional response to the challenge of these crises has focused on the office of the prime minister, who bears full political responsibility in an unequivocal manner and in the most genuine sense of the word *political*, which involves strategic assessment and choice in an uncertain and risky international environment.

This chapter discusses three central problems that were strongly exacerbated by the Greek crisis: the lack of economic rationality of political

DOI: 10.4324/9780429202247-7

decision-making, the neo-Nazi extremism of Chrysi Avgi (Golden Dawn) that emerged as a result of the breakdown of the political system, and the lack of a priori judicial review of the legality of referendums on critical national issues, which dilutes the responsibility of the prime minister, deviating from the main institutional response of Greek constitutionalism to the political challenge of crisis.

The fundamental simplicity of the constitutional relations between the main organs of the state, where the prime minister is the predominant power holder, has been a source of risks for the macroeconomic stability of the country, because there were no sufficient checks and balances to prevent the accumulation of public debt. At the same time this does allow immediate and effective action to be taken to address the Greek crisis in line with the strategic and geopolitical choice of the state to remain in the eurozone.

The development of European economic governance (see Chapter 3 in this volume) in response to the crisis addresses the most severe aspects of macroeconomic stability; it is the government that bears the primary responsibility to meet the country's obligations for membership of the eurozone. Meanwhile, the Golden Dawn trial in 2020 showed that the Greek Constitution can combine extended protection of political parties with defence of democracy against a criminal organization that was operating under the guise of a political party. But the problem of insufficient guarantees for referendums on crucial national matters remains open and imperils the state's geopolitical interests. This institutional aberration highlighted by the crisis needs to be fixed by the introduction of the appropriate legislation.

The institutional simplicity of Greek constitutionalism, the centrality of the prime minister's office and the Greek crisis

The Greek Constitution of 1975 (Art. 1, para. 1) defines Greece as a 'presidential parliamentary republic'. The constitutional identity of the Greek state (Tassopoulos, 2018: 155) has been crystallized through a turbulent historical and political process. The current Constitution of 1975, as amended, goes back to the Constitution of 1864, being formally the outcome of the fifth revision of the latter. Of course, in the meantime, various other regimes (constitutional or dictatorial) have been tried; but it was the Constitution of 1864 that defined the features of the state. The original Constitution of 1864 contains the main structural elements of simplicity: a strict Constitution; popular sovereignty; the unicameral parliament for the representation of the people; and universal suffrage. Greece not only has a very long electoral history (Pantelis et al., 2010: Table 2.1), going back to 1844, but, in addition, universal suffrage has been accepted without back and forth as in France, and even without a long process of 'progressive improvement' as in the United Kingdom (Milet, 2017: 10). A striking feature of Greek constitutional politics is the 'premature' and 'consensual' acceptance (i.e. without strong socio-political opposition) of universal suffrage since the electoral law of

1844 with only a few exceptions (Sotirelis, 1991: 41), and in the Constitution of 1864. This is a contested issue because it involves the 'blurred boundaries' of liberalism and democracy in the country (Tassopoulos, 2007a: 20). It is beyond doubt, however, that this long tradition of elections on universal suffrage gradually consolidated democratic legitimacy as the sole foundation of political legitimacy in Greece. But this has not been a smooth process.

The most important complicating factor in the development of democratic constitutionalism in Greece was the role of the monarchy. During the 19th century, under the reign of King George 1, the monarchy certainly played an important political role, but it adapted, even if with considerable resistance (in the course of the severe political crisis of 1874–1875), to the entrenchment of parliamentarism in Greece, ultimately by appointing Charilaos Trikoupis as prime minister in 1875, and by accepting that the choice of prime minister should be made on the basis of the 'declared confidence' of parliament, i.e. a parliamentary majority. This adaptability of the throne contributed to the development of *inclusive constitutionalism*, which maintained the fundamental political checks and balances associated with the dissolution of parliament on the initiative of the monarchy, in the rare case of a serious conflict between the king and the prime minister on a fundamental issue involving the international position of the country and the national interest. But the experiment of inclusive constitutionalism (Tassopoulos, 2006) broke down when King Konstantinos (Constantine) I tried to impose constitutional enclaves of exclusive royal power beyond the reach of parliamentary majorities and the prime minister on strategic issues directly involving foreign relations and national defence. In 1915, a constitutional crisis erupted between the king and Prime Minister Venizelos regarding the participation of Greece in the First World War.

War and geopolitics were the catalyst for the 'national schism', as the conflict over Greece's participation in the First World War came to be known. The critical constitutional language required reinterpretation according to the principle of popular sovereignty.[1] Consequently, the democratic authority, i.e. the prime minister, rather than the hereditary king, should prevail in the case of disagreement between them, so long as the king had given the people the opportunity to express themselves through the dissolution of parliament (Tassopoulos, 2006: 260). In a book published in 1924, Emmanouel Emmanouelides, who had the extraordinary "good" fortune during those turbulent years to serve both as a deputy from the broader region of Smyrna in the Ottoman parliament of 1914 (Emmanouelides, 1924: 304) and in the Fourth Constituent Assembly in Greece in 1924, aptly summed up national schism thus: 'Greece was organizing elections at a time when the world was fighting one of the most critical conflicts ever mentioned in history' (ibid.: 278).

The great polarization of the national schism undermined and ultimately subverted the minimum consensus required for a system of checks and balances to work properly without threatening constitutional stability and coordination. This situation continued in post-war Greece as well, culminating in a confrontation between the monarchy and the prime minister in 1965, during the Cold War, when the king violated the principle of 'declared confidence' concerning the appointment of the prime minister, in an attempt to shatter the governing parliamentary majority and replace it with another more aligned to the vigorously anti-communist ideology of the Cold War. A military dictatorship under Col Georgios Papadopoulos followed as a consequence of this thorough discrediting of parliamentary governance.

The 50-year-long bitter experience with the undemocratic attitude of the monarchy hastened its abolition and the introduction of the republic in 1974. This resulted in a typical example of what Richard Albert has called 'constitutional dismemberment' (Albert, 2018).[2] A major flank of the 1864/1952 Constitution (the hereditary form of parliamentarism) was left pending, to be decided by referendum, although this was not consistent with the revisionary character of the Assembly, which drafted and enacted the Constitution of 1975. The theory of dismemberment offers a third way to resolve the dilemma between the two extreme poles of a wholly new Constitution, which replaces the older order altogether, and full compliance with the amended provisions of the revised Constitution. The decision to establish a republic in the December 8, 1974 referendum was a huge stride towards further *simplification* of the political regime and the constitutional structure of Greece, in support of democratic consolidation.

However, the Constitution of 1975 tried to combine the removal of the greatest impediment to constitutional stability, i.e. the monarchy, with the entrenchment of sufficient checks and balances which would mitigate the simplicity of Greek constitutionalism by incorporating the traditional prerogative of the head of state to dissolve parliament, and in addition to hold a referendum, whose timing, question and subject would be determined by the president of the republic. Indeed, many considered the ability to hold a referendum as the president's most significant power (Tassopoulos, 2007b: 58–59), because it could establish a bond of direct political legitimacy between the president and the people, even in opposition to parliament and the prime minister. For a decade, however, the Constitution operated as a typical parliamentary republic, with all the power concentrated in the hands of the prime minister.

Nevertheless, the urge for simplicity and the fear that at an opportune time the 'superpowers' of the president could lead to abuses similar to those of the monarchy in the past led to the constitutional revision of 1986, which rendered the office of the president ceremonial in character, thus abolishing the right to dissolve parliament and also the presidential referendum, which was replaced with the governmental referendum. Indeed, the drive for simplicity was so overwhelming that even when the text of the Constitution explicitly allowed the president to exercise mild forms of checks and balances, e.g. in the case of legislative veto, whose consequence was merely to remand the law for a second vote requiring an absolute majority of the total number of votes in parliament (Art. 42, para. 1 of the Greek Constitution), even then the veto power of the president fell into desuetude.

From 1986 to the eruption of the Greek crisis in 2009, the simplicity of Greek constitutional order took the form of the central position of the prime minister in a political system of parliamentary self-regulation whereby the majority party was in full control of the parliamentary game. In addition, the two-party political system was further consolidated by the electoral laws which strengthened the first party (under normal circumstances, at about 10%–15%, over its proportion of the seats) (Clogg, 1987: 201–203) in order to ensure the stability of the government. The only remaining weak counter-weight of power is judicial review, according to the American diffused model, whose origins in Greece go back to 1897. The Greek system of judicial review is dominated by the Council of State, so as to ensure the fundamental rights of the citizens.

The Greek prime minister is simultaneously the head of government, the leader of his or her political party, the leader of the parliamentary majority, and the sole bearer of quasi-direct democratic legitimacy through the holding of general elections (in a country with no tradition of mitigating institutions of direct democracy, e.g. popular initiatives or referendums). The office of the prime minister in Greece has all the critical attributes which give his or her English counterpart a powerful position (Carter, 1956: 331–343). Institu-tionally, the office is the most prestigious one, particularly after the abolition of the president's powers in the 1986 constitutional amendment; the incum-bent prime minister and his or her counterpart in the Opposition, are the dominant personalities who are portrayed as the future leaders of the coun-try, anointed by popular vote. In Greece, political parties are excessively centralized and dependent on their (usually) charismatic leaders with no tradition or practice of intraparty democracy; the political leader can exercise full disciplinary power over dissenting party members, e.g. by preventing them from standing as party candidates in elections, without affording any legal protection to the affected politicians, who are more or less doomed to electoral defeat as a result of such exclusion. The prime minister chooses freely the timing of a snap election, thus denying the ability of members of parliament to dissolve parliament. Finally, the prime minister makes the main political decisions on public policy. In political and constitutional practice, Greek prime ministers have occasionally made full use of all the powers available to them.

During the Greek crisis, the central position of parliamentary elections as a source of political legitimacy was illustrated by the density of political events, in a parallel manner to the intensity of the crisis. Between 2009 and 2019, Greece held six general elections, three elections to the European Par-liament, and one referendum on July 5, 2015. In early 2012, when the poli-tical system was in total disarray, with one of the two dominant political parties losing its central role, as the Panellinio Socialistiko Kinima (PASOK—Panhellenic Socialist Movement) vote plummeted, and with the other (ND) fragmented, new political parties emerged or acquired a central role (Synaspismos Rizospastikis Aristeras—SYRIZA, Coalition of the Radical Left), at the right and left of the political spectrum. However, the most noteworthy development was certainly the rising power of Golden Dawn, an extremist neo-Nazi organization that was active in the political process in the guise of a political party with disruptive parliamentary tactics and violent practices. Evidently, these political developments, in the context of massive unemployment, the loss of about one-quarter of the national income, consecutive cuts in salaries and pensions, combined with heavy taxation, could easily destabilize the country's democratic and constitutional order. After all, the institutional structure of the Constitution depends on the political system, on societal consensus and on international stability. None of these factors existed during the Greek crisis.

And yet the value of simplicity and flexibility helped the constitutional order to survive and to achieve a second major turnover of power from ND (on the right) to SYRIZA (on the left). The Constitution showed surprising resilience (Contiades and Fotiadou, 2016: 106) in times of severe crisis. George Katrougalos, a professor of constitutional law and a minister in the SYRIZA government, argued on several occasions in favour of a constituent assembly which would endow Greece with a new Constitution, through the political participation of the people, in the process of constitution-making (Katrougalos, 2014; for a sympathetic critique see Chrysogonos, 2013: 213–216). But any political momentum for such a proposal evaporated as SYRIZA came closer to power. The simplicity of the constitutional order combined with accumulated authority and established legitimacy is preferable to any uncertain experimentation of constituent power. If the first swing from ND to PASOK, in the historical election of 1981, confirmed the consolidation (Milet, 2017: 265) of the democratic transition from authoritarian democracy under the Constitution of 1952 and dictatorship to full and inclusive democracy, it was the election in 2015 between ND and SYRIZA that belied all the conjecture about Greece sharing the fate of the Weimar Republic, not only because the European context was different, but because Greece had a strong democratic tradition of constitutionally guaranteed elections. The Greek crisis proved that the simplicity of Greece's constitutional design was invaluable.

The geopolitical hard core of the prime minister's powers

If we think of the factors which explain the evolution of the office of the prime minister in Greece we must take into account both the institutional logic of parliamentary government according to the Westminster model (Lijphart, 1999: 10), and the political and constitutional history of the country, described in the previous section.

The power of the Greek prime minister concerns the 'centralization of decisions' (Featherstone and Papadimitriou, 2015: 13). Our focus is not on the power of the prime minister to implement decisions down the bureaucratic ladder. It does not concern *managerial* effectiveness (ibid.: 14). The prime minister's lack of effectiveness as the head of a notoriously inefficient bureaucracy does not come as a surprise. By contrast, his power to *govern* is particularly impressive. The Constitution (Art. 82, para. 1) provides that 'The Government shall define and direct the general policy of the Country, in accordance with the provisions of the Constitution and the laws'. The prime minister came to occupy an absolutely central position in the Greek system of government. Political power and the responsibility of the prime minister for the actions and omissions of the government is not shared under these institutional arrangements: it is historical, 'strategic' (Bobbitt, 2002: 335–336)[3] and personal, resting on the prime minister's shoulders. The prime minister is fully accountable for the consequences of the government's decisions. According to Gaddis,

> grand strategy [is] the alignment of potentially unlimited aspirations with necessary limited capabilities. ... Whatever balance you strike, there'll be a link between what's real and what's imagined: between your current location and your intended destination. You won't have a strategy until you've connected these dots—dissimilar though they are—within the situation in which you're operating.
>
> (2018: 21)

The most suitable contrast is between Greece and Italy, in the light of the strong influence of clientelism in both countries, which 'affects the exercise of leadership' (Featherstone and Papadimitriou, 2015: 17). In Greece, particularly during the Third Greek Republic, i.e. since 1974, the rule is that the prime minister is chosen by the people on the day of a general election, because the electoral law provides that the leading party has, in all likelihood, an absolute majority in parliament, and even if it does not, it will be the predominant political force whose leader will be the next prime minister in a coalition government. By contrast, in Italy, prior to the change in the electoral system in 1993, the political parties chose the prime minister as a result of negotiations among them. Therefore, the legitimacy of the Greek prime minister, being virtually direct, is much stronger than that of his Italian counterpart (Cassese, 2014: 31, 82). This quasi-direct democratic legitimacy of the Greek prime minister is the background to his control over the 'indirizzo politico' (ibid.: 76, 42).[4] In Greece, a crucial part of 'political leadership' (Voulgaris, 2019: 236) concerns *security* (on internal security see Borgeas, 2013; on external security see Dokos, 2016); the impact of the latter on the constitutional power structure has been shaped by historical experience.

Greece emerged as an independent nation out of the disintegration of the Ottoman Empire, and its national integration was inherently associated with the Eastern question, i.e. the post-Ottoman state of affairs. Since gaining its independence in 1830, national integration, i.e. the inclusion of Greek populations within the national borders, has been a central priority of the Greek state, marked by major successes and failures.[5] The small size, the immense aspirations and the geostrategic position of the country at the beginning of the 19th century explain why, among the various forms of interest, be they general, social or public, the *national* interest has traditionally been very effective in Greece.[6] Since 1974, the national policy has been firmly one of stability in accordance with the imperatives of international law (in favour of legality, rather than the realist balance of power) (on human rights in Cyprus see Hathaway and Shapiro, 2017: 382–385).

The renewal of the popular mandate on 'national issues' (e.g. the economy, relations with Greece's neighbours, etc.) offers the usual basis for the dissolution of parliament and the holding of snap elections (Art. 41, para. 2 of the Greek Constitution).Traditionally, an important part of the discussion about national issues takes place in Greece in terms of the country's 'dependence' (Voulgaris, 2019: 145; Reinhart and Trebesch, 2015: 307–328) on the Great Powers, originally European, and then the United States. The focus of this discussion is on their intervention and their political and economic pressure, which distorts the democratic process by pre-empting political decision-making.

But 'dependence' is a very narrow and defensive approach towards a much broader perspective on the influence of *geopolitics* in Greece. Only recently has this issue been identified as a defining factor of Greek political and constitutional life. This theorizing is necessary for a deeper understanding of the forces which shape constitutionalism and explain the performance of democratic institutions in Greece. In an important study, Yannis Voulgaris has put the matter squarely: 'Greece is a geopolitical nation' (2019: 141). Voulgaris argues persuasively that geopolitics played 'a constitutive role' (ibid.: 149) in 19th- and 20th-century Greece. He distinguishes three phases: first, the period 1821–1913 that was dominated by the Eastern question; second, the period 1914–1949 up to 1989 that witnessed the great ideological conflicts of fascism, liberalism and communism that divided the West; and third, the most recent period of globalization that was marked by the development of supra-nationalism in the process of European integration (ibid.: 145).

Of course, the influence of geopolitics is not a peculiarly Greek phenomenon. A typical example of the connection between political institutions and the national problem of a country is offered by the rise and fall of the Weimar Republic, following the humiliating Versailles Treaty, at the end of the First World War. But what is probably less common is the *relative stability* of democratic institutions, and primarily of general elections, in face of the national crises which hit Greece every now and then. As mentioned above, parliamentary elections are the source of political legitimacy under conditions of national unity; and furthermore they are the catalyst that explains the strong position of the prime minister. The so-called political direction, the governmental function, is overwhelmingly important in times of emergency.

The position of the Greek prime minister is weak, as stated earlier, only in the very important aspect of managerial effectiveness for the simple reason that Greek public administration is relatively inefficient and cumbersome (Featherstone and Papadimitriou, 2015). But, in the light of our previous discussion of the character of Greece as a geopolitical nation, even though the British prime minister does play a central role in matters of foreign policy and in war situations (Carter, 1956: 295), nevertheless, the Greek prime minister has a more marked strategic position and role, proportional to differences in the size, strength and geography of the two countries. The Greek prime minister is responsible for the nation and the state in a qualitative manner which seems to combine the powers of the British prime minister with the peculiar responsibility of the French president of the republic (Roussellier, 2015: 590–591) for the vital interests of the state and of the nation, understood over and beyond ephemeral party politics.

It is not an exaggeration to argue that the Greek prime minister is in dialogue with history, and this is a duty and burden that, depending on political events, the prime minister can hardly repudiate. Certainly, this aspect of the office of the prime minister in Greece has its pros and cons. Among the latter is the hubris of excessive power, i.e. the cultivation of traits of personality usually associated with the corruptive effects of concentrated power on a person's character (arrogance, distancing from the common man, distorted sense of mission, vulnerability to flattery, intolerance of institutionalized or personal political dissent, and, of course, the craving for even greater power). Among the former is the sense of responsibility (the burden of historical judgement, the concern for the best exercise of practical reason, the effort to build consensus on the basis of broad deliberation and accurate information, etc.). Evidently, these pros and cons are opposite features, and a major vulnerability of the Greek system is its excessive exposure to, and dependence on, the prime minister's personal traits.

A system of mature constitutionalism should be able to minimize and control the nefarious effects of personality. Seen from this perspective, the notorious procrastination in the labyrinth of Greek bureaucratic legalism and the exasperating inefficiency of Greek bureaucracy may have, at the limit, a 'benign' negative effect, so to speak, by being able to dilute and to downscale inimical reforms, operating as an effective veto. Yet, if one asks how and why the system has evolved to reach this fundamental simplicity regarding grand politics, the answer seems to be concealed, at least in part, in the institutional requirements associated with a state of emergency and severe crisis, impregnated with geopolitical risks. Referring to the prime minister in a state of emergency, Carter writes:

> He would act; he would take responsibility; perhaps he took too much responsibility, but that was infinitely better than a Prime Minister who took little. War requires that the Prime Minister exercise all his power. It is not possible to rely upon brilliant colleagues, for decisions will not

wait for discussion nor will it wait for proposals to go through the 'regular channels.' ... War requires a concentration of power and responsibility.[7]

(1956: 330)

The lack of economic rationality and the development of European economic governance

The interplay between the prime minister's political empowerment and managerial weakness is central to understanding the performance of Greek democracy leading up to and during the crisis. Once the crisis started unravelling rapidly, the effectiveness of invoking the national interest combined with the emergency powers of the executive marks the efforts to tackle the crisis. The most drastic way to pursue reform or to introduce unpopular policies in Greece is through the realistic invocation of the national interest. Indeed, the Greek economic crisis was also a profound national crisis.

Regarding the emergency powers of the executive, the Greek Constitution, in its course towards simplicity, has gone all the way through to the end of this logic, accepting the bitter with the sweet. The executive in the combined form of the president of the republic with the cabinet, upon the proposal of the latter, has the power to legislate by issuing 'Acts of Legislative Content' (Art. 44, para. 1 of the Greek Consitution), in cases of unforeseen emergency, without the intervention of the legislature, which can sanction or annul them within a basic deadline of 40 days following their publication. As a result, during the crisis, Greek governments made excessive use (Chrysogonos, 2013: 57) of their legislative powers by taking the initiative to enact swiftly and summarily thousands of pages of a great variety of austerity measures (Manitakis, 2020: 93). The combination of political legitimacy and extremely drastic legislative means in the hands of the executive explains how the Greek state was able to meet within the framework of the Constitution the unprecedented challenges of the crisis both at the politico-legislative level and at the legal-constitutional one.

If the availability of strong emergency powers is one side of the coin, the other is the political legitimacy to utilize them in order to implement austerity measures. As on other historical occasions, Greece reacted promptly to shaken political legitimacy, because of the unpopular measures of austerity, by holding elections over and again to the bewilderment of many observers, who justifiably considered the disruptive effect of the electoral process on the efforts towards achieving economic recovery (Alcidi and Gros, 2015; Granitsas et al., 2014; Elliott, 2015).[8] But fresh victory in polarized and contested polls animates the traditional political voluntarism of Greek political and constitutional culture (Contiades and Fotiadou, 2016: 78). Associated with the Jacobin ethos (Tassopoulos, 2013: 74), excessive voluntarism relies on a self-referential conception of popular sovereignty, which aims at implementing the political will of the people in a direct and decisive manner.

Accordingly, institutional constraints, state agreements and conditions, which frame and ultimately shape the will of people, tend to be discarded or considered as a sort of undemocratic impediment. The first semester of 2015, when SYRIZA came to power, offered a full-scale view of this mentality, illustrated in the way in which Minister of Finance Varoufakis (2017: 233–238, 386) treated (and was treated by) his colleagues, with nearly catastrophic consequences for Greece's economy and the strategic value of the state's membership of the eurozone.

Jacobin voluntarism withers the resistance of political prudence and leads to flawed judgement. External standards of correctness, regarding the goals of the state (e.g. in maintaining macroeconomic stability; redistributing wealth according to accepted criteria of social justice; and regulating the markets to enhance competitiveness along with environmental protection) tend to be ignored, or subordinated, to political expediency and to the predominant, if not exclusive, political goal of winning elections. As a result, a simplistic and one-sided notion of democratic legitimacy prevails, according to which 'a decision [of the authorities] is right, because it is supported by the majority', instead of a more multifaceted one, according to which 'the majority makes a decision, because the decision seems to be right, for a number of valid reasons'. The Greek crisis was the natural outcome of this declining rationality of political decision-making, under the influence of an idea of political legitimacy that was oblivious to the public interest, which ultimately depends on external criteria of correctness for the resolution of real social problems. Greece's de facto default marked a destructive failure to harmonize politics with the economy (Tassopoulos, 2014: 322, 326).

During the crisis a number of institutions were introduced (see also Chapter 8 in this volume) thus ensuring that the government had all the necessary information and advice to avoid repetition of the catastrophic economic decisions which led to the de facto default of the country in 2009–2010. Greece, being traditionally a parliamentary state, does not hold referendums regarding changes to the European treaties; the process is contained within parliament, and the (usually stable) government exercises almost exclusive control regarding the obligations arising from EU membership, enacting legislation or pursuing specific public policies. To comply with the obligations resulting from the reform of European economic governance,[9] in response to the crisis, Law 4270/2014, Art. 2, created an Independent Administrative Authority, the Hellenic Fiscal Council (HFC), which started its work in November 2015. The HFC reports to the Greek parliament when requested or when required before a Parliamentary Committee. Furthermore, Law 4270/2014, Art. 28 confirmed the parliament's State Budget Office (PBO) established in 2010. The office is responsible for monitoring the implementation of the state budget and assists in the workings of the Special Committee of the Greek Parliament on the Financial Statement and the General Balance Sheet.

To address managerial deficiencies, the third MOU (i.e. that of 2015, following those of 2012 and 2010) set the goal of strengthening the power of the central government and of the public sector more generally (see also Chapter 8 in this volume).[10] The ND government in 2019 immediately introduced legislation establishing the *epiteliko kratos* ('executive state')[11] that enhanced the organization, function and transparency of government, governmental organs and central public administration. The challenge for any reform programme in Greece is for the state to play a directive and coordinating role, without increasing the layers of state bureaucracy or bypassing the ministries.

The inopportune comparisons with Weimar Republic and the Golden Dawn trial

As a result of the crisis, Greek constitutional order faced another novel and major challenge following the electoral success of the far-right party, Golden Dawn. Again, in the spirit of simplicity, the prevailing opinion among the courts,[12] commentators and practice was that the Constitution does not allow the enactment of a statute that outlaws undemocratic political parties, despite the language of the Constitution which provides that the organization and action of political parties must serve the free functioning of democratic government.[13] The rebuff of statutory outlawing of political parties has been regarded as a guarantee of the inclusive constitutionalism inaugurated at the collapse of the military junta in reaction to the post-civil war exclusive constitutionalism, whereby the Communist Party of Greece was outlawed in 1947. In that sense, the broad constitutional protection of political parties has been one of the foundations of the democratic constitutional order since 1974. In the light of this background, the political and legal systems of the country hesitated about how to confront the threat to democracy posed by the neo-Nazi sympathizers.

Golden Dawn is regarded as an ultranationalist political party by its supporters, or as a flagrantly neo-Nazi criminal organization by its opponents, and allegedly undertakes clandestine activities seeking to overthrow the democratic constitutional order. At the general election on May 6, 2012, which shattered the two-party political system dominated by ND and PASOK, Golden Dawn garnered approximately 440,000 votes, and in the two elections of 2015 it emerged as the country's third largest political party. Many observers drew comparisons between Greece and the Weimar Republic, ignoring the former's long tradition with elections. At the election in 2019 Golden Dawn failed to enter parliament.

Golden Dawn escalated the already too high level of political violence in Greece to an unprecedented degree, threatening the legitimate power of the citizenry, which is the negation of violence, as a means to resolve political conflicts. Members of Golden Dawn were responsible for brutal attacks against immigrants and workers, culminating in the murder of an anti-fascist rapper in 2015. The solution to the legal predicament was contained in Article 187 of the Penal Code which outlaws criminal organizations.

The Golden Dawn trial lasted for more than five years and in 2020 its leadership was found guilty and gaoled for directing a criminal organization responsible for a number of crimes, including homicide. The Golden Dawn trial proved that the 1975 Constitution does not leave Greek democracy unprotected against neo-Nazi parties, which organize paramilitary corps and raid battalions, and carry out racist attacks. Precisely because a law that leads to a ban on a political party is not allowed by the Constitution, the effective protection of democracy and fundamental rights requires the correct, fair, but also strict application of penal law prohibiting criminal organizations. The Golden Dawn trial showed the resilience of the Greek Constitution against neo-Nazi political violence.

The need for immediate legislative reform: the experience of the referendum of July 5, 2015

Probably the dramatic peak of the Greek crisis was the referendum of July 5, 2015. The SYRIZA government opted to vote 'no' to the question of whether to accept the terms of the agreement for the third bailout for Greece in a referendum that was hastily organized and held within about a week from its announcement, over a highly technical question, whose timeliness was quite questionable, because the terms of the negotiations had already changed by the time of the referendum. In Greece, the 'no' vote, although overwhelming (61.31%), was not interpreted as a mandate for Greece to leave the eurozone and perhaps the European Union, but as a mandate to negotiate. Allegedly, the referendum strengthened the prime minister's position vis-à-vis the country's European partners. In reality, however, strong cross-party parliamentary support in favour of Greece remaining in the eurozone played a catalytic role in the developments that led to the final agreement on the third bailout of Greece in mid-2015.

The July 2015 referendum had a lot of constitutional problems regarding the validity of the question as well as the short time for deliberation (Contiades and Fotiadou, 2016: 171). But there was no legal basis providing for a priori control of the question and the procedure of the referendum. Consequently, it was hardly possible for any institution of the state (such as the president of the republic or the courts[14]) to stop the 2015 referendum as unlawful. Fortunately, no such attempt was made, which would have rekindled political divisions and discord over democracy and foreign policy. This is because the referendum, in my opinion, sent the message that the period when the people were excluded from foreign policy questions was over; and, instead of the old dependence on foreign powers, which controlled Greek politics, the government had turned to the people, asking them to express their will on a crucial national matter. As a result, the referendum broke a big taboo on the limits of democratization, fortunately without irreparable consequences for the country. Nonetheless, the agreement on the third bailout did eventually test the limits of political voluntarism. The prime minister assumed the historical, political and legal responsibility for holding the referendum and dealing with the outcome.

The problem is that referendums are prone to anti-parliamentary abuses. A comparison of Britain in relation to the Brexit referendum of 2016 and Greece in relation to the referendum of 2015 suffices to show the danger of populist voluntarism that accompanies the institution of referendum. Contrary to Greece, the Brexit vote was interpreted to justify, if not impose, Britain's withdrawal from the EU, whatever the costs and consequences. But to the extent that the cost of Brexit was not known at the referendum, invoking its outcome to justify Brexit *at all costs*, just does not make sense. It is the parliamentary government's responsibility to assess the consequences for the nation.

The referendum is momentary, simplistic and fragmentary; it is institutionally inapposite to address so complex an issue and of such a historical magnitude as the participation of a nation in the process of European integration. Moreover, for a 'geopolitical nation' like Greece, constitutional design on matters of strategy requires strengthening in every possible way the historical and political responsibility of the prime minister and of the governing political majority in parliament, instead of having this responsibility diffused, through the referendum, and evaporating in the name of the 'united and indivisible' popular will. Strategic decisions in a country with serious geopolitical challenges, such as Greece, must entail the corresponding political responsibility of parliamentary majorities, for the ensuing consequences. The great deficit of referendum versus parliamentarism is that parliamentarism retains the political responsibility of the rulers, whereas the referendum offers an alibi to evade it.

Greece must provide for a priori judicial review of the question and the process of the referendum on national matters. This does not require constitutional amendment. The Constitution does not determine the referendum's a priori or a posteriori judicial review. The law[15] provides for ineffective a posteriori judicial review of the validity of the referendum and of its results, by recourse to the Special Supreme Court in accordance with Art. 100 of the Greek Constitution, which operates as a court for electoral disputes. The result of a referendum for a critical national issue is binding (Art. 16, para. 3 of Law 4023/2011), if at least 40% of the electorate goes to the polls.

It is obvious that the regulation of the referendum in Greece is deficient and needs to be revised to ensure that a referendum on national questions is *advisory* [16] and not obligatory; with full and effective a priori judicial review; over a properly formulated question; with ample time for deliberation. But the prime minister and the governing political forces bear full and integral responsibility for the geopolitical consequences of their eventual choice.

Conclusion

The simplicity of institutions and structural relationships has shaped the Greek constitutional order, culminating under the Constitution of 1975 in a self-regulating political system and a strong version of party democracy without checks and balances. The office of the Greek prime minister is crystallized through historical, political and constitutional evolution. The Greek crisis posed for Greek constitutional order at least three major threats and challenges: (1) the disjunction of political decisions from economic rationality, over a period of many years, which resulted into the de facto default of the state in 2010; (2) the challenge of neo-Nazi criminal violence by a political organization, which took advantage of the prohibition of legislation outlawing political parties; and (3) the lack of checks and balances over the conformity of a national referendum with the Greek Constitution. All three of these challenges resulted out the same choice for simplicity, partly explained by the country's strategic and geopolitical exigencies, which necessitate clear-cut and integral political responsibility for decision-making.

European economic governance, as a result of the eurozone crisis, provided the response to the first challenge, i.e. the tendency of the Greek political system to compromise on macroeconomic stability for short-term political advantages. The question remains whether political legitimacy requires rationality and efficiency for the acceptability of political decisions. Owing to the Jacobin element of Greece's political and constitutional culture, the mere fact of establishing institutions with the task of enhancing the economic rationality of political decisions is by no means a guarantee of their success.

The challenge of anti-democratic political parties in a way consistent with the fundamentals of the Constitution was met successfully from within the legal system, as shown by the historic Golden Dawn trial. But the last remaining open question still lacks a satisfactory answer: whether it is valid for institutional checks and balances to secure a priori judicial review of advisory referendums, without offering the prime minister an opportunity to shift the burden of responsibility for geostrategic choices from his or her shoulders to the people.

Notes

1 Art. 31 of the Constitution 1864/1911 provided that 'The king appoints and dismisses his ministers'.
2 Albert (2018: 4): 'A constitutional dismemberment alters a fundamental right, a load-bearing structure, or a core feature of the identity of a constitution. It is a constitutional change understood by political actors and the people to be inconsistent with the constitution at the time the change is made. To use a rough shorthand, the purpose and effect of a constitutional dismemberment are the same: to unmake a constitution'.
3 Bobbit (2002: 353): 'By "strategic" I do not mean simply "planned" or "economic", but rather an approach that focuses on the use of force as the principal arbiter of international affairs'.
4 Barbera and Fusaro (2012: 252): 'Guidare verso il perseguimento di determinati fini di carattere generale una comunità politica – vale a dire imprimere a essa un determinato *indirizzo politico* – comporta poter incidere sia sulla produzione dei commandi normativi sia sulla loro successiva esecuzione. Guidare politicamente una comunità, se non vuol dire esercitare entrambi i poteri (di fare re leggi e di

attuarle), vuol dire certamente influire in misura determinante sull'uno e sull'altro'. Bin and Pitruzzella (2011: 77): 'Percio, si afferma una quarta funzione, che è la funzione di indirizzo politico. Esse consiste nella determinazione delle linee fondamentali di sviluppo dell'ordinamento e della politica interna ed esterna dello stato e nella cura della loro coerente attuazione'.

5 For example, the Balkan Wars (1912–1913), Asia Minor (1922). The geostrategic dimension has nourished Greek political romanticism. Spyridon Zambelios, who coined the term 'Greek-Christian', which became part of the official doctrine of the nation's cultural identity under the Constitution of 1952 (Art. 16), following the Civil War, was writing in 1857 (Zambelios, 1999: 686–687) that modern Greek life, more than any other medieval one, owed its existence and progress to reactive force against the East and the West.

6 See the invocation of an imperative national interest in the judgement upholding the constitutionality of the Memorandum of Understanding (MOU) for the first Greek bailout (2010), Council of State (*in pleno*) 668/2012 (para. 10).

7 The failure of the Karamanlis government to take adequate measures when the Greek crisis was imminent in 2008 confirms the position about the perils of inaction. Greece suffered from the inertia of the prime minister. For some early descriptions of the Greek crisis in the Athenian press, in December 2008, see Tassopoulos (2014: 317–318).

8 For an academic view of the impact of the 2014 polls, see (Sotiropoulos, 2014): 'While Greece survived a wave of economic and political shocks in 2010–2014, in the coming year political conflicts may put recent economic accomplishments at risk'.

9 Regulation (EU) No 473/2013 of the European Parliament and of the Council of May, 21, 2013 on common provisions for monitoring and assessing draft budgetary plans and ensuring the correction of excessive deficit of the member states in the euro area: Art.e 5 (independent bodies monitoring compliance with fiscal rules).

10 www.consilium.europa.eu/el/policies/financial-assistance-eurozone-members/greec e-programme/.

11 Law 4622/2019.

12 See in particular Areios Pagos 590/2009.

13 Art. 29, para. 1 of the Greek Constitution.

14 Council of State 2787/2015 (*in pleno*).

15 According to Law 4023/2011, the voter's preference is expressed on the question of the referendum, decided by parliament. The question must be stated in a clear and concise manner (Art. 3). There must be public dialogue with the participation of political parties and civil society (Art. 5). The ballot takes place 'within 30 days' from the publication of the presidential decree proclaiming the referendum, but the law does not set the minimum time of deliberation. Recourse is accepted within ten days following the publication of the referendum's final results in the *Official Gazette* (Art. 35, para. 5 of Law 345/1976).

16 The July 2015 referendum was treated as advisory. There is disagreement over the advisory or binding character of a referendum on a national matter; see e.g. Pantelis (2018: 447) on advisory, and Spyropoulos (2006: 196) on binding. In my opinion, it is legally advisory, but of course with very important political weight (a sort of a 'rebuttable presumption').

References

Albert, R. (2018). Constitutional amendment and dismemberment. *Yale Journal of International Law*, 43, 1–84.

Alcidi, C., and Gros, D. (2015). *The Greek Elections and the Third Bailout Programme: Why It Could Work This Time Round*, CEPS Commentary, September 21.

www.ceps.eu/wp-content/uploads/2015/09/Commentary%20CA+DG%20Greek%20 elections.pdf.

Barbera, A., and Fusaro, C. (2012). *Corso di diritto Costituzionale*, 2nd edn. Bologna: il Mulino.

Bin, R., and Pitruzzella, G. (2011). *Diritto Costituzionale*. Turin: Giappichelli.

Bobbitt, P. (2002). *The Shield of Achilles*. London: Penguin.

Borgeas, A. (2013). The evolution of Greece's security legislation and policy. *Journal of International and Comparative Law*, 3(2), 161–208. https://scholarship.law. stjohns.edu/cgi/viewcontent.cgi?article=1018&context=jicl.

Carter, B. (1956). *The Office of the Prime Minister*. Princeton, NJ: Princeton University Press.

Cassese, S. (2014). *Governare gli Italiani*. Bologna: il Mulino.

Chrysogonos, K. (2013). *The Circumvention of the Constitution*. Athens: Livanis (in Greek).

Clogg, R. (1987). *Parties and Elections in Greece*. London: Hurst.

Contiades, X., and Fotiadou, A. (2016). *The Resilience of the Constitution*. Athens-Thessaloniki: Sakkoulas (in Greek).

Dertilis, G. (2009). *History of the Greek State*, vol. 1. Athens: Estia (in Greek).

Dokos, T. (Ed.). (2016). *White Book on Greek Foreign Policy, Defence and Security*. ELIAMEP. Athens: Sideris (in Greek).

Elliott, L. (2015). Greece: The election is over, the economic crisis is not. *The Guardian*, September 20. www.theguardian.com/world/2015/sep/20/greece-the-election-is-o ver-the-economic-crisis-is-not.

Emmanouelides, E. (1924). *The Last Years of the Ottoman Empire*. Athens: Kallergis (in Greek).

Featherstone, K., and Papadimitriou, D. (2015). *Prime Ministers in Greece*. Oxford: Oxford University Press. doi:10.1093/acprof:oso/9780198717171.001.0001.

Gaddis, J.L. (2018). *On Grand Strategy*. London: Penguin.

Granitsas, A., Bouras, S., and Forelle, C. (2014). Greek vote for President fails, reviving uncertainty in London. *The Wall Street Journal*, December 29.www.wsj. com/articles/greece-to-face-early-elections-after-presidential-vote-fails-1419850337.

Hathaway, O., and Shapiro, S. (2017). *The Internationalists and Their Plan to Outlaw War*. London: Penguin.

Katrougalos, G. (2014). *A Way out from the Crisis*. April 12. www.Katrougalos.gr (in Greek).

Lijphart, A. (1999). *Patterns of Democracy*. New Haven, CT: Yale University Press.

Manitakis, A. (2020). *At the Twilight of 'Metapolitefsi'*. Athens: Epikentro (in Greek).

Milet, M. (2017). *La démocratie en Europe. Trajectoires et Enjeux*. Paris: Ellipses.

Nikolaidou, E. (2016). The role of military expenditure and arms imports in the Greek debt crisis. *The Economics of Peace and Security Journal*, 11(1), 18–27. http://dx.doi.org/10.15355/epsj.11.1.18.

Pantelis, A. (2018). *Manual of Constitutional Law*, 4th edn. Athens: Livanis (in Greek).

Pantelis, A., Koutsoubinas, S., and Gerapetritis, G. (2010). Greece. In D. Nohlen, and P. Stöver (Eds.), *Elections in Europe* (pp. 807–872). Baden Baden: Nomos.

Reinhart, C., and Trebesch C. (2015). The pitfalls of external dependence: Greece, 1829–2015. *Brookings Papers on Economic Activity*, 307–328). www.brookings.edu/ wp-content/uploads/2015/09/ReinhartTextFall15BPEA.pdf.

Roussellier, N. (2015). *La force de gouverner*. Paris: Gallimard.

Sotirelis, G. (1991). *Constitution and Elections in Greece 1864–1909*. Athens: Themelio (in Greek).

Sotiropoulos, D.A. (2014). Aftershocks: The political fallout of Greece's economic crisis. *World Politics Review*, November 18. https://greece-s-economic-crisis.

Spyropoulos, P. (2006). *Introduction to Constitutional Law*. Athens-Thessaloniki: Sakkoulas (in Greek).

Tassopoulos, I. (2006). The experiment of inclusive constitutionalism, 1909–1932. In P. Kitromilides (Ed.), *Eleftherios Venizelos: The Trials of Statesmanship* (pp. 251–272). Edinburgh: Edinburgh University Press.

Tassopoulos, I. (2007a). The ideological conversion to National Unity under the Greek Constitution of 1864. In A. Frangoudaki, and C. Keyder (Eds.), *Ways to Modernity in Greece and Turkey: Encounters with Europe 1850–1950* (pp. 9–25). London: Tauris.

Tassopoulos, I. (2007b). *Institutional Checks and Balances and Constitutional Revisions*. Athens-Thessaloniki: Sakkoulas (in Greek).

Tassopoulos, I. (2013). On the Jacobin dimension of Greek Constitutional tradition. In A. Triandafyllidou, R. Gropas, and H. Kouki (Eds.), *The Greek Crisis and European Modernity* (pp. 59–88). Basingstoke: Palgrave Macmillan. https://doi.org/10.1057/9781137276254_4.

Tassopoulos, I. (2014). *Popular Sovereignty and the Challenge of Impartiality*. Athens: Kritiki (in Greek).

Tassopoulos, I. (2018). From economic crisis to the crisis of parliamentarism? The incomplete social integration and the unnecessary revision of the constitution. *Social and Political Representation* (pp. 151–180). Athens: Scientific Foundation of Parliament (in Greek).

Tassopoulos, I. (2020). Political emergencies as challenges to the impartiality of Public Law. In R. Albert, and Y. Roznai (Eds.), *Constitutionalism Under Extreme Conditions* (81–100). Cham: Springer. https://doi.org/10.1007/978-3-030-49000-3_6.

Varoufakis, Y. (2017). *Adults in the Room*. London: Penguin.

Voulgaris, Y. (2019). *Greece: A Country Paradoxically Modern*. Athens: Polis (in Greek).

Zambelios, S. (1999). *Byzantine Studies*. Athens: Karavias (in Greek).

6 Greece and the EU

Official discourse and public opinion in the aftermath of the crisis

Calliope Spanou

Introduction

Over the past four decades Greece's position vis-à-vis the EU has experienced various ups and downs. The early strategic orientation in favour of the European Economic Community (EEC) was meant to offset its political and security vulnerability due to its geographic isolation in the context of a wider geopolitical conflict and the ensuing Cold War (Verney, 1987: 253–255). On such political considerations the then conservative Prime Minister, Constantinos Karamanlis, initiated the 1961 Association Agreement, which was frozen during the military junta (1967–1974), but confirmed by the same prime minister (1974–1981) following the return to democracy. Greece's membership of the EEC was a combined response to security, democracy and economic prosperity for the country in a troubled region (ibid.: 259; 1993: 132; Kazakos, 2001: 325–328). However, in economic terms expectations were politically divided: overcoming economic backwardness or widening a development gap transforming the country into 'a new colony' (Kazakos, 2001: 238, 243–246).

Ten months after the start of full membership of the EEC (January 1981), a change in government brought to power the Panellinio Socialistiko Kinima (PASOK—Panhellenic Socialist Movement), which had strongly opposed membership of the EEC while in opposition. Prime Minister Andreas Papandreou had argued that Greece could not avoid an unequal relationship with the European Community (EC), which would only perpetuate its political and economic weaknesses (Kazakos, 2001: 341). The early years of membership were therefore characterized by a rather defensive attitude, with the country trying to avoid the negative effects of membership while benefiting from the resources made available to it; this resulted in inadequate adjustment, delays and violations of EC rules that gave Greece the image of an unreliable partner (Verney, 1993: 143; Ioakimidis, 1994; Kazakos, 2001: 372; Frangakis and Papayannides, 2003). However, in the mid-1980s, Papandreou made an impressive U-turn and began to take the next steps in the integration process (Verney, 1993: 145–148; Ioakimidis, 1996: 39–40; Kazakos, 2001: 374).

In the 1990s, the EU project established its hegemony with the support of successive Greek governments (Nea Demokratia—ND, New Democracy

DOI: 10.4324/9780429202247-8

1991–1993 and PASOK 1993–2004); both opted for joining Economic and Monetary Union (EMU). Public opinion appeared to accept the terms set by the Maastricht Treaty (Ioakimidis, 1994: 146; Kazakos, 2001: 525–527). Under Prime Minister Simitis (1996–2004), Europeanization became synonymous with economic, political, administrative and social modernization. He maintained that 'a strong EU is a condition for a strong Greece'. This included a strategy to recognize the notion of 'EU external borders' (Simitis, 2005: 128–129), an objective which later assumed even greater importance. During this time, Greece actively and consistently supported deepening political union and the EU Constitution, which it was among the first to ratify. Eurozone membership in 2001 was a further step in this direction. It would provide a strong currency, greater international leverage, thereby overcoming 'the myth of a weak country', one that was known as the constant laggard (ibid.: 169, 330). Opinion polls also showed a high degree of acceptance of EMU (Kazakos, 2001: 508–509).

These positive expectations from joining the EC/EU and later EMU were supported by high growth rates, abundant resources from structural funds and lower borrowing rates for sovereign debt. A united Europe was seen as a 'safe haven' providing democratic consolidation, security, economic development and institutional modernization.

The economic crisis was therefore a critical test for this positive image of the EU. The harsh austerity measures and the pressure of the adjustment programmes on Greek society revived controversies about the costs and benefits of membership that for a long time had seemed appeased. The way that the EU managed the financial and refugee crises contributed to a growing Euroscepticism. However, the low point in Greece-EU relations seems to have been left behind. Pro-Europeanism is slowly returning, albeit accompanied with disenchantment. During 2020, a security crisis along the eastern border and a health crisis due to the outbreak of the coronavirus (COVID-19) pandemic provided further opportunities to test trust in EU and possibly to improve its image in public opinion. However, their effects have yet to be seen.

The chapter, organized in two parts, examines the evolution of the image of the EU in Greece during the past decade by following the rhetoric of prime ministers and the trends in public opinion. First, the official declarations of (elected) Greek prime ministers[1] are analysed, and second, trends in Greek public opinion as reflected in opinion polls and selected Eurobarometer indicators are examined.

The official discourse[2]

The political context

When the sovereign debt crisis broke out, the new PASOK government had only been in office for a few months. Prime Minister George Papandreou argued that the euro crisis was a systemic problem that extended beyond

Greece and its domestic weaknesses and therefore a 'European solution' was necessary. He put the blame on unaccountable speculators and rating agencies as well as on previous governments, which did not have the diligence required to prevent such a crisis. However, the slow and difficult European response to the economic crisis hardly acknowledged the European dimension of the problem. Abroad, Greece continued to be seen as the main culprit in official declarations and the media. When at last the first economic adjustment programme was instigated and the corresponding Memorandum of Understanding (MOU) signed, the government was heavily criticized domestically for 'bringing the Memorandum' and the IMF into the country (see Chapter 2 in this volume). Opposition parties portrayed the government as 'traitors' who had facilitated a new kind of 'occupation' of the country. After two years of extreme pressure owing to fiscal consolidation and unpopular reforms, in October 2011[3] Papandreou attempted to clear the air by calling a referendum,[4] but met the hostility of the EU leaders. His position was weakened, even losing support within his own party; coming under considerable pressure to revoke the referendum, he subsequently resigned. A coalition government was then formed under a 'technocrat' Prime Minister, Loukas Papadimos, with a short-term mandate, followed by elections in May 2012 resulting in a hung parliament. New elections were held in June 2012.

In the meantime, as the major opposition party under Antonis Samaras, ND had opted to join the 'anti-MOU' side, thereby denying its governmental responsibilities during the pre-crisis period (2004–2009). Its main argument was that the policies included in the first MOU were wrong. A 'different policy mix' should be adopted. This disagreement was instrumental to opposition politics, exploiting popular discontent without actually blaming Europe. In June 2012, Samaras became prime minister, heading a coalition government (with PASOK from 2012–2015 and the Dimokratiki Aristera, DIMAR—Democratic Left) during its first year in office). He agreed to comply with the requirements of the second economic adjustment programme, which included further austerity measures and a long list of reforms.

The initial stance of ND under Samaras was radicalized by Synaspismos Rizospastikis Aristeras (SYRIZA—the Coalition of the Radical Left), which under Alexis Tsipras was to upset the party landscape in the 2012 (early) elections. It criticized the 'neo-liberal Europe' and nurtured to some extent Eurosceptic positions, showing an overall ambivalence regarding euro membership. The party finally came to power after the (early) elections of January 2015, and formed a coalition government with Anexartitoi Ellines (ANEL—Independent Greeks), a small right-wing populist party. Having promised to give back to the Greek people their 'dignity and pride', the Tsipras government set out to renegotiate the existing MOU. The risk of a Greek default (or 'Grexit') was implicitly used as leverage in order to reach a 'mutually beneficial agreement' with Europe, while looking for alternative financial assistance outside the EU (e.g. the Russian Federation or the People's

Republic of China). When developments proved this strategy unrealistic, he called a referendum in July 2015, which he won, but fear of 'Grexit' made him change course and sign the third adjustment programme.

Defending the EU

On April 23, 2010, Papandreou announced that Greece had requested the activation of the European Support Mechanism. Describing the EU and membership of the euro as a 'safe haven', he emphasized unity and solidarity between Greece and its European partners, which provided 'a common defence front against markets and speculators threatening the Euro'. He avoided references to disagreements with Greece's EU partners, who 'ignored the international roots of the crisis, the dubious role of the markets and the rating agencies' or had 'different approaches' to the 'cure' applied.[5] The EU remained an environment that could contribute to rationalization and modernization. Euro membership was never called into question, but it was stressed that it also includes obligations.[6] Papandreou defended Europe against simplistic and complacent 'conspiracy theories', namely 'that the IMF or the European Commission deliberately want to harm Greece'.[7]

Putting the blame on the PASOK government was for Samaras part of a political strategy. Focusing on the 'wrong policies of the (first) MOU' agreed by the PASOK government allowed him to side with popular discontent while preserving pro-EU positions.[8] For the rest, membership of Greece in the eurozone and the EU were strongly supported. Moreover, ND was founded by Prime Minister Karamanlis, who led Greece into the EC, and who would not 'gamble with the European perspective of the country'.[9]

Both Europe and the eurozone represented safety.[10] Hence, strengthening the position of Greece in Europe and in the euro was a priority.[11] Moreover, both Europe and Greece were being threatened by the markets, which amounted to a 'positive sum game',[12] since a 'Grexit' would leave Europe in unchartered waters.[13] At the same time, Samaras appeared to defend national dignity and sovereignty vis-à-vis foreigners who 'dictate conditions',[14] a direct response to the criticisms expressed by Tsipras as leader of the increasingly popular SYRIZA.

During Samaras's time in office, large migration and refugee flows across the Aegean became an ever greater problem.[15] Although disproportionally affecting EU border states, migration was a regional security-related issue, a common European problem calling for a European solution.[16] It required solidarity, co-responsibility for the protection of European borders and proportional burden-sharing.[17] And Greece needed assistance in order to effectively 'protect itself and Europe at large'.[18]

Differences between the rhetoric of prime ministers Papandreou and Samaras essentially concerned domestic politics and political stakes. Nevertheless, they both maintained a positive view of the EU, and stressed the need for further integration, although with different emphasis. For

Papandreou, the European construction was at its most critical moment. The way forward should be 'strong economic and political governance, at least for Eurozone countries'. This was essential in order to avoid a breakdown of its political, economic and social cohesion. The creation of Eurobonds was an example of such deeper integration. Greece should maintain its voice and credibility as an equal partner and be part of an alliance for a *different Europe*, the Europe of the citizens and of the peoples against rising nationalism and introversion.[19]

For Samaras, next to 'prosperity, solidarity, democracy', Europe should rise to the common challenge of economic competitiveness, as a complement to its social dimension. The 'competitiveness discrepancy' among EU countries undermines the Union[20] and a 'quick fix', such as 'Grexit', is not a real solution.[21] The crisis has shown the need for 'more and better Europe'. The 'ever closer Union' is the means to defend Europe against crises. More Europe means social justice, opportunities for all, as well as prosperity and prospects for future generations.[22]

Saving the 'good EU'

Tsipras's rhetoric combined elements of both Papandreou and Samaras's rhetoric adding a radical twist in line with his party's profile. It hardly referred to the benefits of the EU and eurozone membership, and indeed appeared rather ambivalent towards the latter—at least during his first term in office (January–September 2015)—and was open to Euroscepticism. Building on Samaras's (initial) rejection of the MOUs, Tsipras targeted 'neoliberal Europe' and the 'unaccountable technocrats' who drive austerity policies at the EU level[23] and exclude any other alternatives.[24] His statements were at times quite harsh:

> [T]he Europe of the Enlightenment has become a social and labour Middle Ages. ... The risk is that the Europe of democracy and solidarity, of values and of the peoples, cedes its place to a Europe of terror, of strife, of punishment and finally of generalized destabilization.[25]

Putting forward an ideological-political criticism of the EU did not, however, exclude a potential positive image: an EU that respects its founding principles and its distinctive social model is opposed to a 'bad' EU that sacrifices them on the altar of the austerity dogma.[26] This 'good EU', i.e. 'a return to the founding principles' of Europe, is an objective to pursue for a wider alliance with other European forces. It is 'a Europe of solidarity and democracy' versus 'a divided Europe, a Europe of harsh fiscal discipline, of hard punishment of those who are not disciplined'.[27]

Attributing the difficulties faced during the 2015 renegotiation process to the hostilities vis-à-vis the SYRIZA-led Greek government,[28] this rhetoric raised the issue of respect of democracy and the will of the people by the EU partners. 'A basic principle of the United Europe is respect for the democratically expressed will of its people'.[29] Therefore, European treaties, founded on the universal value of democracy and the principle of popular sovereignty, are (currently) 'violated'.[30]

It was in this context that the July 2015 referendum took place, and was intended to be the answer to the blackmailing 'ultimatum' sent by the EU asking Greece 'to surrender'.[31] The 'no' vote was presented as an act of resistance, of dignity and pride, and as a sacred duty of the Greek people towards its history and future generations.[32] However, Tsipras sought to reassure voters that it was 'not a decision to break with Europe' but rather 'with practices that insult Europe'.[33] It also defended 'the vision of great European leaders, such as Adenauer, Helmut Schmidt, Willy Brandt, Mitterrand, Spinelli, Berlinguer', against the IMF and the Eurogroup. The referendum, a 'battle for democracy, dignity and hope', was presented as having wider implications for the course of European integration.[34]

The escalating refugee crisis[35] offered Tsipras a further opportunity to criticize 'Europe', this time on moral grounds. While Greece as a government and society showed solidarity, upholding humanitarian values and respecting international obligations vis-à-vis the asylum seekers, other EU countries were xenophobic, 'raised walls and built wired fences'. A 'Europe- fortress' cannot 'keep its borders open to austerity and closed to people who run away from war seeking hope and a lifeboat'. A 'different EU'[36] is sought in the 'moral foundation of European integration'.[37]

The twin crises, financial and refugee, showed that 'Brussels is weak when dealing with common challenges'. The search for a European solution called for stronger EU authority, including imposing sanctions on countries that do not respect rules and agreements regarding the refugee relocation process.[38]

Through the refugee and migration crisis, Tsipras sought a way back onto the European scene, posing as a defender of European values. This also allowed to Greece to build new alliances with Germany in the EU negotiations on the migrant issue. Gradually, the initial anti-Europeanism met the pragmatic acceptance of the importance of the EU and criticism shifted towards the Eurosceptic extreme-right parties in Europe,[39] which gained in strength as a result of 'economic orthodoxy technocrats' and their political management of the (economic) crisis.

Public opinion

Once the Greek society entered the troubled waters of the sovereign debt crisis, the pro-EU attitudes that had dominated up until then were deeply affected. Until 2009, Greek public opinion, as reflected in Eurobarometer surveys, showed levels of support for EU membership that were higher than across the EU as a whole (Clements et al., 2014). Greece was seen as having benefited from EU membership and trust in the Union was higher than in domestic institutions. The June 2009 Standard Eurobarometer data (EB 71)[40] reveal the level of trust and hope placed in the EU. Some 38% of Greeks responded to the survey (by far highest in EU-27) that among the various global actors (such as the G20, the United States, the IMF, etc.) the EU was best able to take collective action against the effects of the financial crisis.

The crisis period was clearly a game-changer. One of the most pro-EU societies lost faith in the European integration and trust in European institutions was eroded (Verney, 2015: 281). The expectation of economic prosperity was belied by a dramatic decline in living standards. While the complexity of EU-Greece relations increased, the crisis management of EU institutions was disappointing (Tsoukalis, 2011, 2014). The EU was part of the 'troika', which imposed harsh austerity and reversed past achievements that were positively associated with the EU, e.g. in terms of social rights.

Within just two years (2009–2011) the negative image of the EU more than tripled, while the number of those who tended not to trust the EU and believed that the EU was going in the wrong direction more than doubled (Clements et al., 2014: 4). Those who agreed that Greece had not benefited from membership almost doubled from 27% in 2008 to 50% in 2011. Meanwhile, in the EU countries, this figure only rose from 31% to 37%. As a result, Greek popular Euroscepticism, that for two decades had been consistently below the EU average, now significantly exceeded it, even surpassing the level of traditionally Eurosceptic countries, such as the United Kingdom (Verney, 2015). Greece showed the most pronounced increase in Euroscepticism (Serricchio et al., 2013: 57).

Standard Eurobarometer data (EB 85, May 2016)[41] show that trust in EU institutions such as the European Parliament, the Commission and the ECB had fallen sharply and was the lowest among member states (25%, 19%, 15%, respectively). Only 6% of Greeks considered that 'things go in the right direction in the EU' versus 76% thinking the opposite. While Europe was seen to represent freedom of movement and the euro, it was also associated with unemployment (34%). According to an October 2016 opinion poll in Greece,[42] demand for Europeanization was no longer dominant among the middle and lower social classes (Malkoutsis, 2016).

In contrast, though fluctuating from the initial enthusiasm to scepticism in the mid-2000s, attitudes towards the euro proved more positive. An early 2011 opinion poll in Greece showed that despite the crisis and the MOU, the euro was supported by almost 60% of the population, with 55% against leaving the eurozone (only 16% were in favour) (Marantzidis, 2017: 17–18). The 'Greek paradox' (Clements et al., 2014) opposed declining general support for the EU to increasing support for the euro. While in 2009 support for the euro stood at 62%, according to Standard Eurobarometer (EB 71) data and remained at this levels for some time, in 2015 (EB 84)[43] it had reached 70%. This was seen as a sign of a 'soft variety of Euroscepticism' that did not go so far as to advocate a break with European integration (Verney, 2015). It was, however, observed that in 2016 consensus on the euro appeared more and more fragile; a steady decline of support showed that it could not be taken for granted (Malkoutsis, 2016). In any case, far from the initial enthusiasm, support for the euro now appeared to be a safety option.

Euroscepticism peaked during the period 2015–2017, which corresponded with the clash between the EU institutions and the then Tsipras-led coalition government. The referendum had created intense social and political polarization, while the initial ambivalence of the SYRIZA-led government regarding the euro had legitimized the discussion about a possible 'Grexit'. The last-minute U-turn by Tsipras (see Chapter 5 in this volume) and the signature of the third adjustment programme and corresponding MOU were presented as a new episode of foreign 'occupation' that stimulated negative attitudes.

A series of annual opinion polls carried out by the independent, private, non-profit research organization diaNEOsis followed these trends in society. In April 2015, 69% of Greeks assessed membership of the EU as positive; in December 2016 this number fell to 54%, while negative assessments rose significantly (up from 30% to around 44%). One year later, in 2017, the Greek society appeared to be split; thus, 47% of the population believed that the structures and interests of the EU do not favour Greece, compared to 49% who believed that the EU represents progress and that it is necessary that Greece remains a member (Marantzidis, 2017: 12–13).

A slow reversal of this trend could be ascertained in 2018. With the gradual normalization of relations between the Greek government and the EU institutions and the prospect of exiting the third economic adjustment programme, Euroscepticism seemed to be weakening. According to dia-NEOsis,[44] in 2018 68% of Greeks assessed EU membership positively, compared to 31% who viewed it negatively. Furthermore, 67% of Greeks saw the EU as representing progress and believed that Greece should remain a member. On the downside, 28% believed that Greek interests were not represented in the EU and that Greece should leave. Still, while 66% (59.6% at the end of 2016) were in favour of the euro and 26.3% wished for a national currency (33.1% at the end of 2016), 57% believed that the decision to join the euro currency was a mistake.

Selected indicators based on the Standard Eurobarometer paint a similar picture, with the additional advantage of the comparison with wider trends within the EU.

As Table 6.1 shows, in June 2009 'trust in the EU' was at a rather high level of 55%, well above the EU-27 average (47%), the highest being 68% in Estonia. The image of the EU was positive, at 45%, similarly to the EU-27 average. Additionally, as already mentioned, Greece had the highest percentage of people (38%) who saw the EU as being more capable of dealing with the financial crisis than any other global player.

The comparison with the responses to the May 2016 Eurobarometer polls is devastating. Trust was at 17% and distrust at 82%, making Greece the country with the lowest trust and the most negative trust ratio in the EU-27, significantly below the UK (30%) and Italy (29%).

Table 6.1 Selected indicators of the Standard Eurobarometer

	Ref. 71, June 2009	Ref. 73, May 2010	Ref. 78, Nov. 2012	Ref. 81, May 2014	Ref. 84, Nov. 2015	Ref. 85, May 2016	Ref. 90, Nov. 2018	Ref. 91, June 2019	Ref. 92, Nov. 2019	Ref. 93, July 2020
Trust (%)	55	42	19	24	18	17	26	32	34	32
Distrust (%)	31	56	79	75	81	82	70	66	62	66
Image										
Positive (%)	45	38	–	22	22	16	25	33	31	27
Negative (%)	–	24	49	44	38	51	35	28	32	32

Source: Standard Eurobarometer.[45] https://europa.eu/eurobarometer/surveys/browse/all/series/4961.

This seems to have been the lowest point in the period under examination. In November 2018 and June 2019 (EB 90 and EB 91)[46], [47], things slowly started to change. In March 2018 (EB 89),[48] Greece still presented the lowest levels of trust (26% trust compared to 70% distrust) and the most negative ratio. In November 2019 (EB 92),[49] trust in the EU reached 34% compared to 62% distrust (EU average 43% trust compared to 47% distrust), the last being the UK with 29%. In July 2020 (EB 93),[50] it seemed slightly worse, with 32% trust compared to 66% distrust (EU average 43% compared to 48%), with Italy appearing lowest, with 28% 'trust'.

Regarding the 'image of the EU', in June 2009, the proportion of respondents who had a positive image of the EU stood at 45%, equivalent to the EU-27 average. By May 2016 the positive image had plummeted to 16% and Greece stood out as being the only country to have a negative image of the EU-27 (51% negative compared to 16% positive), both in absolute terms and in terms of the positive-negative ratio. The negative image was confirmed in the subsequent surveys (carried out between November 2016 and March 2018), with Greece standing out among other EU members in this respect, although there are some indications of a slow change. In the November 2018 Standard Eurobarometer, a relative majority (39%) had a neutral image of the EU, while 25% had a positive image and 35% a negative image. One year later, in the November 2019 Eurobarometer, Greece was the only country where more than three in ten respondents had a negative image of the EU (32% compared to 31% positive, with an EU average of 42% compared to 20%), although a relative majority (37%) had a neutral image of the EU. There is hardly any difference in the 2020 data, which showed that 32% of respondents had a negative image of the EU, 27% had a positive image and 41% a neutral image.

Eurobarometer indicators reflect the disappointment of Greek citizens in the de facto relegation of Greece to a second-class EU member during this period. In November 2015 (EB 84) only 16% of respondents felt that 'their voice counts', compared to 83% who did not feel that this was the case (EU average 'does not count' 54% versus 39% 'counts'). Greece was in the last position among the EU-27 and presented the most negative ratio in this respect. Again, this appears to start changing slowly in November 2018 (EB 90), with 19% and 79%, respectively, which was still the worst result in the EU-27 (EU average 'does not count' 47% versus 49% 'counts'). This finding remained the same in November 2019 (EB 92), although in absolute terms there was some improvement ('does not count' 30% versus 60% 'counts').

Furthermore, in November 2018 (EB 90), 48% of respondents did not feel that they were 'citizens of the EU' compared to 28% EU-average and just above Bulgaria (47%). In November 2019 (EB 92), this score was 49% (compared to 51%) i.e. the worst among EU countries, with an EU average of 29%. In July 2020 (EB 93), it appeared even lower (46% versus 54%), but this time Greece is not last, since Italy (51% versus 48%) appears at the bottom of the scale (possibly after the dramatic experience of the pandemic).

The data from these various opinion polls reflect the effects of the deep crisis in the attitudes of Greek citizens to the EU and the trauma resulting from it. Compared with the lowest scores registered during 2015–2016, there are signs of a slow but fragile recovery. Greece remains well below the EU average regarding indicators such as 'trust in the EU' and (positive) 'image', and clearly far below the corresponding pre-crisis levels.

In contrast, support for the euro is impressively higher. In November 2018, 67% of respondents supported the euro, compared to 30% who did not (EB 91); one year later, in November 2019, (EB 92) this figure increased to 70% (versus 26% against) and was surprisingly higher than the EU average (62% versus 29%). In 2020, it even reached 75%, presenting one of the largest increases (up by 5%). Despite Greek citizens' disillusionment with the EU, there is still a high level of support for the euro.

However, it is interesting to note that regarding the role of the EU in fighting the pandemic, results in Greece are significantly better and closer to (though below) the EU average. More specifically, in November 2020, 41% (versus 55%) of respondents were satisfied with the actions taken by the EU (EU average 45% versus 44%), and 51% (versus 47%) of respondents trusted the EU to make the right decisions in the future (EU average 62% versus 36%) (EB 92).

Conclusion

The chapter examined the official discourse of the Greek prime ministers and the trends in Greek public opinion regarding the image of the EU during the past decade. It is difficult to assess how much the rhetoric of the prime ministers has actually influenced public opinion and vice versa. Other factors need to be taken into account, such as the role of the national and international media, social, economic and political conditions, and the perception of various types of risks involved. However, it may be asserted that the effects of the negative official discourse on public opinion prove stronger than any positive message it could convey, such as the humanitarian and democratic European values, the 'safe haven' or the a clear pro-EU stance of the prime ministers. This point is supported by the fact that while currently the image of the EU in the official discourse is far from negative, the recovery of the image of the EU in public opinion is very slow and uncertain.

What also emerges is the fragility of the EU integration project. Having remained a top-down, elite-driven project (Frangakis and Papayannides, 2003: 175), it does not seem to have impregnated society. Public opinion has proved to be very sensitive to the negative tones of the political rhetoric as well as to tangible aspects of economic and social prosperity. Although this is not necessarily an exclusively Greek characteristic, the traumatic effects of the sovereign debt crisis and of its management by the European institutions account for the extremely low levels of trust in the EU and its difficult recovery, which is still below EU average even after the conclusion of the adjustment programmes and the heavy presence of the troika.

However, the other side of the coin points to a different perspective. Through the hardships of the crisis and its legacies, membership of the EU and the euro, as well as the need for further integration, were confirmed at the political level. The testing events of mid-2015 threatened but did not reject the long-standing strategic orientation of the country that started in 1960s. Moreover, while the relevance of the EU for domestic politics seemed to be diminishing, the crises that appeared in early 2020 revived the awareness of the importance of Greece's EU membership.[51] The migration flows continue to put pressure on the Greek border, but it is increasingly acknowledged that this is also an EU border requiring a common European response. Moreover, this issue is at times associated with a security threat not only against Greece but Europe as a whole. Finally, the COVID-19 pandemic presented an opportunity for European policies to overcome the dogma of fiscal rectitude. Faced with the symmetrical shock engendered by the pandemic, the EU managed to reconsider its fiscally minded reflexes and recognized the need to provide a common pool of resources under mild conditionality in order to confront the serious effects of the health crisis on national economies.

To what extent the EU will continue to attract domestic political controversy or improve its standing in public opinion now also depends on the developments in two new problem areas: the position of the EU regarding the East Mediterranean security issue and the EU's role in fighting the COVID-19 pandemic. After some initial nationalist reactions, the EU introduced initiatives to ensure the implementation of common policies to contain the pandemic based on the solidarity of its members and free from antagonistic national policies. But the road is still long and the next steps may prove slippery. At mid-2021, the EU was facing criticism for delays in the authorization of the COVID-19 vaccines and the rollout of the vaccination programme, when compared with the United States or the UK. Furthermore, it had yet to adopt a common position on developments in the Eastern Mediterranean.

Notes

1 Between 2009 and 2015, the country experienced five general elections, three elected prime ministers, six governments—one under a technocrat prime minister—and a referendum. After exiting the third economic adjustment programme in August 2018, elections held in July 2019 heralded a new government under ND leader Kyriakos Mitsotakis.

2 The material cited below comes from the archives of George Papandreou (http://archive.papandreou.gr) and the official website of prime ministers Anthonis Samaras (2012–2015) and Alexis Tsipras (2015–2019) (http://primeminister.gr).

3 This took place after the agreement for a second adjustment programme was reached at the European Summit of Cannes, in October 2011.

4 See, Second intervention during the parliamentary debate on the vote of confidence, November 4, 2011. http://archive.papandreou.gr.

5 Response to Tsipras. February 25, 2011. Response to Samaras June 4, 2010. http://archive.papandreou.gr.

6 Parliamentary debate on the vote of confidence regarding Papandreou's initiative, November 3, 2011. http://archive.papandreou.gr.
7 Parliamentary discussion on the 2011 budget, December 22, 2010. http://archive.papandreou.gr.
8 'Economic Ideas Forum', Centre of European Studies. June 7, 2013. http://prim eminister.gr.
9 Parliamentary discussion, November 7, 2012; '40 years of New Democracy', September 27, 2014. http://primeminister.gr.
10 Interview, *The Washington Post*, September 15, 2012. http://primeminister.gr.
11 Programmatic statements of the government, July 6, 2012. http://primeminister.gr.
12 Interview, *The Washington Post*, September 15, 2012; Interview after the European Summit in Brussels, March 14, 2013, March 15, 2013; 'Economic Ideas Forum', Centre of European Studies June 7, 2013; Press conference after the Tripartite Summit, Greek presidency, March 20, 2014; Plenary Session of the European Parliament, January 15, 2014. http://primeminister.gr.
13 Interview, *The Washington Post*, September 15, 2012; Speech at the IHT Conference October 4, 2012. http://primeminister.gr.
14 Parliamentary discussion, November 7, 2012. http://primeminister.gr.
15 Interview after the Brussels Summit, December 14, 2014. http://primeminister.gr.
16 Common statements by Samaras and President Hollande, February 19, 2013; Meeting of Samaras with Van Rompuy, September 7, 2012. http://primeminister.gr.
17 Closing speech of the Greek presidency, July 1, 2014. http://primeminister.gr.
18 'Economic Ideas Forum', Centre of European Studies. June 7, 2013.
19 Parliamentary discussion on the 2011 budget, December 22, 2010; Second intervention at the parliamentary discussion on the bill of the Ministry of Finance, June 29, 2011. http://archive.papandreou.gr.
20 Annual conference of *The Economist*, April 17, 2013. http://primeminister.gr.
21 Parliamentary discussion, November 7, 2012; Speech at the IHT Conference October 4, 2012. http://primeminister.gr.
22 Press conference with Martin Schulz, January 15, 2014. http://primeminister.gr.
23 Plenary session of the European Parliament, July 8, 2015. http://primeminister.gr.
24 Programmatic statements, February 8, 2015; Parliamentary group of SYRIZA February 17, 2015. http://primeminister.gr.
25 OECD, March 12, 2015. http://primeminister.gr.
26 Parliamentary discussion, July 23, 2015. http://primeminister.gr.
27 Parliamentary discussion, June 6, 2015. http://primeminister.gr.
28 Parliamentary discussion, July 11, 2015. http://primeminister.gr.
29 Parliamentary discussion, June 6, 2015. http://primeminister.gr.
30 Programmatic statements, February 8, 2015. http://primeminister.gr.
31 Address of Tsipras to the people concerning the referendum, June 27, 2015; Parliamentary discussion, June 28, 2015. http://primeminister.gr.
32 Greeting the rally in favour of the 'no' vote, Syntagma Square, July 4, 2015. http://primeminister.gr.
33 Parliamentary discussion, June 28, 2015. http://primeminister.gr.
34 Parliamentary discussion, June 28, 2015; Greeting the rally in favour of the 'no' vote, Syntagma Square, July 4, 2015. http://primeminister.gr.
35 First Council of Ministers, September 25, 2015. http://primeminister.gr.
36 'Q&A' session in parliament, October 30, 2015; Programmatic statements October 5, 2015. http://primeminister.gr.
37 International conference on 'Alliance against Austerity, for Democracy in Europe', March 19, 2016. http://primeminister.gr.
38 Commons statements by Tsipras and Donald Tusk, March 3, 2016; European summit on migration, April 24, 2015. http://primeminister.gr.

39 Interview, Bloomberg, June 27, 2018; Speech at the Congress of the SPD, November 10, 2018; Speech at the conference on 'Prosperity for All in a Sustainable Europe', March 5, 2019. http://primeminister.gr.
40 https://europa.eu/eurobarometer/surveys/detail/829.
41 https://europa.eu/eurobarometer/surveys/detail/2130.
42 Kapa Research. *To Vima*, November 6, 2016: A16.
43 https://europa.eu/eurobarometer/surveys/detail/2098.
44 Opinion poll carried out by diaNEOsis. www.dianeosis.org/research/tpe-2018/; see also www.dianeosis.org/2018/03/greeks-believe-2018/.
45 http://ec.europa.eu/commfrontoffice/publicopinion/index.cfm/Survey/index#p=1& instruments=STANDARD.
46 https://europa.eu/eurobarometer/surveys/detail/2215.
47 https://europa.eu/eurobarometer/surveys/detail/2253.
48 https://europa.eu/eurobarometer/surveys/detail/2180.
49 https://europa.eu/eurobarometer/surveys/detail/2255.
50 https://europa.eu/eurobarometer/surveys/detail/2262.
51 See for instance statements by Prime Minister Mitsotakis: Interview of Prime Minister Mitsotakis with the French daily *Le Figaro*, October 9, 2020. https://primeminister.gr/2020/10/09/24996. See also the press conference of Prime Minister Mitsotakis after the European Council, December 11, 2020. https://primeminister.gr/2020/12/11/25423.

References

Clements, B., Nanou, K., and Verney, S. (2014). We no longer love you, but we don't want to leave you: The eurozone crisis and popular Euroscepticism in Greece. *Journal of European Integration*, 36(3), 247–265. doi:10.1080/07036337.2014.885753.

Frangakis, N., and Papayannides, A. (2003). Greece: A never-ending story of mutual attraction and estrangement. In W. Wessels, J. Mittag, and A. Maurer (Eds.), *Fifteen into One? The European Union and its Member-states* (pp. 166–183). Manchester: Manchester University Press. https://doi.org/10.7765/9781526137364.00016.

Ioakimidis P.C. (1994). The EC and the Greek political system. In P. Kazakos, and P.C. Ioakimidis (Eds.), *Greece and EC Membership Evaluated* (pp.139–153). London: Pinter.

Ioakimidis, P.C. (1996). Contradictions between policy and performance. In K. Featherstone and K. Yfantis (Eds.), *Greece in a Changing Europe: Between European Integration and Balkan Disintegration* (pp. 33–52). Manchester: Manchester University Press.

Kazakos, P. (2001). *Between State and Market. Economy and Economic Policy in Post-war Greece, 1944–2000*. Athens: Patakis (in Greek).

Malkoutsis, N. (2016, November 11). *Are We Taking the Greeks' Devotion to the Euro for Granted?* www.macropolis.gr/?i=portal.en.the-agora.4739.

Marantzidis, N. (2017). Greeks change ideas on Europe and the world. *diaNEOsis, March* (in Greek). www.dianeosis.org/wp-content/uploads/2017/10/TPE_2017_Ekthesi_Marantzidis.pdf.

Serricchio, F., Tsakatika, M., and Quaglia, L. (2013). Euroscepticism and the global financial crisis. *Journal of Common Market Studies*, 51(1), 51–64. https://doi.org/10.1111/j.1468-5965.2012.02299.x.

Simitis, C. (2005). *Policy for a Creative Greece*. Athens: Polis (in Greek).

Tsoukalis, L. (2011). The JCMS Annual Review Lecture: The shattering of illusions – and what next. *Journal of Common Market Studies*, 49(1), 26–44. https://doi.org/10.1111/j.1468-5965.2011.02185.x.

Tsoukalis, L. (2014). *The Unhappy State of the Union: Europe Needs a New Grand Bargain*. London: Policy Network.

Verney, S. (1987). Greece and the European Community. In K. Featherstone, and D. K. Katsoudas (Eds.), *Political Change in Greece: Before and After the Colonels* (pp. 253–270). London and Sydney: Croom Helm.

Verney, S. (1993). From 'special relationship' to Europeanism: PASOK and the European Community 1981–89. In R. Clogg (Ed.), *Greece 1981–89: The Populist Decade* (pp. 131–153). London: Macmillan.

Verney, S. (2015). Waking the 'sleeping giant' or expressing domestic dissent? Mainstreaming Euroscepticism in crisis-stricken Greece. *International Political Science Review*, 36(3), 279–295. https://doi.org/10.1177%2F0192512115577146.

Part II

Looking ahead: opportunities and challenges

7 Public sector restructuring and marketization reforms

Manto Lampropoulou

Introduction

In the course of the three economic adjustment programmes of Greece (2010–2018) a large-scale reorganization of the public sector took place. An important element of the reform agenda was the restructuring of critical sectors of the national economy such as energy, transportation, water supply and other networks as well as the management of infrastructure and public property. In these policy fields, the tone was set by a notable intensification and acceleration of market-oriented reforms, such as privatization and liberalization, along with a reorganization of the corresponding administrative structures via agencification. While privatization and liberalization have been a common trend in the EU (Hermann and Verhoest, 2014) and the rationales for state ownership and privatization paradigms are changing world-wide (OECD, 2019), the restructuring and marketization of the Greek public sector presents certain specificities, due to the policy environment imposed by policy conditionality (Spanou, 2016).

This chapter explores the process of the restructuring and marketization of the public sector during the sovereign debt crisis and seeks to address its outcomes and future prospects in the post-crisis era. While most studies focus on the economic impact of these reforms, in the analysis that follows the emphasis is placed on their implications for public policy and administration. It is suggested that market-oriented reforms have important implications for the structure and organization of the public sector as well as for public service provision. Major shifts have occurred at the policymaking level, which have led to subsequent transformations of the administrative apparatus, the market and ownership structures, the role of state-owned corporations and the service production and provision mechanism.

The restructuring and marketization reforms are analysed with reference to the following interrelated criteria: (i) government intervention and public policy; (ii) role and governance of state-owned enterprises; and (iii) market structure and service delivery. The analysis seeks to explore the positive and negative effects of the reforms and to point out their strengths and weaknesses. At the same time, it provides some explanations for the observed

DOI: 10.4324/9780429202247-10

failures and tries to discern the opportunities opened up by the reforms, beyond the constraints caused by the crisis. The findings are based on a synthesis of existing literature, policy documents, reports and empirical research.

The rest of the chapter is structured as follows: in the first section the conceptual and theoretical background of public sector restructuring and marketization is presented in relation to the eurozone and the Greek sovereign debt crisis. The second section provides a detailed account of the reform goals, measures and outcomes in the area of network industries and the management of public property. In the third section the empirical findings are discussed, highlighting policy successes and failures and pointing out the constraining factors as well as the challenges and future prospects of the reforms. The concluding section summarizes the impact of the reforms that were introduced during the crisis and suggests some longer-term research questions beyond the context of the fiscal adjustment.

The conceptual background of public sector restructuring and marketization

Public sector reform via restructuring and marketization is linked to a range of policy tools and options, including privatization, liberalization, corporatization, deregulation, downsizing, divestiture, decentralization, de-bureaucratization, agencification, contracting-out, commodification and commercialization. The common denominator of these policies is the idea of enhancing the efficiency and effectiveness of the state machinery via the infusion of market techniques in the public sector. Their theoretical underpinnings can be traced back to the analytical framework of New Managerialism (Painter, 2011) and to economic schools of thought that promote the market model as an alternative to the traditional bureaucratic organisation.

The criticism of public choice theory, the ideas of New Institutional Economics and the influence of New Managerialism have largely inspired the reform of the state apparatus in line with the concept of the competitive market (Self, 1993). From this point of view, the market becomes the reference model for the organization and function of government, introducing techniques such as contractualism and agencification, with the aim of achieving budget discipline and result-orientation and to enhance user satisfaction (Torfing et al., 2020: 13). A key tool of the New Public Management agenda has been the marketization of public services (Pollitt and Bouckaert, 2004; Painter, 2011: 238), which promotes the adoption of private sector concepts and commercial-style practices. The idea of marketization is primarily linked to the neoliberal economic theory and since the late 1970s has inspired many reforms that seek to 'roll back' the state (Bevir, 2009: 128–129) and downsize the public sector.

Despite their common theoretical underpinnings, the agenda and tools of public sector restructuring and marketization vary significantly among countries and over time. Privatization and market-driven reforms are typical elements of financial support and bailout packages that entail reform programmes under policy conditionality (Edadan, 1997; Brune et al., 2004). In the context of the eurozone crisis, member states' policy responses to the crisis depended considerably on the debt level and the robustness of the national economies as well as on the degree of external lending. Hence, the countries of the European periphery, such as Greece, Portugal and Ireland, were forced to introduce massive privatizations as a result of the restructuring programmes imposed by external actors (e.g. the 'troika', EU institutions); on the contrary, in countries of continental Europe, such as France and Germany, the management of state assets was based on domestic decisions (Christodoulakis, 2015: 109).

Greece adopted the heaviest and longest adjustment path, and experienced a high level of turbulence in the implementation of the agreed reform plan. During the three economic adjustment programmes (2010–2018) the domestic public sector experienced wide-ranging transformations which aimed primarily at reducing its size and cost. The policy mix was a combination of different policies and measures. In the network industries the tone was set by privatization and liberalization along with the introduction of market techniques and a reorganization of the corresponding administrative structures.[1] Furthermore, new structures and policy tools for the management of state property were introduced, on the basis of the supremacy of technocracy and business-like administration over traditional bureaucracy. These measures were not new to the public sector reform agenda; previous or ongoing reforms had already transformed many of the traditional state monopolies to competitive markets (telecoms, energy) and state-owned enterprises (SOEs) into corporatized and/or (partly or wholly) privatized entities (Lampropoulou, 2018), while several administrative and regulatory powers have been delegated to arm's-length bodies. However, during the crisis period the intensity and the scale of the required changes were unprecedented and the prioritization of the components and instruments of the policy mix was revised.

Public sector reform during the crisis: goals, measures and outcomes

Government intervention and public policy

Over the past decade the landscape of the domestic public sector has changed significantly. Along with policy reform in communications, energy, transport and other major economic sectors, a large-scale restructuring of the machinery of government was required in order to support the implementation of the measures included in the Memoranda agreements. The restructuring of the network industries and the reform of the management of state assets were accompanied by a widespread reshuffling of the corresponding government and administrative structures. At the government level, the responsibility for the restructuring and privatization has been assigned to the Interministerial Committee for Restructuring and Privatization (ICRP), while during the third economic adjustment programme the privatization agenda was upgraded to the level of the Government Council for Economic Policy (GCEP).

The role of the Ministry of Finance has been pivotal in the formation and implementation of the reforms and its position was strengthened vis-à-vis line ministries. An in-depth reorganization of its internal units and a reallocation of competences took place. In 2011, a new General Secretariat for Public Property was established,[2] while the Special Secretariat for Privatizations and the Special Secretariat for SOEs were abolished in 2012. Two years later, the unit responsible for monitoring the finances of SOEs was moved to the General Accounting Office (GAO). Most of the asset management competences were transferred to arm's-length bodies, namely the Hellenic Republic Asset Development Fund (HRADF, established in 2011), the Public Properties Company and their parent company, the Hellenic Corporation of Assets and Participations[3] (HCAP, established in 2016), which has become the key administrative agency for the implementation of the envisaged reforms.

HCAP is a sovereign wealth fund that gathers under a single institutional structure the responsibilities for the operation and exploitation of state assets, real estate properties and state's participation in SOEs. It has three direct subsidiaries: (i) the Hellenic Republic Asset Development Fund (privatizations); (ii) the Hellenic Financial Stability Fund (HFSF) (banking system, shares in systemic banks); and (iii) the PPC (real estate assets),[4] and other subsidiaries that include its participation in SOEs. HRADF runs the privatization programme and PPC manages real estate assets, while HCAP has the overall responsibility for the long-term strategic planning, management, exploitation and monitoring of the performance of state assets (HCAP, 2018: 33). These new agencies are sociétés anonymes (SAs) and operate in line with technocratic-managerial criteria. The Ministry of Finance represents the Greek government and provides the strategic guidelines to HCAP, as its sole shareholder. However, its political role has been weakened, as the transfer of state assets management to arm's-length bodies aimed at the depoliticization of public administration and the limitation of political influence on SOEs.

The centralization of ownership from line ministries to arm's-length bodies in the form of sovereign wealth funds had important implications for policymaking. Within the market logic, this form of agencification is based on the separation of policy and management (Cox, 1999: 40) via the creation of semi-autonomous entities for the management of state assets. Agencification shifted the exercise of ownership rights from the Ministry of Finance to HCAP (and its subsidiaries) and changed the character and standards of policy implementation. The latter have been reoriented towards managerial and market values, as reflected in the agencies' mission, goals and operational standards. The new entities are not part of the public sector, are subject to corporate laws (as SAs) and operate in line with business-type standards. Contrary to the traditional bureaucratic structures, their mission, structure and governance have been defined in accordance with international best practice for companies and commercial principles (European Commission, 2017: 60, 162), reflecting a marketization of government structures via decentralization and agencification.

At the same time, in the network industries decentralization of regulatory powers led to a proliferation and strengthening of independent agencies. In the course of the economic adjustment programmes, new regulatory agencies were created, such as the Regulatory Authority for Railways (RAS), the Regulatory Authority for Ports (RAL) and the Regulatory Authority for Passenger Transport (RAEM) while existing agencies were strengthened, namely the Hellenic Telecommunications and Post Commission (EETT) and the Regulatory Authority for Energy (RAE). These agencies were assigned the responsibility for the regulation of the restructured and marketized parts of the public sector.

Role and governance of SOEs

A major goal of the public sector restructuring programme has been to reduce state ownership of SOEs via downsizing and privatization. The restructuring of the SOEs aimed to decrease their cost[5] and has led to notable cutbacks in expenditures, a revised wage grid and an overall reduction in their workforce. Regarding SOEs' ownership, sales, liquidations and transfers of state assets to private investors led to full privatization or mixed ownership regimes, along with other privatization methods. Some SOEs were or will be wholly privatized (OTE, TRAINOSE, EESSTY, DEPA Infrastructure) or partially privatized (DESFA, Athens International Airport, DEPA Commercial, OLP, OLTH) via shares transfer. For other SOEs and public infrastructures, along with the potential sale of shares, concession agreements and lease contracts (development and operation rights) were or will be used (Athens International Airport, regional airports, Egnatia SA, regional ports). In some cases, the structural separation of SOEs was required via the unbundling of infrastructure (which remains in state ownership) from commercial activities, for instance the demerger of Public Gas Corporation (DEPA)'s activities in 2019.[6]

Marketization has further penetrated the management and governance of SOEs. According to the measures agreed in the Memoranda of Understanding and the economic adjustment programmes, each enterprise is obliged to prepare a statement of commitments setting out its financial, operational and other objectives, submit business plans as well as to sign performance contracts with the supervising ministries[7] (HCAP, 2018). The compliance of SOEs with these measures as well as their performance will be monitored in line with 'robust and commercial benchmarks' that sets out the ministerial guidance (European Commission, 2020a: 69). The importation of private sector techniques is also reflected in the empowerment of corporate governance of SOEs through their appointment procedures,[8] reviews of their boards of directors, and internal and external audits (European Commission, 2020b: 90–91).

At the same time, an in-depth organizational and corporate restructuring took place in the SOE sector. In 2011, mergers and transfers of the transport companies led to a rearrangement of existing SOEs (ETHEL, ILPAP, AMEL, ISAP, TRAM, OASA) and the establishment of new parent companies (OSY, STASY). In other sectors, some units were hived off from the parent company, for instance the DG Distribution in DEI (DEDDIE S.A., 2011), which is in the process of partial privatization, and the competent structure for rolling stock maintenance from OSE (EESSTY SA, 2013), which has been fully privatized. In addition, several functions were assigned to external companies along with a strengthening of SOEs' collaboration with the private sector. For instance, typical market-based practices such as outsourcing, contracting-out and public-private partnerships for the management of certain operations, the provision of services and the construction of infrastructure (see United Nations, 2008: 33–34) have gradually gained ground in most network industries.

Market structure and service delivery

The restructuring of network industries was deemed necessary prior to privatization in order to establish an appropriate regulatory and institutional framework that would lead to the development of a competitive environment (OECD, 2019: 45–49). A key goal has been the abolition of state monopolies. In view of market opening and privatization, several adjustments were made in order to motivate private investors and to safeguard the competitive environment, such as the separation of structures, ownership rights and functions. Unbundling has led to changes in the structure of ownership, the separation of competitive and non-competitive segments, the establishment of independent system operators (electricity/gas), the separation of infrastructure management and service provision (railways), etc. (European Commission, 2014).

However, the restructuring and opening up of network markets to competition has so far brought about modest results. Market structure varies from state monopolies (urban transport) to competitive oligopolies (telecoms, energy) or less competitive markets (railways). As competition increases, a gradual decrease of market shares of the incumbents has been observed, but concentration is still high. The effect of the crisis on market liberalization and competition seems weak, as the main priority has been the transfer of ownership and privatization proceeds. The communications sector was already a liberalized market (oligopoly) before the crisis. Competition in the energy sector was introduced a decade before the crisis, but has encountered many problems and only in recent years some positive prospects for competition have been gradually shaped up. In the transport and infra-structure sector (rail, ports, airports), the crisis reforms were not primarily aimed at introducing market competition, but the main goal was market restructuring for privatization. In some cases (regional ports and airports) concessions were preferred instead of direct ownership transfer. In short, the crisis has generally led to the further privatization of most SOEs and has reduced or eliminated the state's participation in their share capital (TRAI-NOSE, DEI, DEPA, DESFA, ELPE, OTE, OLP, OLTH, EESSTY, EYATH, EYDAP, El. Venizelos), not necessarily in connection with market liberalization.

The restructuring of the production and provision mechanisms in network industries has changed the tools for service delivery accordingly. Service marketization, as a form of the commercialization process (United Nations, 2008: 32–33), has shifted the criteria of service provision and even the very perception of utilities services. Public utilities in the EU constitute a distinct category known as 'services of general economic interest' (SGEIs). In many countries they were previously considered to be quasi-public goods and/or public services. In view of the market-oriented reforms, public service or universal service obligations have been (re-)defined at the EU level, setting out some minimum fundamental principles for the provision, access, afford-ability and quality of services, which are specified by the member states (European Commission, 2007: 71). In Greece, no uniform framework existed for SGEIs or public/universal services prior to the crisis, as they were defined in an ad hoc manner in each sector. In the current circumstances, mainly as a result of the creation of HCAP, some public service obligations apply hor-izontally to network industries via the 'Co-ordination Mechanism'[9] and 'special obligations', which are part of the performance contracts signed between SOEs and the Greek state. While these provisions offer a systematic and organized framework of co-operation between the state and public enterprises, the implementation of the Co-ordination Mechanism is still pending and has encountered important limitations and obstacles.

Regarding the public service criteria, the introduction of private sector techniques in the network industries has moved the utilities' sector one step closer to commercialization. Restructuring policies such as privatization alter not only the character of public service delivery and the relationship between the government and the citizenry (Gilmour and Jensen, 1998: 247), but also the perceived role of citizens vis-à-vis SOEs (Lampropoulou, 2020). The emergence of the notions of 'customer', 'client' and 'consumer' is linked to market-type reforms in the public sector (OECD, 1988; Cox, 1999; Alford, 2002; Spanou, 2003), which are built upon the central idea of the empower-ment of service recipients via the freedom of choice (Tummers et al., 2014). However, beyond the consistency of their rhetoric with these ideas, most of the reforms that took place during the Greek crisis only partially meet the criteria of the empowered 'citizen-consumer', as they have resulted in the transformation of state monopolies in mixed or private monopolies and not in competitive markets. In competitive sectors such as telecommunications

Table 7.1 Restructuring and marketization reforms during the crisis

	Restructuring and marketization agenda	Policy programmes and reforms	Policy tools and measures
Government intervention and public policy	Ownership restructuring	Privatizations Divestment Share of public ownership Shareholding reform Property rights shift	Abolishment of state monopolies and nationalized industries Partial/whole transfer of shares/assets to private investors Strategic investors in state corporations Concessions
	Management and control marketization	Depoliticization Managerialism	Technocracy Entrepreneurial values Shareholder rights Economic efficiency
	Administrative restructuring	Structural reorganization Agencification De-bureaucratization Decentralization	Centralization of ownership and management in a single agency (HCAP) Creation of arm's-length bodies (state assets management) Decentralization of regulatory powers Proliferation and strengthening of regulatory agencies
		Restructuring of the Ministry of Finance	Abolition of general and special secretaries for SOEs and privatizations Creation of the General Secretariat for Public Property
Role and governance of SOEs	Restructuring of SOEs	Financial restructuring Business restructuring Organizational restructuring Corporate restructuring Corporatization	Cost reduction/increase in revenues (improve financial situation/economic performance) Unbundling of ownership/structure/activities (split ups) Mergers (transport) Employment: payroll downsizing Public-private partnerships Outsourcing/Contracting out
	Marketization of SOEs	Management and governance standards of SOEs Commercial restructuring Corporate Governance	Appointments from the private sector Managerial reorganization Corporate/shareholders' control Business-like criteria Performance contracts

Restructuring and marketization agenda		Policy programmes and reforms	Policy tools and measures
Market structure and service delivery	Market/sector restructuring	Liberalization (Re-)regulation Functional unbundling (separation of activities)	Institutional and regulatory adjustment Break-up of vertically integrated monopolies Opening up of state monopolies to competition
	Service marketization	Marketization Commercialization SGEI framework	Commodification Commercial criteria of service provision Special obligations

Source: author's elaboration.

and energy, choice was the result of the liberalization process (coupled with the technological progress and globalization), which was accelerated during the crisis, but had begun long before the crisis erupted.

Taking stock of the reforms: challenges, constraints and opportunities

Reform gains and future prospects

Despite the drawbacks and difficulties encountered along the way, the reforms enacted during the crisis via restructuring and marketization have brought about some positive changes in the domestic public sector. At the policy level, for the first time an organized effort was made to manage state assets in an orderly and coordinated manner. The previously scattered and uncharted public property is currently in the process of registration, clearance and organization. Regarding the management of state assets, the creation of a special-purpose body for their management and exploitation (HCAP) has led to the centralization and concentration of the relevant competences, which is expected to lead to better coordination, monitoring and economies of scale. The establishment of uniform standards, measurable deliverables and horizontal performance criteria for all SOEs has strengthened the consistency and the uniformity of SOEs' policy. In the same direction, the set of uniform standards for SGEIs and the establishment of a specific framework for the definition of 'special obligations', which since the abolition of cross-subsidizations has remained vague, shows signs of a more consistent policy for public service obligations in the utilities sector. However, state aids still subsidize a considerable percentage of service providers, even in cases where the provider is a private firm (for instance the non-profit lines in rail transport), and no proper mechanism for the overall planning and monitoring of these services exists.

The reform of the SOEs has also led to certain improvements. It is estimated that their commercial restructuring has improved governance methods and has contributed to the depoliticization of their management (European Commission, 2017: 60, 167). The introduction of corporate standards and governance rules has enhanced transparency and contributed to the (economic-technical) rationalization of the management and control of SOEs. As regards market performance, a positive effect of marketization has been the notable decrease in the price of utilities in competitive sectors, which is mostly observed in telecoms. As experience suggests, in the market environment demand becomes more individualized (Laperche and Uzunidis, 2003: 6) and tariffs tend to decrease. While it is difficult to isolate the effect of the market-driven reforms from that of technological advancement and globalization, liberalization has offered consumers more choice and indicates a positive outlook for the quality and cost of services. Along with market advantages, a noteworthy initiative has been the establishment of a legal framework for energy communities and the encouragement of social economy,[10] which, despite the limited development so far, opens up prospects for greater community participation, beyond the usual 'state versus market' (pseudo-)dilemma about the provision of services.

Reform failures and constraints

Privatization and liberalization advocates argue that competition and private sector techniques will improve efficiency and service quality. However, no conclusive evidence supports this hypothesis in the case of Greek public sector marketization, especially regarding the reforms that were initiated in the context of the economic adjustment programmes. Besides, no systematic assessment of their impact has (yet) taken place at the domestic level. An explanation behind the modest results is the lack of 'rationality' in the design, goals and implementation of the privatization programme and the 'suboptimal' decisions on the management of state assets, due to the lack of a successful macro-economic plan and the short-sighted approach adopted by the 'troika' (or 'institutions') towards privatization proceeds (Christodoulakis, 2015). Accordingly, the tight time frame has been a constraining factor for the proper preparation and implementation of these reforms. Reform outcomes have been negatively affected by the depressed prices of assets and the unfavourable financial environment, the weak operational performance of some SOEs and the opposition from the political system and the general public (OECD, 2016). The privatization process has been characterized by delays and disruptions, proceeds are well below expectations (along with the unrealistic initial goal of €50 billion) and allegations of 'fire sales' have often accompanied the transfer of state assets to private investors.

A gap between formal and actual compliance has been observed in many reform areas. For instance, despite the attempted depoliticization, government intervention in SOEs remains intense, raising concerns about their autonomy and professionalism, especially regarding the appointment of senior management (OECD, 2016). In addition, several structural measures were adapted and implemented hastily in order to 'tick the box', due to policy conditionality pressure, without adequate preparation of the competent institutions to support market reforms. The case of the RAEM is an illustrative case of a 'ghost' institution that was legislatively established in response to the external obligations but has remained practically inactive. The weak domestic 'reform ownership' is a typical explanation for the low take-up of the agreed reforms and their modest outcomes. Similarly to other externally imposed reforms, i.e. those that were not introduced on the Greek government's own initiative (including those that were initiated long before the crisis, such as the prerequisites for entry to the EU single market in the 1990s), the reforms included in the rescue packages and dictated by the countries' lenders did not win sufficient domestic support.

From an administrative-organizational perspective, the proliferation of structures, levels and agencies involved in policymaking and policy implementation (central government, line ministries, HCAP and its sub-sidiaries, regulatory authorities, systems operators, etc.), coupled with the disintegration of vertically integrated functions and structures of utilities markets, have caused institutional fragmentation and severe policy co-ordination problems. A particularly problematic area is the Coordination Mechanism, which has faced numerous obstacles and has not (yet) been in effective operation. While the Coordination Mechanism was consistently and clearly defined in the agreements between the Greek government and the EU insti-tutions, the transition from theory to practice was not smooth. Its heavy design and complex procedures did not manage to deal with the existing fragmentation and coordination problems of the domestic public sector, while the capacity of the involved institutions has been over-estimated. Similar negative results may arise as a result of the structural and functional disintegration of markets and SOEs, as unbundling helps to prevent dis-criminatory and anti-competitive conduct, but may lead to the loss of potential synergies that arise from vertical integration (European Commission, 2007: 31).

A broader issue is the compatibility of market techniques with the pre-servation of public service values, which has not been effectively clarified at the policy level. For instance, the management of public property, national infrastructure and natural resources cannot be solely based on economic-technical criteria of efficiency, which were prioritized in the reform agenda of the crisis period. The appropriateness of commercialized criteria for public policy in the SOE sector is questionable with reference to social and envir-onmental concerns (Self, 1993: 215–217) as well as social rights and tradi-tional democratic decision-making (Claassen, 2017). Relevant constitutional issues arose regarding the transfer of the majority shares of the Water Supply and Sewerage Companies of Athens and Thessaloniki (EYDAP, EYATH) in HCAP in view of their planned (partial) privatization, which were ruled unconstitutional by the Council of State.[11] In addition, marketization tech-niques usually lead to a weakening of political/parliamentary control and imply a 'minimal' democratic accountability of agencies and private sector organizations (Gilmour and Jensen, 1998; Bevir, 2009: 130). While these issues appeared in the domestic political debate, they were absent from the official policy programmes for public sector reform and may hamper their long-term viability.

Trade-offs and open questions

Restructuring and marketization reforms aimed at a range of social, political and economic goals that in many cases have been conflicting. Regarding policy directions, the key performance indicators of SOEs that are monitored by HCAP include economic and public value, financial performance, corpo-rate governance, quality of services, operational efficiency and innovation (European Commission, 2020a: 69). They also embrace environmental concerns, sustainable growth, unemployment, knowledge and information issues (HCAP, 2018). Notwithstanding the advantages of this holistic approach, in practice the combination and balancing of the different goals remain vague. This set of goals has been defined in a rather disjointed way, as a sum—not a synthesis—of external demands and the wants of the Greek government. Hence, they have not been specified, prioritized or evaluated on the basis of potential synergies, complementarity or incompatibility. In addition, the agenda of HCAP includes wide and very optimistic targets/ objectives, while it is doubtful that can be implemented by the SOEs and the competent administrative structures, as recent experience and pilot efforts show.

An interesting illustration reflecting the different motives and priorities of the reform agenda is the contrasting focus of the crisis-related documents and other legal/institutional provisions. The former (for instance the MOUs, the Compliance Reports and the Enhanced Surveillance of the European Commission), which mainly reflected the demands and views of the external actors, place emphasis on the technical and economic aspects of privatizations. On the contrary, HCAP's Strategic Plan, which was drafted by the Hellenic Authorities, introduces broader policy goals including issues of public interest, public value, social accountability, social and territorial cohesion, social awareness, employment and sustainability. Similarly, the assessments of the compliance reports regarding the performance of SOEs mainly refer to their fiscal sustainability and efficiency, while service quality and user satisfaction have not yet been given much, if any, attention.

Beyond the direct financial effect of the reforms, namely the envisaged proceeds for the reduction of public debt, privatization procedures also entail considerable financial, working and administrative costs (Bastian, 2011). For instance, the agencification of the Greek asset management institutions has led to a notable proliferation of external assignments for the preparation and implementation of the restructuring and privatization programmes. Apart from the remuneration and expenses of the managers and employees of the new structures, the commissioned services of consulting groups, banks, law firms, economic, legal and technical consultants to HCAP and HRADF came at a considerable cost, which is covered by the state budget.

Further trade-offs may arise between the direct short-term effects and the indirect long-term wider socio-economic impact of restructuring and marketization. Notwithstanding the economic benefits accompanying liberalization (tariffs/prices), experience shows that a decline in investments often occurs after the opening up of utilities markets to competition (Pelkmans and Luchetta, 2013: 43). A major challenge is therefore to put private firms on the track of competition and investments and to avoid the risk of cream-skimming (Painter, 2011: 248). In the Greek case, the incentives provided are still weak in sectors that have opened up to competition during the crisis, while certain investments by the private firms have been delayed and not been implemented according to the agreed plans (for instance in the rail sector).[12]

The business-like approach to public service may also come into collision with public policy questions of social justice, fairness, openness, collectivity and environmental protection as well as public interest and citizenship values (Cox, 1999). The conciliation of conflicting goals, for example between market competition and ecological concerns (Besselink and Yesilkagit, 2020), remains a puzzling issue that does not seem to have been resolved by the recent and ongoing restructuring and marketization policies. In the same vein, marketization has brought about a more active role for citizens as market consumers but has weakened certain citizenship aspects. The distance between 'happy consumers' and 'involved citizens' (Cox, 1999: 35) indicates the different conceptualization of users of utilities within the context of the market and that of public provision. The latter does not mean exclusively state-owned utilities, but implies a broader perspective on stakeholders' involvement in utilities policy (local government, users, society, etc.). In the Greek case of restructuring and marketization, service users were obviously not the main concern of the crisis' reforms, especially from a political/citizenship perspective.

Conclusion

As Greece emerges from the sovereign debt crisis and after the conclusion of the three economic adjustment programmes, the legacy of the restructuring and marketization reforms becomes increasingly apparent. The integration of managerial and market techniques in the public sector was primarily aimed at reducing its size and cost and enhancing its efficiency. However, the effect of the reforms has been much broader. The reform agenda encompassed a great variety of measures, including privatization, divestment, liberalization, reorganization and agencification. The impact and the outcomes of these policies vary significantly and were highly affected by external pressure and policy conditionality requirements.

Regarding the achievements of the reforms, the restructuring and marketization programmes have brought some improvements in the organization and function of the public sector. A positive effect of the restructuring measures has been the rationalization of the competent government structures via the creation of a single agency for the management of state assets and the systematization of the procedures of co-operation and collaboration between the involved parties (state-public administration, HCAP, SOEs). The strengthening and proliferation of regulatory agencies was also an important step towards the effective transition from state monopolies to competitive markets and the modernization of utilities sectors. However, these new institutional arrangements have caused fragmentation and coordination problems and brought about institutional 'confusion' regarding the allocation of policy tasks across public sector bodies, levels and agencies. At the same time, the transfer of powers to arm's-length bodies raised considerable democratic control and accountability issues.

The impact of marketization reforms is not yet clear and it is doubtful that they have brought about the anticipated benefits. Privatizations were mainly (if not exclusively) driven by revenue targets, while their contribution to long-term investment goals has yet to be seen. The prioritization of the fiscal-oriented goals by the external lenders coupled with the constraints of policy conditionality often led to a short-sighted approach, focusing excessively on the proceeds from the sale of state assets. Accordingly, emphasis was placed on market restructuring for privatization rather than on market restructuring for competition and many of the agreed investments have been delayed or are pending.

Certain trade-offs exist between the short- and long-term impact of the reforms and their economic and sociopolitical implications. The limitations and risks of introducing market techniques in government activities were also highlighted. Beyond the criticism, it should be noted that marketization does not necessarily cause conflicts between political and economic values; on the contrary, if certain conditions are met regarding the quality of policy design and implementation, market-type mechanisms may actually 'work well' for public services (Dan and Andrews, 2016). However, it is doubtful that these conditions were met in the Greek case, as policies were formulated and implemented hastily way, under constant pressure of raising revenue for debt reduction, while the tight timeline undermined the proper planning and design of the reforms. The direct results were modest (proceeds), while the long-term prospects (investments) are still uncertain.

Beyond the above-mentioned limitations, the restructuring and market-ization reforms have changed not only the boundaries and the allocation of powers between the public and the private sector, but also the type, organi-zation and powers of the competent government and administrative struc-tures. Notwithstanding that much was achieved, the results, so far, have been uneven compared with the anticipated benefits. The implementation and viability of the reforms in the post-crisis era remains an open question, as the gradual loosening of policy conditionality and fiscal recovery may provide an opportunity for their effective implementation and better adaptation to the domestic policy agenda.

Notes

1 These processes relate to one another but are not identical. In short, liberalization implies the opening up of markets to competition, while privatization mainly refers to the shift from public to private ownership and control of state assets. Marketization is related to both privatization and liberalization, also including the process of infusing market elements in public services, such as contracts, competition, flexible procedures, business-like management and economic effi-ciency criteria (Laperche and Uzunidis, 2003: 5–6; Savas, 2005: 32; Whitfield, 2006: 4; Hermann and Verhoest, 2014: 25).
2 Currently the General Secretariat of Tax Policy and Public Property.
3 These institutions were partly inspired by existing foreign agencies, namely the German Treuhandanstalt in the case of HRADF (Bastian, 2011; Christodoulakis, 2015) and the French Agence des participations de l'État in the case of HCAP (EDIS).

4 Initially, a fourth subsidiary was established—the Public Holdings Company (EDIS) —which would manage the state's shares in SOEs and would be involved in broader public policy issues, including special obligations and services of general economic interest (SGEI); however, it was quickly abolished.

5 See, for instance, the ongoing reform of the Hellenic Post (ELTA).

6 DEPA Commercial SA and DEPA Infrastructure S.A.

7 However, it should be noted that the obligation to submit strategic and business plans as well as management/performance contracts has been established since the 1990s (Law 2414/1996).

8 Top managers come from the private sector and are hired on a contract basis.

9 The Coordination Mechanism defines the framework for the cooperation of the state, HCAP and SOEs and the procedures and deliverables expected by SOEs (HCAP, 2018: 37, 45, 96–98).

10 Law 4513/2018.

11 Decisions 1223/2020 and 1224/2020.

12 See the planned €500 million investment of TRAINOSE by 2020 (https://m.na ftemporiki.gr/story/1570598 and www.europeandatajournalism.eu/eng/News/Data -news/Railways-in-Greece-poor-service-no-competition).

References

Alford, J. (2002). Defining the client in the public sector: A social-exchange perspective. *Public Administration Review*, 62(3), 337–346. https://doi.org/10.1111/1540-6210.00183.

Bartle, I. (2011). Utility regulation and NPM. In T. Christensen, and P. Laegreid (Eds), *The Ashgate Research Companion in Public Management* (pp. 193–206). Farnham: Ashgate.

Bastian, J. (2011). Is 'Greece Inc.' ready for privatization? Lessons learned from the German Treuhandanstalt, *poleconomix.gr*. www.poleconomix.gr/portal/pages/1934.

Besselink, T., and Yesilkagit, K. (2020). Market regulation between economic and ecological values: Regulatory authorities and dilemmas of responsiveness. *Public Policy & Administration*. https://doi.org/10.1177/0952076719827630.

Bevir, M. (2009). *SAGE Key Concepts: Key Concepts in Governance*. London: SAGE.

Brune, N., Garrett, G., and Kogut, B. (2004). The International Monetary Fund and the global spread of privatization. *IMF Staff Papers*, 51(2), 195–219.

Christodoulakis, G. (2015). Privatization of state assets in the presence of crisis. In G. Christodoulakis (Ed.), *Managing Risks in the European Periphery Debt Crisis* (pp. 108–123). London: Palgrave Macmillan.

Claassen, R. (2017). Markets as mere means. *British Journal of Political Science*, 47 (2), 263–281. https://doi.org/10.1017/S0007123415000113.

Cox, R. (1999). Running Government like a business: Implications for public administration theory and practice. *The American Review of Public Administration*, 29(1), 19–43. https://doi.org/10.1177%2F02750749922064256.

Dan, S., and Andrews, R. (2016). Market-type mechanisms and public service equity: A review of experiences in European public services. *Public Organization Review*, 16, 301–317. https://doi.org/10.1007/s11115-015-0310-6.

Edadan, N. (1997). Privatisation strategies in developing countries: External debt and domestic economic prospect. *Economic and Political Weekly*, 32(27), 1906–1919.

European Commission (2007). Evaluation of the performance of network industries providing services of general economic interest. *European Economy*, 1.

European Commission (2014). Market functioning in network industries: Electronic communications, energy and transport. *European Economy Occasional Papers*, 204 (December).

European Commission (2017). *The ESM Stability Support Programme for Greece. First and Second Reviews: July*. Background Report. Luxembourg: Publications Office of the European Union.

European Commission (2020a). Enhanced Surveillance Report: Greece. *European Economy Institutional Paper*, 123, February.

European Commission (2020b). Enhanced Surveillance Report: Greece. *European Economy Institutional Paper*, 127, May.

Gilmour, R., and Jensen, L. (1998). Reinventing government accountability: Public functions, privatization, and the meaning of 'State action'. *Public Administration Review*, 58(3), 247–258. https://doi.org/10.2307/976565.

HCAP (2018). *Strategic Plan of the Hellenic Corporation of Assets and Participations*. Athens: HCAP.

Hermann, C., and Verhoest, K. (2014). The process of liberalization, privatization and marketization. In C. Hermann and J. Flecker (Eds.), *Privatization of Public Services: Impacts for employment, working conditions, and service quality in Europe* (pp. 6–32). London: Routledge.

Lampropoulou, M. (2018). State-owned enterprises in Greece: The evolution of a paradigm. *Annals of Public and Cooperative Economics*, 89(3), 491–526. doi:10.1111/apce.12174.

Lampropoulou, M. (2020). Utilities policy and reform: The changing relationship between citizens and State-Owned Enterprises. In P. Bance, M. Florio, and B. Sak. (Eds), *The Routledge Handbook of State-Owned Enterprises* (pp. 479–498). London and New York: Routledge.

Laperche, B., and Uzunidis, D. (2003). *Etatisme et marchéisation du secteur public*. Laboratoire Redéploiement Industriel et Innovation, Document de Travail No. 63. Dunkirk: Université du Littoral Côte d'Opale.

Pack, J.R. (1987). Privatization of public-sector services in theory and practice. *Journal of Policy Analysis and Management*, 6(4), 523–540. https://doi.org/10.2307/3323506.

Painter, M. (2011). Managerialism and models of management. In T. Christensen, and P. Laegreid (Eds.), *The Ashgate Research Companion in Public Management* (pp. 237–249). Farnham: Ashgate. doi:10.4324/9781315613321.ch16.

Pelkmans, J., and Luchetta, G. (2013). *Enjoying a Single Market for Network Industries?*Paris: Institut Jacques Delors.

Organisation for Economic Co-operation and Development (OECD) (1988). *The Administration as Service: The Public as Customer*. Paris: OECD Publishing.

Organisation for Economic Co-operation and Development (OECD) (2011). *Government at a Glance 2011*. Paris: OECD Publishing.

Organisation for Economic Co-operation and Development (OECD) (2016). *Greece Policy Brief. Corporate Governance: Reforming the State-Owned Enterprises Sector*. Paris: OECD Publishing.

Organisation for Economic Co-operation and Development (OECD) (2019). *A Policy Maker's Guide to Privatisation: Corporate Governance*. Paris: OECD Publishing.

Pollitt, C., and Bouckaert, G. (2004). *Public Management Reform: A Comparative Analysis*. Oxford: Oxford University Press.

Savas, E.S. (2005). *Privatization in the City: Successes, Failures, Lessons*. Washington, DC: CQ Press.

Self, P. (1993). *Government by the Market? The Politics of Public Choice.* London: Palgrave Macmillan.

Spanou, C. (2003). *Citoyens et administration: Les enjeux de l'autonomie et du pluralisme.* Paris: L'Harmattan.

Spanou, C. (2016). *Policy Conditionality, Structural Adjustment and the Domestic Policy System: Conceptual Framework and Research Agenda.* Research Paper No. RSCAS 2016/60. Florence: European University Institute, Robert Schuman Centre for Advanced Studies. https://dx.doi.org/10.2139/ssrn.2872090.

Torfing, J., Andersen, L.B., Greve, C., Klausen, K. (2020). *Public Governance Paradigms: Competing and Co-Existing.* Cheltenham: Edward Elgar Publishing.

Tummers, L., Jilke, S., and Van de Walle, S. (2014). Citizens in charge? Reviewing the background and value of introducing choice and competition in public services. In Y.K. Dwivedi, M.A. Shareef, S.K. Pandey, V. Kumar (Eds). *Public Administration Reformation: Market Demand from Public Organizations* (pp. 9–26). New York and London: Routledge. https://doi.org/10.4324/9780203694428.

United Nations (2008). *Public Enterprises: Unresolved Challenges and New Opportunities.* New York: United Nations.

Whitfield, D. (2006). *A Typology of Privatisation and Marketisation.* Research Report No.1. European Services Strategy Unit. https://european-services-strategy.org.uk. archived.website/publications/essu-research-reports/essu-research-paper-1/essu-research-paper-1-2.pdf.

8 Reversing policy legacies

The significance of administrative reforms

Calliope Spanou

Introduction

With the onset of the crisis, the public sector was held 'responsible for many of Greece's woes'. The country was found to 'underperform in virtually all policy areas relative to the EU average'. An overstaffed public administration, complex, burdensome and lengthy administrative procedures, and a lack of consistent policy implementation 'stifled competitiveness'. A reform of public administration was therefore 'urgently needed and a key element of the programme' (European Commission, 2010: 20–23). These few sentences describe the low administrative capacity, which constituted the point of departure for reform requirements under all three adjustment programmes. Low capacity was systematically repeated as a diagnosis, as a risk for the consistent implementation of the programme, and as an explanation for delays.

Administrative reform became a solid part of any sectoral structural reform. During the crisis, long overdue reforms were linked to the new fiscal policy priorities. They fed the conditionalities for the disbursement of loan instalments and were subjected to close monitoring, detailed guidance and tight deadlines. Downsizing and reorganization, merger or abolition of various entities were all to be considered. A wide range of further actions included the introduction of new legislation and regulations, drafting reports on the state of affairs and devising action plans for the necessary changes, data collection and processing, developing technological infrastructure, the creation of sectoral or cross-sectoral bodies, and the redeployment of human resources.

However, horizontal administrative reforms gradually occupied a larger part of the agenda. Some were directly linked to the crisis and the management thereof, others were rather an expression of the 'crisis as opportunity' mantra. The reform agenda was essentially set by a mapping of problems provided by the Organisation for Economic Co-operation and Development (OECD) Review of the Central Administration (OECD, 2011), which was included as a requirement of the first adjustment programme.

The diagnosis was by no means new and it was not the first time that these issues had been raised. The new element was the 'big bang' character of the

DOI: 10.4324/9780429202247-11

administrative reform agenda, whose realism can be seriously questioned. However, the overpowering fiscal priority, especially of the first two programmes, did not allow sufficient scope for meaningful administrative reform. In mid-2014, a certain shift towards 'qualitative reforms' was detected but the change of government in 2015 interrupted this process. Only the third adjustment programme covering the period 2015–2018 announced a belated concern for qualitative reforms, for 'a modern state and public administration', once staff numbers and the public wage bill had been reduced by 26% and 38%, respectively, compared to 2009. This shift can be seen as an acknowledgment of their negative impact on administrative capacity (European Commission, 2017: 137; Almunia, 2020).

Among the reforms included in the adjustment programmes, budgeting and fiscal management reform was of primary importance, since public finances and related inaccurate data were at the centre of the storm. Meanwhile, the size of the public workforce and the public wage bill were also major areas of concern, particularly because reliable data was missing. In both areas better allocation and use of (financial and human) resources were required, entailing different management rules, procedures and tools. Both areas had for a long time avoided or neutralized built-in constraints and countered general rules. Moreover, in both areas deep changes were necessary, exceeding by far practical arrangements. Human resources (HR) and fiscal management not only defined critical aspects of administrative capacity, understood as 'the ability to manage efficiently the human and physical resources required for delivering the outputs of government' (Painter and Pierre, 2005: 2), but also touched upon core aspects of state operation in Greece (Spanou, 2020c). They represented two areas where the political personnel had successfully managed to preserve discretion in handling (financial or human) resources. The notorious lack of reliable fiscal and HR data is hardly a coincidence. In that sense, examining and comparing reforms in these two areas helps to highlight reform dynamics under the three adjustment programmes, which test perennial trends of the political administrative system.[1]

To clarify the perspective of this chapter, reforms are to be understood as marking 'significant departures from the status quo' (Peters, 1996: 9), i.e. as challenging the existing explicit or implicit arrangements or systems in a substantial way. There are various ways to assess the significance of policy change. For example, it can be seen as a paradigm change (Hall, 1993); as a change in the sets of ideas which comprise the overall goals and the framework guiding action (Halligan, 1997: 19); or as a major change that challenges or destabilizes established policy preferences, as reflected in statutes, processes and practices (Sabatier and Jenkins-Smith, 1999: 147). The concept of the 'policy frame' condenses the above aspects. It points to the underlying assumptions which serve to select, organize, interpret and make sense of a complex reality, and therefore define and legitimate action and remedies (Rein and Schön, 1993: 146). In a nutshell, policy change requires a 'frame shift' at the level of legislation as well as implementation. The assessment of the reforms under examination will therefore include two dimensions: *policy regime*, as reflected in the old and new policy frames, and *policy implementation*, namely policy as adopted and implemented (Boyne et al., 2003: 29–30).

The chapter undertakes a brief assessment of two groups of reforms, which can be distinguished by their closer or looser links to the priorities of fiscal consolidation. It shows that while the crisis provided an opportunity for reform in one area, it proved incapable of bringing about significant change in the other. The chapter is structured in three parts. The first section, 'Counting the numbers', deals with reforms directly linked to fiscal consolidation. The second section, 'Questioning civil service rules and practices', turns to major human resources management (HRM) issues as part of 'qualitative' reforms. The third section, 'Comparing reforms', discusses the significance of changes and the outcome of the confrontation between old and new policy frames. The chapter concludes by speculating on the future.

Counting the numbers

Fiscal management: from inertia to radical reform

Public financial management (PFM) can be described as the 'black box' of government in Greece. Lack of central monitoring, coordination and control coexisted with insufficient information and unreliable data, as well as fragmented and uncontrolled practices by various state entities (Hellenic Observatory, 2014). Budget formulation was excessively decentralized while budget execution was excessively centralized. The minister of finance appeared— somewhat paradoxically—to be isolated, if not weak. The incumbent minister appeared unable to either monitor centrally and in real time more than 60% of general government expenditure or to intervene in case of deviations. Thus, various state entities (local authorities, insurance funds, hospitals and public utilities) were taking on financial obligations (e.g. wage policies, loans, procurement, etc.) which resulted in budget overruns, deficits and expenditure that were not registered in the budget. Transparency and accountability were equally poor.[2] Above all, there was no balance sheet showing the precise state of the public finances, while parliament was unable to examine and approve the entire fiscal activity (Rapanos, 2007: 48–53).

During the 2000s, converging recommendations for radical reform were put forward by international organizations, such as the OECD (2008) and the IMF (2006). However, little actually changed.[3] At the end of that decade, fiscal management was undoubtedly ripe for reform direction. But awareness of the problem was restricted to domestic experts and within Ministry of Finance circles. It had not been accorded priority status on the government's agenda, nor had it provoked any public debate and its political and financial implications continued to be ignored (Spanou, 2020b).

With the onset of the global financial crisis in 2008, the fiscal management deficiencies could no longer be swept under the carpet. Their consequences were exposed in the form of high levels of budget deficits and sovereign debt, and a fundamental lack of reliable statistical data (Kaplanoglou and Rapanos, 2013). Addressing chronic distortions in PFM was a most urgent priority (OECD, 2011: 14 and 71–79). The objective was to discipline fiscal behaviour in order to meet strict fiscal targets, as well as to systematically monitor budget execution and produce accurate and timely fiscal reports.

The crisis constituted an external shock, which entailed a radical change of perspective. The introduction of a coherent fiscal management system was launched in January 2010 with the technical assistance of the IMF (Papaconstantinou, 2016: 197; Ministry of Finance, 2009: 26–27). Subsequent legislative initiatives came about as a result of structural fiscal reforms included in all three programmes but also through changes in European regulations that were introduced from 2011 onwards. The whole budgeting system was remodelled in terms of formal structures, procedures, rules and standards.[4] The reform unfolded along the lines proposed earlier by the IMF and the OECD, with the exception of programme budgeting, which was seen as a subsequent stage. The role of the Ministry of Finance as the central actor in budget formulation and execution was considerably strengthened as was its grip on expenditure by other ministries and public entities. New instruments were developed, such as the Medium-Term Fiscal Framework (MTFS), which defines the general strategy and serves as the point of reference for annual budgets; top-down budgeting processes with binding expenditure ceilings per central administration body for the entire general government; the Expenditure Commitment Register and corrective mechanisms to address cases of deviation from agreed fiscal targets; and new fiscal reporting obligations for various public entities organized in line with the European time frame and standards (the so-called European Semester).

The strengthened central functions of the Ministry of Finance essentially relied on the leading policy role of the General Accounting Office (GAO). This was complemented by the parallel strengthening of the financial management capacity and responsibility of ministries. The establishment of a network of new General Directorates of Financial Services (GDFS) in 'spending' ministries under the guidance of the GAO illustrates the new division of responsibilities for the entire budgeting process (formulation, execution, control and reporting). The general directors took on a 'custodian' role regarding the expenditure ceilings and commitments, as well as ensuring sound fiscal management. They were expected to serve as a counterweight to political leadership and hence their significance extends far beyond fiscal management to touch upon the relationship between politics and administration (see below). Additionally, a major shift from ex ante to ex post controls of expenditure rendered the GDFS primarily responsible for ex ante controls, while the Hellenic Court of Auditors (HCA) was to concentrate on ex post controls and the GAO gradually moved towards spending reviews.

Fiscal transparency was equally reinforced by institutional reforms, such as the transformation of the statistical services into an independent authority in 2010 (the Hellenic Statistical Authority—ELSTAT). Furthermore, the creation of the Parliamentary State Budget Office (PBO) was meant to provide support for an enhanced role of parliament in the budgetary process. Soon afterwards, the Hellenic Fiscal Council (HFC) was established as an independent authority to monitor compliance with fiscal rules[5] (following Directive 2011/85 and the Fiscal Compact). Last but by no means least, the public sector accounting system changed (or, better still, is changing) to comply with European and international standards. It established a common way of representing economic data for all general government entities, replacing the—until recently—five different, fragmented and non-compatible systems of functional data classification (see Miliakou et al., 2017; OECD, 2019: 64).

Budgeting and fiscal management reform epitomize a belated but radical policy shift in a highly problematic sector of the Greek political-administrative system. The breadth and depth of the reforms are acknowledged as being impressive (OECD, 2019: 6, 37–40, 58, 66, 76). There is no doubt that the sovereign debt crisis served as a focusing event, an external shock that exerted a forceful pressure for change. At the same time the subjection of the country to the adjustment programmes and their policy conditionalities did not allow any other option. Obstacles and political resistance from individual ministers became practically irrelevant.

The most impressive aspect, nevertheless, rests in the fact that this has been one of the few reforms that presented continuity beyond the term of individual ministers and governments. The constant presence of, and coaching by, the IMF in its double role as technical assistance provider and a tough member of the so-called troika cannot be underestimated. Domestically, this continuity may be also attributed to the political leadership of the Ministry of Finance during this period. As one of the signatories of the Memoranda of Understanding (MOUs) and aware of the stakes involved, the ministry was responsible not only for meeting fiscal targets but more generally for the implementation of its terms. These reforms allowed it to claim the central role it ought to have played by right and to remedy its past weaknesses (Spanou, 2020b).

HR data

The immediate need to contain public expenditure required reliable data on the wage bill and the size of the public workforce. The 'unusually high degree of uncertainty affecting public employment data, particularly beyond central government' was highlighted by the OECD Review (OECD, 2011: 59). Long-standing issues came to the fore, such as the wide diversity of employee status and regime, unregulated hiring of personnel on fixed-term contracts as well as a hazy picture regarding the number and expediency of various state entities. The number of public sector employees and entities were a terra incognita for the Greek political-administrative system.

This priority was immediately addressed by the Ministry of Finance, essentially through launching a census of the public sector personnel and entities, as well as with the establishment the Single Payment Authority (EAP) for all kinds of payments. The continued implementation of these two initiatives was later incorporated into the structural reforms required by the programme (European Commission, 2010: 47–48 and 67).[6]

This endeavour was not only complex but also met with resistance. Creating a Human Resources Register for the entire public sector required the collection and verification of information on total personnel per public body, employment status, and so forth, and it required the parallel inventory of public entities; both had frequently failed in the past. Resistance among the wider public sector has been significant, judging from the series of legislative measures that provided for sanctions against those who would not comply (public entities, political leaders and public employees).

Notwithstanding the difficulties and delays, this reform bore fruit. It laid the foundations for the rationalization and better utilization of HR. The Register facilitates not only a quantitative but also a qualitative overview and monitoring of public employment. It thus develops into a broader instrument for HRM wage policy planning, as well as for increased transparency and accountability. A 'Digital Organigram' was built using the census database, reflecting in real-time the structure of the general government and the allocation of human resources, positions and corresponding requirements.

Beyond the pressure of the troika, the main actor in the above-mentioned reforms was the Ministry of Finance, which was aware of the stakes of such reforms, less dependent on other actors, and disposed of effective means of pressure. More generally, the narrow fiscal focus on quantitative aspects had a powerful—though negative—influence on HRM, essentially through downsizing. At the same time, however, it required a reliable organizational and technological infrastructure to control expenditure and provide accurate data.

Questioning civil service rules and practices

Regarding the more substantial aspects of HRM, there have been instances of reform over-reach and blind spots. As HRM rules had turned into state resources at the discretion of politicians (recruitment, career prospects, allowances, etc.), past reforms were often repetitive, and effected little substantial change. Rather than building an efficient and reliable state machinery, HRM issues were seen as a process of 'distribution of privileges' to various groups of public employees. This perception was part of the existing policy frame that tended to guide policy and counter or prevent administrative modernization. A selective 'reform over-activity' (Spanou, 2010) and an—apparently paradoxical—coexistence of formalism with by-passing of rules and procedures had shaped and sustained a 'symbiotic relationship' between politics and administration (Spanou, 2001 and 2014b). This describes a mutually beneficial relationship that keeps the administration at a low level of independence and expertise and provides the basis of the 'public service bargain' (Hood and Lodge, 2006).

In the crisis context, the administrative capacity in general and HRM in particular became a major area of reform (Featherstone, 2015). The 2011 OECD review stressed the urgency of qualitative aspects of HRM reforms, thus setting the essence of the agenda, which, during the first and second programme, continued to be overshadowed by downsizing (Spanou, 2014a and 2015). To illustrate the rationale behind the HRM reforms that were undertaken, a few examples will be discussed below, including HRM rules (mobility, performance appraisal) and the relationship between politics and administration (selection and status of senior civil servants and board-level executives).

Mobility

Over several decades, mobility was systematically sidelined. Its absence had become a distinctive feature of the Greek administration. The numerous obstacles it faced resulted from the mode of recruitment that tied public employees to a specific ministry or body, and from the fragmented system of job classifications and employment status. The absence of general rules for organizing mobility led to a total reliance on individual decisions, something that had as a major consequence the qualitative and quantitative misallocation of personnel.

The issue was given particular prominence in the 2011 OECD review (2011), which recommended opening up mobility across the entire general government (i.e. including regional services and all state entities). A critical condition for this was the creation of a single system of classification of employment positions, drastically reducing its 'branches', and streamlining them on the basis of job descriptions.

Mobility was nevertheless not treated as an HRM instrument per se, but rather as a means of curtailing public employment. Only later did attention shift to the restructuring of ministries (2014 and 2017/2018) and the introduction of job descriptions. A new mobility system was eventually introduced (Law 4440/2016) covering the entire general government. It rationalized the length of temporary secondments and created a centrally managed mobility mechanism. Uniform rules, regular publication of available openings, an electronic platform and the use of job descriptions as criteria to match supply and demand were its main innovative tools. These also provided transparency and predictability. However, mobility still relied on the initiative of the employee and suffered from numerous exceptions to general rules, while it proved difficult to reform branches of the old job classification system.

Performance appraisal

Personnel evaluation had been repeatedly highlighted as being of limited value. The plethora of top-level scores neutralized its significance as a tool for career development and for managing human resources (motivation, promotion, etc.). Since the early 1990s, the issue remained off the government agenda, despite widespread awareness regarding its limits. During the crisis it only reached the agenda of the adjustment programme associated with downsizing.

Although in 2012 a new appraisal system was being developed, it did not see the light of day. In 2014, a comparative assessment method was tentatively introduced (Law 4250/2014) with an aim to contain top-level ratings. However, not only did it represent too radical a shift but was also perceived by public employees as an immediate threat of dismissal. The insecurity resulting from parallel downsizing measures fuelled intense opposition from public employees and their unions and it proved impossible to implement. After this experience, a new bill did not find its way to parliament because of the snap elections of January 2015. The issue remained pending and was included in the requirements of the third programme. The new appraisal system that was eventually introduced (Law 4369/2016) represented little more than a combination of old and new regulations, without actually remedying the long-standing deficiencies.

During the period 2010–2018 various attempts were made to introduce a new appraisal system, but they were abandoned by successive ministers and governments. The lack of continuity as well as downsizing policies delayed and even neutralized change. Party controversies and ministerial inconsistencies were at the root of this. Thus, the final reform output resulted in only a few marginal changes compared to the former unsatisfactory system, while the procedure was modernized only in technical terms (e.g. use of electronic forms).

Depoliticization

The selection of managers has constantly been suspected of political partiality, while neglecting considerations of merit. The imbalance between politics and administration constitutes a major obstacle to the development of a professional and independent civil service, as highlighted in the 2011 OECD review. Depoliticization in the sense of strengthening the senior civil service vis-à-vis political appointees was one of its essential recommendations (OECD, 2011). It was meant to clarify the division of labour, address the perennial imbalance in politics-administration relationships (Sotiropoulos, 2007) and ensure institutional continuity.

However, this issue had often been on the reform agenda given that the grade and career systems were 'reformed' seven times in less than 20 years (1999–2016), thus marking a striking lack of awareness of the consequences of such instability (Wettenhall, 2013: 160). Formalism and standardization were the main ways to respond to criticisms of party-political bias in the selection of senior managers. However, changes had a minimal added value while transitional provisions left the administration in limbo throughout the crisis period (with often discretionary temporary assignments in management positions). What was systematically underestimated is that frequent changes in the career rules and selection procedures undermined the development of an independent and professional civil service.

The new system for the selection of managers (Law 4369/2016) essentially constituted a combination of previous provisions. It adopted a rather complicated point system with four sets of diverse, variably weighted criteria: (a) formal qualifications and vocational training; (b) work experience and responsibilities; (c) evaluation; and (d) structured interview. Based on these, a shortlist of seven candidates were interviewed to decide the finalist. The reform was essentially a replay of the past. The emphasis remained on formal qualifications as a symbol of merit; the length of service of senior managers was again limited to three years resulting in a frequent turnover of personnel and keeping prospective senior officials on the party-political hook while weakening hierarchical authority; and the core issue of the respective roles of senior civil servants and political appointees was left untouched. Nothing like the above-mentioned general directors of financial services was even envisaged. The whole exercise remained within the same policy frame. Fluidity of rules, formalistic criteria and the three-year 'rotation' constitute major problems for the civil service system that politicians as well as public servants were not eager to address, because they define the terms of their 'symbiotic relationship'. A significant reshaping of the politics-administration nexus would require a shift away from the constant manipulation of career rules, a substantial redefinition of respective roles and responsibilities and the use of substantive (non-formalistic) criteria of selection.

Another dimension of depoliticization concerned senior executive positions in specific sectors where credibility and efficiency depended on distance from government influence. These include the National Statistical Service, which became an independent authority (Hellenic Statistical Authority, ELSTAT, Law 3832/2010) and the General Secretariat of Taxation and Customs that became in 2012/2013 the semi-autonomous General Secretariat of Public Revenue (GGDE, Law 4093/2012) and was succeeded in 2016/2017 by the Independent Authority for Public Revenue (AADE, Law 4389/2016) (Dimitrakopoulos and Passas, 2020). The third programme extended this requirement to all executive positions, including the politically appointed and freely revocable general and special secretaries in the government ministries and the heads of public entities.

These changes were ushered in by Law 4369/2016 (and its subsequent amendments) which established a four-year term of office (instead of revocability) for senior executive positions, and introduced a procedure for the assessment of qualifications that was meant to reduce government discretion. The

National Register of Executive Staff, which was electronically compiled by the Supreme Council for Civil Personnel Selection (ASEP), served as a quite large pool of interested candidates mainly from the public but also from the private sector. Vacancies were publicly advertised and candidates were assessed by a Special Board for the Selection of Executive Staff that had to shortlist three candidates. Ministers were able to choose from among the three at their discretion.

Such a change can be considered as a radical shift of approach. Against absolutely discretionary appointment and revocability, it attempted to rationalize and standardize the selection of senior executives and to guarantee them a four-year term of service. In other words, it subjected political discretion to institutional constraints. However, the implementation of this reform pointed to a different direction. Not only because it was delayed, leaving the discretionary political appointees in place until the 2019 general elections, but also for another major reason: approximately one-third of all advertised vacancies outlining the requirements for the position of administrative secretary promoted informally preselected candidates. Hence, this reform stands out for compromising its depoliticization objectives from its inception. Under the surface of a strictly regulated process, a wide margin was left informally to influence the selection outcome beyond what is institutionally allowed. As the European institutions requested to restart the selection process, it became evident that the new policy frame was visibly and immediately captured by pre-existing patterns of political behaviour.

The emblematic reform of the third programme also highlights the incongruence with the political culture, which managed to absorb and neutralize its innovative elements at the implementation stage. Whereas government discretion in selecting senior executives is acceptable in numerous administrative systems, the programme imposed in disregard a different option; thus, attention was diverted from the real stakes of depoliticization, i.e. civil service empowerment. In the absence of an operational redefinition of tasks, the reform was devised in terms of status and selection procedures which are known to be easily manipulated.[7] The strengthening of the senior civil service vis-à-vis politics was not simply ignored but further undermined by the ambivalence of the (political or administrative) role of the new 'depoliticized' senior executives.

Comparing the significance of reforms

Looking at the ambitious administrative reform agenda of the three adjustment programmes, there are some striking differences. First, some reforms were more closely related to the crisis and were better defined than others; certain issues reached the agenda for the first time (i.e. budgeting reform, mobility, performance appraisal, depoliticization of executives); while others had a long history of previous repeatedly inconclusive or symbolic reforms (career and selection of managers); still some other issues never really made it onto the agenda (three-year term of office, mobility as part of staff career development, etc.).

Second, the outcomes in terms of a significant departure from the status quo were clearly uneven. Moreover, the continuity of reforms was uneven, despite the politically restricted framework of the time and the close monitoring by international and European lenders. In certain cases they unfolded in a consistent manner, while in others the well-known pattern of discontinuity prevailed, following the frequent changes of governments and of ministers.

Policy frames: prevalence or capture?

Did the new policy frames prevail in their competition with established ones? As shown above, the most consistent and radically new frame characterizes reforms related to fiscal management and HR data. These developed rather consistently under the three adjustment programmes and related MOUs, and their content clearly demarcates them from past patterns of operation. New fiscal management mechanisms, procedures and rules were introduced to overcome fragmentation, increase central control, as well as produce reliable data and transparency. An innovative role was assigned to the general directors of financial services that could potentially reshape the politics-administration relationship—although no similar redistribution of roles has taken place in other areas of the civil service. Similar observations can be made regarding the collection of HR data, the long-standing absence of which mirrors the unreliability of economic and statistical data. Thus, the *terra incognita* was replaced by the systematic monitoring of public sector expenditure, including personnel numbers and the overall wage bill. The common element in these two cases is their importance for achieving fiscal targets.

By contrast, HRM reforms seem intermittent and erratic, constantly experimenting with different solutions and delaying the production of results. No doubt the HRM agenda was formed gradually, while parallel downsizing policies affected its content as well as the conditions of its implementation. However, it is important to highlight that past practices were not actually reconsidered. HRM reforms managed to reproduce the status quo or to indirectly neutralize any substantial innovation at the implementation stage. Old policy frames remained active permeating or even capturing at various degrees the new ones.

Fiscal pressure was in this case indirect; it mainly took the form of downsizing measures that rendered the environment of HRM reforms more difficult and affected the capacity of corresponding ministers to promote them. Beyond that, it hardly influenced the substance of reforms. Despite policy conditionalities, significant room was left for domestic influence on policy preferences. The representatives of the lenders practically delegated the specification of solutions to outside experts who were increasingly involved in the provision of technical assistance,[8] which did *not* have a directive (i.e. executive) role.

The 'paradigmatic shift' proved ambiguous or uncertain (Featherstone, 2015: 311; Ladi, 2014; Lampropoulou and Oikonomou, 2018). The wider margin of discretion that was left to domestic actors in the area of HRM reform is an important factor accounting for the differences observed when compared with those in fiscal management. It is reflected in the continuation of party competition and symbolic policies (Spanou, 1996), with constant doing and undoing, delaying reform outputs, not to say outcomes, and wasting large amounts of time and energy. It is also reflected in the perpetuation of the old policy frames. What seems to have been underestimated by the troika/'institutions' (and the technical assistance) is that the Greek political system thrives on changing civil service rules, thereby (re-)distributing public resources in terms of status, remuneration and career prospects. It readily took the opportunity offered to play the new game by the old rules. Business went on as usual: it meant fine-tuning existing practices without significantly departing from, nor challenging, the core of pre-existing policy arrangements.

One case stands out for not complying with this pattern: the introduction in 2014 of the comparative assessment. Such a radical policy shift—which was briefly possible as a result of domestic discretion—is a clear illustration of the incompatibility and ultimately the clash between the old and the new policy frames. It is also a confirmation *a contrario* of the prevalence of the old public service bargain in all other areas of HRM. Not only did frame incompatibility turn in to a clash, but contrary to other cases, this took place in the open, despite the politically restrictive framework of the time. Such a development was facilitated by imminent elections (in January 2015) and the expected change of government.

Secondary changes and the 'invisible game'

Another factor that has to be taken into account is reform dynamics within the specific policy area. Beyond domestic discretion concerning the content of reforms, a critical factor for uneven outcomes is their capacity for obstruction or influence. In the case of fiscal management reform and data collection, unprecedented constraints were introduced, processes were rearranged, responsibilities and supervision were tightened. However, these did not particularly affect the status and career prospects of public employees. Opposition came primarily from political officials defending their margin of freedom. However, their capacity for resistance vis-à-vis the Ministry of Finance was limited during those times.

In contrast, HRM reforms directly concerned public employees and even required their cooperation (e.g. performance appraisal, mobility, etc.). They affected their status, remuneration and career prospects, while they were running the risk of drastic downsizing. This exacerbated struggles among various groups of public employees fighting for limited resources.

The availability of domestic discretion combined with the need to compensate public employees or in some way secure their cooperation (Spanou,

2020a) provided opportunities for the survival of the old policy frame, whereby public resources are distributed as 'privileges'. This perception prevailed in HRM, passing its core elements on to the reforms and allowing only secondary changes to be made. Even when potentially new ideas appeared, possibilities were left wide open by design to be exploited by older rationales at the implementation stage. Senior administrative officials influenced new policy choices, thus exchanging their cooperation for favourable regulations. In a nutshell, the symbiotic relationship between politics and administration survived and reproduced the terms of the existing 'public service bargain'.

In such conditions, an invisible game was played among those groups of public servants who had better access to the shaping of policy choices. They did not act as a single actor. On the contrary, various policy choices bear the mark of the differential treatment of specific sub-groups; middle- and lower-level employees were more affected than senior civil servants in terms of remuneration and were more exposed to downsizing measures. In terms of remuneration, senior public servants were comparatively much better off than before, while the remainder of the civil service was subjected to drastic cuts under the unified salary scheme. Civil servants with higher postgraduate degrees even improved their future career prospects, based on the perpetuation and intensification of formalistic selection criteria. While the restructuring of the 'branches' proved to be the most complicated reform endeavour, since it involved too many competing corporatist interests and affected the whole public service, related obstacles were selectively lifted to the exclusive benefit of the graduates of the School of Public Administration who could compete for positions of director general outside of the rule of 'branch' that applied to all others. This invisible game may also account for the policy discontinuities in HRM reforms: the change of ministers revived expectations and offered opportunities to various groups of public servants for influencing the content of related policies.

The consensus on instruments

The focus of the troika's monitoring methods and of the technical assistance actors on instruments represented a further push in the direction of visible secondary changes regarding instruments rather than in the direction of policy core issues. Given the pressure for reform and the complexities surrounding it, this was the easiest part. It provided a basis for consensus that veiled or sidelined potentially new and divergent policy approaches. This may be seen as a form of goal displacement. Rather than contesting deeper rationales, policy issues were reframed in a way that emphasized their preconditions in terms of instruments. When ambitious reform goals are translated into useful instruments (rules, procedures, technological infrastructure, etc.), all parties in the reform process can claim that there is change, independently of its significance. Instruments represent convenient tangible effects. They can easily be observed and checked as 'deliverables' during the monitoring process. Furthermore, the level of instruments is the privileged terrain of technical assistance, which may have a limited understanding of deeper deficiencies, of related stakes and past experiences, but also a limited influence on policy choices.

Such a focus also suits those domestic political actors who are not prepared (politically or intellectually) for deeper changes; under the surface of novelties, it shields the most important elements of pre-existing policies (as evidenced by marginal changes in personnel appraisal, selection of managers, in the employee-centred mobility and the preservation of the 'branches'). For instance, new techniques and infrastructure were meant to change the terms of the politics-administration nexus and preclude the use of HR issues from being used as 'distribution of privileges', but were isolated from this major policy objective and lost their ambition. This is not to say that more sophisticated and modernized tools are not important. But they do not necessarily lead to significant change to the extent that the policy frame remains unchallenged.

Conclusion: legacies and prospects

The reform agenda induced by the OECD and inscribed in the three programmes challenged entrenched core policy arrangements but with uneven results. The reform dynamics emerging from this brief analysis point to a complex set of determining factors. The overpowering fiscal priority favoured certain reforms but proved insufficient—if not unfavourable—for others that were only loosely related to it. With regard to fiscal management, the crisis served as a critical juncture and opened a policy window that allowed changes to be made that hitherto had not been possible, to the point that a change of paradigm occurred. In the area of HRM, changes were unambitious, half-hearted and inconsistent. In short, policy legacies proved much stronger in this case than policy conditionality requirements.

However, administrative reform is a much more complex process than it is often thought to be. Therefore, before drawing any dark conclusions, it is worth speculating about the future. Experience shows that a change of government is often accompanied by new reform initiatives. This is what happened soon after the new government took office in 2019. In the area of fiscal management, any new initiatives built upon previous arrangements and achievements (European Commission, 2020b: 52; 2020c: 8, 34). This continuity may be seen as the common result of domestic policy learning and of the fact that budgeting and fiscal management are part of the European economic governance system. In the area of HRM reforms, various aspects were reconsidered. Policy continuity is observed in the further development of digital instruments supporting the HRM system, such as the digital organigram and related job descriptions, something that represents a tangible gain from past reforms (European Commission, 2020c and 2020d: 71).

Although some of the changes in HRM exhibit an incremental approach, correcting and adjusting existing arrangements (e.g. selection of managers and strengthening the ASEP), others stand out because they reverse past reforms. This marks a return to the Greek tradition of politically appointed general secretaries in government ministries. This reversal was essentially pre-announced by the then leading opposition party, when the attempted depoliticization process was compromised in practice. Additionally, the selection process for senior executives in public entities was revised. While the process essentially remained along the lines of the 2016 reform, the new selection body includes the presence of government appointees, who participate as ex officio members.[9] The message is clear: while accepting the main idea of a competitive pre-selection process, the political dimension of these positions is openly acknowledged.[10]

However, there is more to it than that. A parallel significant change was introduced in the direction of depoliticization: general secretaries as political appointees in ministries are now sitting across from permanent secretaries, who exclusively come from the career civil service. They are selected by a special committee of the ASEP for a three-year term. As senior career officials coordinating the administrative machinery, they potentially strengthen the role of the higher civil service vis-à-vis politics. They are also endowed with a series of delegated decision-making powers. Although these arrangements need time to be tested in practice, they represent a big step towards the essence of the recommendations of the 2011 OECD report. They introduce a more balanced and clearer division of labour between politics and administration, something that was acknowledged by the European Commission (2019: 75 and 2020a: 27–30). Furthermore, they seem to be better adapted to the Greek political culture, an aspect that increases their chances of taking root.

An overall assessment of these developments shows that even with twists and turns, there is an implicit process of maturing and of growing awareness, i.e. of learning, which is essential for the domestic reform dynamics. From now on, this needs to evolve independently from any outside pressure in order to become sustainable. To risk a final guess, these developments may prove to represent a case of 'institutional layering' (Thelen, 2004), whereby despite policy legacies change comes gradually as a result of new elements attached to existing institutions.

Notes

1　The chapter draws on the findings of an empirical research study entitled Reforms in Public Administration under the Crisis, conducted with the support of the A.G. Leventis Foundation Research Chair of the Hellenic Foundation for European and Foreign Policy (ELIAMEP). See Spanou (2019). The full report is available in Greek at www.eliamep.gr/wp-content/uploads/2018/11/metarrythmiseis-sth-dim osia-dioikisi-sti-diarkeia-tis-krisis.pdf. A previous version of this paper was presented at the Conference 'Greece and the Euro: From Crisis to Recovery',

Fletcher School, Boston, April 12, 2019, co-organized by Tufts University and the Hellenic Observatory, LSE.

2 According to a report of the European Commission (2007) covering 18 countries belonging to the Economic and Monetary Union, Greece ranked highest in terms of centralization of budget execution, last in budget transparency, and last but one in terms of the top-down budgeting process.

3 Pilot projects for programme budgeting were launched by the Ministry of Culture in 2008. PFM reform appeared in the electoral programme of the Panellinio Socialistiko Kinima (PASOK—Panhellenic Socialist Movement) in the 2007 and 2009 elections.

4 Major legislative stages in this process are Laws 3871/2010, 4270/2014 incorporating European Directive 2011/85/EU (L 306/45), and 4337/2015.

5 The PBO and the HFC have partly overlapping fiscal oversight functions which need to be streamlined in the medium term (OECD, 2019: 74).

6 Laws 3845/2010 and 3870/2010. A General Directorate of Remunerations was legislated in May 2009 (N.3763/2009) but had not advanced until then.

7 This is confirmed by the earlier experience of the resignation of the first (2014) and the dismissal of the second (2015) General Secretary of Public Revenue, who—on the insistence of the troika—were selected through a special competition process and were provided with a 'guaranteed' five-year term.

8 First, it was within the Taskforce for Greece, created in September 2011 by the EU Commission, when France was designated as the 'domain leader' or 'reform partner' in administrative reform; later, from 2015 onwards, by the French technical cooperation agency Expertise France.

9 The pre-selection process is carried out by a five-member committee, chaired by a vice-president (or counsellor) of the ASEP. A counsellor from the Legal Counsel of the State, and three ex officio members complete the selection body, i.e. two general secretaries (from the Presidency of the Government and from the Ministry of the Interior) and the President of the National Centre for Public Administration and Local Government. The committee shortlists three people, and the relevant political authority (ministers, Council of Ministers) then selects and appoints one of them for a three-year term (Law 4735/2020).

10 The European Commission has 'welcomed' this development 'as it is expected to contribute both in terms of the transparency and efficiency of this reform. The central role foreseen for the ASEP in the selection process is also welcomed, in particular in terms of contributing to the further depoliticization of the public administration' (European Commission, 2020b: 98, 2020d: 72).

References

Almunia, J. (2020). *Lessons from Financial Assistance to Greece*, Independent Evaluation Report. Luxembourg: European Stability Mechanism.

Boyne, G.A., Farrell, C., Law, J., Powell, M., Walker R.M. (2003). *Evaluating Public Management Reforms*. Buckingham: Open University Press.

Dimitrakopoulos, D.G., and Passas, A.G. (2020). *The Depoliticisation of Greece's Public Revenue Administration: Radical Change and the Limits of Conditionality.* Cham: Springer.

Edelman, M. (1988). *Constructing the Political Spectacle*. Chicago: University of Chicago Press.

European Commission (2007). Public Finances in EMU 2007. *European Economy Occasional Papers*, 3.

European Commission (2010). The Economic Adjustment Programme of Greece. *European Economy Occasional Papers*, 61.

European Commission (2017). The ESM Stability Support Programme for Greece, First and Second Reviews July 2017. Background Report. European Commission DG ECFIN, *Institutional Paper*, 64, November.

European Commission (2019). Enhanced Surveillance Report: Economic and Financial Affairs Greece. *European Economy Institutional Paper*, 116, November.

European Commission (2020a). Enhanced Surveillance Report: Greece. *European Economy Institutional Paper*, 123, February.

European Commission (2020b). Enhanced Surveillance Report: Greece. *European Economy Institutional Paper*, 127, May.

European Commission (2020c). Enhanced Surveillance Report: Greece. *European Economy Institutional Paper*, 134, September.

European Commission (2020d). Enhanced Surveillance Report: Greece. *European Economy Institutional Paper*, 137, November.

Featherstone, K. (2015). External conditionality and the debt crisis: The 'troika' and public administration reform in Greece. *Journal of European Public Policy*, 22(3), 295–314. https://doi.org/10.1080/13501763.2014.955123.

Hall, P. (1993). Policy paradigms, social learning, and the State: The case of economic policymaking in Britain, *Comparative Politics*, 25(3), 275–296. https://doi.org/10.2307/422246.

Halligan, J. (1997). New public sector models: Reform in Australia and New Zealand. In J.E. Lane (Ed.), *Public Sector Reform: Rationale, Trends and Problems* (pp.17–46). London: SAGE.

Hawkesworth, I., Bergvall, D., Emery, R., Wehner, J. (2008). Budgeting in Greece. *OECD Journal on Budgeting*, 3, 70–119. doi:10.1787/budget-v8-art12-en.

Hellenic Observatory (2014). *Administrative Reform in Greece*. A Report on a Keynote Policy Symposium of the Hellenic Observatory (April 11, 2014). London: London School of Economics and Political Science. www.lse.ac.uk/europeanInstitute/research/hellenicObservatory/CMS%20pdf/Various/Administrative-Reform-in-Greece-%E2%80%93-A-Report-on-a-Keynote-Policy-Symposium-of-the-Hellenic-Observatory, -LSE.pdf.

Hood, C., and Lodge, M. (2006). *The Politics of Public Service Bargains*. Oxford: Oxford University Press.

International Monetary Fund (IMF) (2006). *Greece: Report on Observance of Standards and Codes*. Fiscal Transparency Module. Country Report no. 06/49. Washington, DC: IMF.

Kaplanoglou, G., and Rapanos, V. (2013). Fiscal deficits and the role of fiscal governance: The case of Greece. *Economic Analysis & Policy*, 43(1), 5–27. doi:10.1016/S0313-5926(13)50001-4.

Ladi, S. (2014). Austerity politics and administrative reform: The Eurozone crisis and its impact upon Greek public administration. *Comparative European Politics*, 12 (2), 184–208. doi:10.1057/CEP.2012.46.

Lampropoulou, M., and Oikonomou, G. (2018). Theoretical models of public administration and patterns of State reform in Greece. *International Review of Administrative Sciences*, 84(1), 101–121. https://doi.org/10.1177%2F0020852315611219.

Miliakou, S., Pappa, A., Tetorou, K., Tserkezis, E. (2017). *Greece: Recent Developments in Public Financial Management*. Athens: Ministry of Finance, General Accounting Office, General Secretariat for Fiscal Policy.

Ministry of Finance (2009). *Introductory Report to the Budget for 2010.* Athens: Ministry of Finance.

Ministry of Finance (2017). *Introductory Report to the Budget for 2018.* Athens: Ministry of Finance.

Moretti, D., Keller, A., and Chevauchez, B. (2019). Budgeting in Greece. *OECD Journal on Budgeting,* 2, 3–83. doi:10.1787/2f5e7d7a-en.

Organisation for Economic Co-operation and Development (OECD) (2011). *Greece: Review of the Central Administration.* Paris: OECD Publishing.

Painter, M., and Pierre, J. (2005). Unpacking policy capacity: Issues and themes. In M. Painter, and J. Pierre (Eds.), *Challenges to the State Policy Capacity* (pp. 1–18). Basingstoke: Palgrave Macmillan. https://doi.org/10.1057/9780230524194_1.

Papaconstantinou, G. (2016). *Game Over: The Inside Story of the Greek Crisis.* Athens: Papadopoulos.

Peters, B.G. (1996). *The Policy Capacity of Government.* Research Paper no. 18. Ottawa, ON: Canadian Centre for Management Development. http://publications. gc.ca/collections/Collection/SC94-61-18-1996E.pdf.

Rapanos, V. (2007). *Drafting and Execution of the State Budget: European Experience and Greek Reality.* Working Paper. Athens: IOBE (in Greek).

Rein, M., and Schön, D. (1993) Reframing policy discourse. In Frank Fischer, and John Forester (Eds.), *The Argumentative Turn in Policy Analysis and Planning* (pp. 145–166). London: UCL Press.

Sabatier P.A., and Jenkins-Smith, H.C. (1999). The Advocacy Coalition Framework: An assessment. In P.A. Sabatier (Ed.), *Theories of the Policy Process* (pp. 117–167). Boulder, CO: Westview Press.

Sotiropoulos D.A. (2007). A case of amateurs and professionals: The role of the Greek senior civil service. In E.C. Page, and V. Wright (Eds.), *From the Active to the Enabling State: The Changing Role of Top Officials in European Nations* (pp. 15–37). Basingstoke: Palgrave Macmillan.

Spanou, C. (1996). Penelope's Suitors: Administrative Modernization and Party Competition in Greece. *West European Politics,* 19(1), 97–124. doi:10.1080/01402389608425123.

Spanou, C. (2001). (Re)shaping the politics-administration nexus in Greece: The decline of a symbiotic relationship? In B.G. Peters, and J. Pierre (Eds.), *Politicians, Bureaucrats and Administrative Reform* (pp. 106–115). London: Routledge.

Spanou, C. (2010). Inability for self-correction: Factors undermining rationalization. In C. Spanou (Ed.), *Public Policies in Greece: Facets and Contradictions* (pp. 285–317). Athens: Papazisis (in Greek).

Spanou, C. (2014a). Administrative elites and the crisis: What lies ahead for the senior civil service in Greece? *International Review of Administrative Sciences,* 80 (4), 709–725. https://doi.org/10.1177%2F0020852314533453.

Spanou, C. (2014b). La haute fonction publique hellénique: La permanence du pro-visoire. *Revue Française d'Administration Publique,* 151–152, 645–661.

Spanou, C. (2015). Administrative reform and policy conditionality in Greece. *Administration and Public Employment Review/Revista de Administração e Emprego Público,* 1, 31–54.

Spanou, C. (Ed.) (2019). *Reforms in Public Administration under the Crisis, Executive Summary.* Athens: Papazisis. www.eliamep.gr/wp-content/uploads/2019/02/Reforms-In-Public-Administration_translation.pdf.

Spanou, C. (2020a). External influence on structural reform: Did policy conditionality strengthen reform capacity in Greece? *Public Policy and Administration*, 35(2), 135–157. https://doi.org/10.1177%2F0952076718772008.

Spanou, C. (2020b). Between domestic learning and external coercion: Budgeting and fiscal management reform in Greece. *South European Society and Politics*, 25(1), 1–26. https://doi.org/10.1080/13608746.2020.1762372.

Spanou, C. (2020c). Constant elements in the functioning of the political-administrative system and governance capacity. In Y. Voulgaris, K. Kostis, and S. Rizas (Eds.), *The Great Transformation: Politics and the State in Greece during the 20th and 21st Centuries* (pp. 410–437). Athens: Patakis (in Greek).

Thelen, K. (2004). *How Institutions Evolve: The Political Economy of Skills in Germany, Britain, the United States, and Japan*. Cambridge: Cambridge University Press.

Wettenhall, R. (2013). A critique of the 'administrative reform industry': Reform is important but so is stability. *Teaching Public Administration*, 31(2), 149–164. https://doi.org/10.1177%2F0144739413488904.

9 Attracting FDI in Greece

China's growing footprint since 2009

Jens Bastian

Introduction

Attracting a higher share of foreign direct investment (FDI) to Greece is a recurring theme of policymakers, corporate representatives and analysts alike. During the past decade, when Greece was subjected to three macro-economic adjustment programmes by international creditors, the issue of FDI featured prominently in quarterly reviews. Increasing FDI was repeatedly linked to achieving high(er) economic growth and creating sustainable new employment opportunities. Equally, leading items such as the ease of acquiring business licenses, the duration of decision-making in public tenders and legacy issues facing Greek banks' capacity to rebalance their balance sheets following non-performing loan exposure are frequently voiced as existing obstacles to attracting higher volumes of FDI.

For a real economy that in 2019 was gradually emerging from a decade of austerity policies but that must now confront the fiscal and economic challenges of the coronavirus (COVID-19) pandemic, caution in how to move forward on the investment front is paramount. The same also holds true as a benchmark for those institutions that are considering investing in Greece. Making Greece a more 'investment-friendly' environment still constitutes a recurring theme at business and economist conferences in Athens and at international roundtables. There is a community of foreign investors in Greece (e.g. Watsa, 2019) who have incurred substantial losses during the past decade, but they continue to hold out for the recovery story to take root.[1]

Against this background of challenges and potential opportunities in the field of FDI, one development during the past decade is noteworthy. While many US and European investors have been hesitant to commit substantial financial resources to Greece during this period, one country in particular has filled the void. The willingness of the People's Republic of China to enter the Greek market before[2] and during the aforementioned twin crises signalled an unprecedented development in Sino-Greek political economy relations. During the past decade Chinese companies and financial institutions have invested almost €10 billion in Greece.[3]

DOI: 10.4324/9780429202247-12

In what follows this contribution seeks to explain the rationale for Chinese investments in Greece. Over time these investments have diversified across sectors and grown in volume. They are not speculative; they display a long-term perspective; and they have received political support from different Greek governments during the past decade. Belatedly, the European Commission and the US Administration are beginning to react to this widening Sino-Greek engagement. The former is introducing regulatory conditions for the bilateral investment cooperation, while the latter is challenging Chinese FDI in Greece by advocating US investments in port infrastructure. It cannot be in Greece's interest to become a battleground for Sino-American investment rivalries and geopolitical competition.

But the evolving nature of Sino-Greek economic relations over the course of the past decade is also important because it tells us how a number of Chinese companies were allowed to purchase key assets in Greece during the implementation of the three macroeconomic adjustment programmes mandated by its international creditors. This development raises some critical questions about the responsibility of European policymakers who have assisted in opening the investment door for China in Greece. Some answers to these questions are debated in the conclusion to this chapter.

Greece: China's gateway to Europe

The politico-economic importance that both Beijing and Athens attach to China's investment drive in Greece has repeatedly been articulated by its respective government representatives. During his visit to Athens and the Port of Piraeus in June 2014, the Chinese Premier Li Keqiang called Greece 'China's gateway to Europe' (Maltezou, 2014). Five years later, the Greek Minister for Development and Investments, Adonis Georgiadis, emphatically took stock of Sino-Greek relations:

> We really admire China in Greece. The People's Republic of China is one of the biggest investors in Greece and in the last ten years we made together many stories of success. Even more investments from China are very welcome in Greece.
>
> (*Xinhua*, 2019)

Such ambitious rhetoric culminated in a plethora of superlatives in November 2019. The three-day state visit of China's President Xi Jinping to Athens (November, 10–12) was termed a 'vote of confidence' for Greece. Prime Minister Kyriakos Mitsotakis emphasized that Greece and China were bound together by their cultural heritages, linking ancient civilizations of the West and East, respectively. For his part, President Xi described China's initial investment in the Port of Piraeus as the 'biggest project of the One Belt, One Road Initiative' (OBOR).[4] Beijing and Athens spoke of transforming Piraeus into the 'biggest' port in Europe. The presence of the state-owned China

Ocean Shipping Company (COSCO), the majority owner of the Piraeus Port Authority (OLP), was termed 'the head of the dragon' by President Xi (*Kathimerini*, 2019b).

The extent to which China has penetrated the Greek economy is best illustrated by its multi-year investments in port facilities. China's gateway to Europe was first established by COSCO's decision in 2009 to lease container terminals in Piraeus under a 35-year concession agreement with the Greek government. This initial cooperation can be interpreted as an anchor investment in Greece which established material facts on the ground and provided substance to the 'gateway' rhetoric. In April 2016, as part of the mandatory privatization obligations in the third macroeconomic adjustment programme, the government of then Prime Minister Alexis Tsipras selected COSCO's subsidiary—COSCO Shipping—as the new majority owner (51%) of OLP, the management company responsible for the operation of the maritime facility.[5]

COSCO's follow-up investment in 2016 signalled its determination to stay the course at a time when other foreign investors were reluctant to consider Greece a suitable destination. While European countries were lecturing Greek policymakers about the virtues of 'structural reforms', 'policy ownership' and the continued need for 'fiscal rectitude', Beijing was busy identifying further investment opportunities in Piraeus and beyond. In September 2019, the Port Planning and Development Commission (ESAL) approved COSCO's proposed €800-million investment plan for the Port of Piraeus. COSCO's master plan includes the construction of a fourth container terminal,[6] the transformation of the dock currently used for ship repairs into a new car terminal, enlargement of the cruise passenger handling terminal, additional storage facilities, four hotels, a logistics and a commercial centre.

COSCO'S expanding involvement in the Port of Piraeus is a long-term investment. It includes clear strategic objectives (as illustrated by its master plan) and the capacity to mobilize considerable investment volumes. In terms of measurable outcomes, the results speak for themselves. Ten years after the initial investment, the Port of Piraeus is highly profitable and has become the largest port (by container traffic, i.e. TEU[7]) in the Mediterranean, overtaking the Port of Valencia in Spain in 2019 (Maundrill, 2020). This 'success story' notwithstanding, COSCO's expanding investment strategy is also a reflection of the degree to which Greece has become dependent on Chinese FDI.

Moreover, COSCO's anchor investment in Piraeus is part of China's extensive European outreach strategy in port facilities. Apart from COSCO, the Shanghai International Port Group and the China Harbour Engineering Company have invested in port infrastructure ranging from Egypt (Suez Canal Container Terminal), Turkey (Kumport Ambarli), Israel (Haifa Port) to Germany (Duisport in Duisburg), Italy (APM Terminals Vado), Albania (Port of Shengjin), the Netherlands (Euromax Terminal Rotterdam), Bulgaria (Black Sea ports of Varna and Burgas), Spain (Noatum Port Holdings Container ports in Valencia and Bilbao) and Belgium (Port of Zeebrugge).

This Chinese portfolio of port facilities stands in marked contrast to the reverse observation. Over the past decade, Chinese investors have expanded their ports portfolio in Europe, Africa and the Middle East. However, not a single European company has become a shareholder in, let alone a majority owner of, a port facility in China.

In retrospect (see Table 9.1), we can argue that COSCO's arrival in Greece served as a catalyst for Chinese investment. Not only did it have positive knock-on effects on the wider Athens area, it also impacted Greece's real economy, the shipping sector, the labour market, tourism and commercial trade. Most importantly, with the gateway firmly established, other Chinese companies started to invest in different sectors of the Greek economy. Table 9.1 illustrates the extent of this magnetic pull factor since 2016 when COSCO Shipping became the majority owner of OLP.

While COSCO Shipping is returning the Port of Piraeus 'to its glory as a Mediterranean hub' (Yongxin, 2019), this development should not obscure the fact that there have also been some notable setbacks and one explicit failure of Chinese investments in Greece. China's ambassador to Greece, Zhang Qiyue, cannot simply compile a dossier of various success stories. Her FDI brief should also include some lessons learned in Greece. There are a number of corporate examples which illustrate that China's growing investment footprint

Table 9.1 Selected Chinese investments in Greece since 2009

Year	Chinese company	Investment in Greece	Sector
2009; 2016	COSCO	Majority shareholding in OLP €1.4 billion: concession/equity/investment	Ports
2017	State Grid Corp.	24% shareholding in ADMIE*	Energy
2017	Shenhua Group	75% stake in four wind farms belonging to the Copelouzos Group	Energy
2018	Fosun International	16.4% shareholding in Folli Follie	Retail
2019	DeepBlue Technology	Memorandum of Cooperation with the Aristotle School of Informatics	Artificial intelligence
2019	Bank of China Industrial; Commercial Bank of China	Branch opening in Athens Branch opening in Athens	Banking
2014– 2020	Chinese Retail Investors	Golden Visa Programme €1.4 billion	Real estate
2020	ChemChina**	Alfa Agricultural Supplies SA (acquisition)	Agriculture
2020	Geek+	FDL Group (exclusive cooperation)	Logistics

Source: compiled by the author.
Note: * ADMIE (Independent Power Transmission Operator). ** The acquisition was executed through the Israeli company Adama which is fully controlled by ChemChina.

in Greece is *not* a linear path to success. Some ambitious projects either remain at the planning stage or have failed, while others have been delayed despite the vibrant promotional rhetoric between Athens and Beijing. Consider the following cases (for more details see Bastian, 2019b):

- Fosun International Ltd's investment in Folli Follie has turned into a bitter lesson learned for the Chinese company. In May 2011, Fosun initially acquired a 9.5% stake in the Greek luxury jewellery and handbag maker for €84.6 million. In 2014, the Chinese group boosted the stake further to 13.9% and subsequently raised it to 16.4% in 2018. Two years later the second largest shareholder in Folli Follie had lost most of its equity investment as the Greek company and many of its former executives were under investigation for share manipulation, fraud, money laundering and issuing false financial statements.
- In February 2018, the tender for the operating concession of Dimosia Epicheirisi Ilektrismou (DEI—Public Power Corporation)'s four lignite-powered plants at Melitis and Megalopolis failed. Three Chinese companies had bid for the sale-and-purchase agreement.
- In early 2018, Shanghai-based Fosun Investment and Gonbao Investment came up short in their bid to buy National Bank of Greece (NBG)'s insurance unit Ethniki Asfalistiki. NBG's subsidiary is Greece's largest insurer.
- Greece's marquee privatization project at Athens' former international airport Ellenikon took a surprise U-turn in September 2019. China's Fosun and Eagle Hills from Abu Dhabi, both partners in the project's consortium since 2014 (together with Greece's Lamda Development), unexpectedly pulled out.

These examples highlight that project delays, their cancellation or outright failures have been part and parcel of the Sino-Greek investment story during the past decade. They also illustrate the complexities of navigating Greek politics and overcoming administrative obstacles. They also shine a light on the fact that Chinese companies can become the victims of fraud and manipulation, despite carrying out due diligence. Finally, these examples signal a broader trend in Sino-Greek relations, namely that the initial honeymoon period for Chinese companies is coming to an end. EU-mandated investment screening procedures are being introduced (see next section). Chinese companies are applying lessons learned in terms of corporate scrutiny and public tender details. Furthermore, Greek stakeholders, be they from politics, the media, non-governmental organizations or investigative authorities, are scrutinizing Chinese investment initiatives in terms of transparency, origin of financial resources and the material additionality these activities can provide for the local economy.

But the lessons learned—and this is the flipside of the argument—do not deter interested Chinese companies from seeking further avenues of cooperation in Greece. This is a major difference to many European companies who are willing to invest in Greece but who withdraw at the sight of the first hurdles appearing along the way. By contrast, Chinese companies view these hurdles as obstacles that can be overcome in the short-to-medium term. Nowhere is this more apparent than in the area of 'soft issue' cooperation. This engagement can be seen as a lubricant or test case for other joint ventures in the near future. The following are examples of such initiatives:

- China was the honoured country at the 82nd Thessaloniki International Fair (TIF) in September 2017.
- In mid-2018, the Shanghai University of Traditional Chinese Medicine (TCM) and the University of West Attica launched the Taiji (Tai Chi) Health Center in Athens.
- On the occasion of his state visit China's President Xi officially endorsed Greece's decades-long demand for the return of the Elgin Marbles from the United Kingdom's British Museum.
- In January 2020, the Sino-Hellenic Investors' Confederation was established in Athens.
- In September 2020, China's Sichuan Province and the region of Attica signed a twining agreement to enhance bilateral cooperation in tourism, commercial trade, educational exchange programmes, etc.

The COVID-19 pandemic has provided further opportunities for China's engagement in and cooperation with Greece. New inroads are being made in the health sector. Since March 2020, Chinese companies, state-sponsored foundations and ministries have repeatedly donated and/or provided medical supplies and laboratory testing equipment to Greece during the pandemic.[8] These Sino-Greek efforts are embedded in the terminology of jointly building 'a community with a shared future' and alleged 'win-win cooperation' (Qiyue, 2020). Chinese corporates that are invested in Greece such as COSCO Shipping, State Grid, Bank of China and Huawei are also mobilizing or financing the shipment of medical resources.

There is another aspect worth considering when Chinese cargo planes land in Greece and in other countries in south-eastern Europe loaded with face masks, pharmaceutical supplies and protective gear. They illustrate China's capacity to intervene in European countries' medical supply chains. China's 'donation diplomacy' widens its perimeter of engagement in Greece and beyond. Such 'politics of generosity'[9] signals to an international audience that China has acquired leverage in the provision of health equipment and medical supply chains in European countries during the pandemic.

Greece's Golden Visa programme and China

During the past decade Greece's efforts to attract strategic investments in key sectors of its economy has also included initiatives hitherto unthought of. In mid-2013, the then government of Prime Minister Antonios Samaras sought to attract new sources of revenue from abroad. Included in the Invest in Greece bill was a new residence permit scheme entitled 'Golden Visa'. The timing of the visa scheme was initiated during the execution of the second macroeconomic adjustment programme.

The timing of the visa programme is instructive. In 2013, the sovereign debt and economic crises were growing in intensity. The political authorities in Athens attempted to square fiscal austerity requirements from the country's international creditors with the new revenue streams, particularly from non-EU citizens. It was again China which grasped the opportunities and quickly took the lead as regards investors' interest in the Greek Golden Visa scheme.

The Greek Golden Visa programme offers a five-year renewable residency permit to non-EU citizens. It requires the investor to buy, or rent, a local real estate property of a definite value of at least €250.000.[10] The Greek legislation further provides for a 'strategic investment' without defining the concept, e.g. the creation of jobs (as in Croatia, Bulgaria and Portugal) or the requirement of a business project of 'general interest' as in Spain. Similarly to other EU member states (e.g. France, Ireland or Latvia) the Greek investor residence scheme does not require continuous physical residence in the country. The law only requires the investor's presence on the day of application (European Commission, 2019a).[11]

From the outset of the programme Chinese buyers have dominated this part of the Greek real estate market. Since the launch in 2013, more than €2 billion have been invested by non-EU citizens. Chinese nationals represent

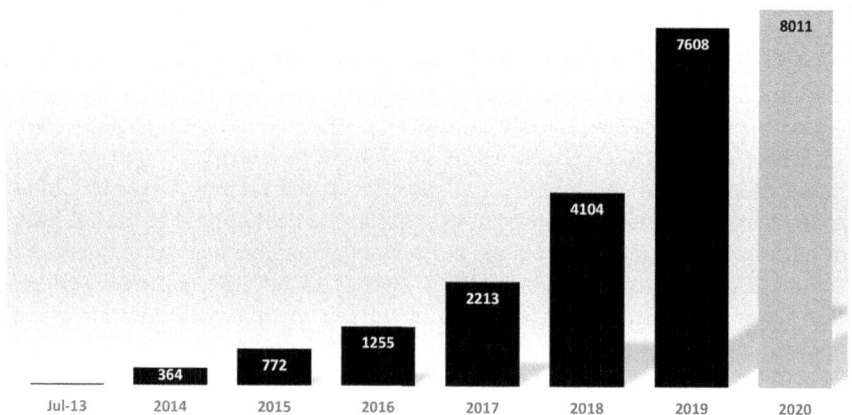

Figure 9.1 Total number of Golden Visas issued in Greece, 2013–2020
Source: Transparency International Hellas (2021).

the single largest constituency by country. They accounted for 73.9% of all Golden Visas issued in Greece (5,869 out of a total of 7,903 until September 2020).[12] This share was equivalent to more than €1.4 billion of Chinese investment in the programme.

In November 2019, a joint ministerial decision by the government of Prime Minister Kyriakos Mitsotakis broadened the criteria for non-EU citizens seeking a Golden Visa. The amendment to existing FDI legislation foresees new permits being issued for third country nationals (and their families) who invest a minimum of €400,000 in Greek securities of at least three years' duration through a Greece-based bank. Similarly, non-EU nationals can also obtain the permit with an investment of €800,000 in stocks or corporate bonds in the Greek capital markets.

However, the apparent 'success story' of Greece's Golden Visa programme has been negatively impacted by the COVID-19 pandemic. In 2020, only 403 Golden Visas were issued in Greece. This pandemic year was the first to record an annual decline since the launch of the programme. Primarily due to national lockdowns in Greece and China as well as foreign travel restrictions, the Golden Visa scheme came to a virtual standstill in 2020. In order to stimulate further interest in the programme remote applications for Golden Visas can now be made directly to the Hellenic Ministry of Migration via authorized attorneys.

Golden Visa programmes facilitating residency in EU countries and in some cases (e.g. Cyprus and Malta) even granting citizenship rights illustrate how such rights become tradeable commodities in Europe. Luring wealthy Chinese real estate investors to Greece proved politically controversial neither for the Samaras government nor for the Synaspismos Rizospastikis Aristeras (SYRIZA—Coalition of the Radical Left)-led administration of former Prime Minister Alexis Tsipras. Continuity across the political spectrum, usually in low supply in Greek politics, greatly benefited Chinese investors who purchased apartments and houses in Athens and on the Greek islands, only to convert most of them into Airbnb facilities. The consequences for the rental market in parts of Athens and on high-profile islands such as Santorini or Mykonos were significant. Greek Airbnb with 'Chinese characteristics' attracted foreign tourists who guaranteed a higher rate of return on investments rather than offering longer-term rental contracts for Greek citizens.

Lessons learned from Sino-Greek investment cooperation

One year after COSCO's first investment foray into Greece the Chinese premier Wen Jiabao offered in October 2010 to buy Greek government bonds when Athens resumed the issuance of sovereign debt. As Greece was excluded from international capital markets after the signing of the first macroeconomic adjustment programme in early May 2010 such a statement from China was a rare sign of public endorsement for Athens. While European institutions and EU member states were arguing among each other and with the International Monetary Fund (IMF) about the need for debt restructuring and severe fiscal austerity in Greece, Chinese policymakers offered to buy Greek debt in the event of a return to capital markets. In other words, through the COSCO investment Beijing established facts on the ground and the eventuality of acquiring Greek debt came at a time when euro area countries and US investment funds considered such paper highly toxic.[13]

Greece's growing investment partnership with China is not limited to ports, the energy sector and Golden Visas. It has diversified across sectors and led to eminent political consequences. In 2018, Greece applied to join the then-existing 16+1 Network.[14] On the occasion of the annual Central and Eastern European Countries-China summit in Dubrovnik (Croatia), Greece was admitted as the 17th European member, thereby changing the name of the network to '17+1'. Greece's membership of the network was driven by the then Greek Prime Minister Alexis Tsipras. His successor in office, Kyriakos Mitsotakis, has continued Greece's membership in the 17+1 Network thus lending bi-partisan political support on the subject matter of greater Sino-Greek cooperation.

COSCO's multi-year investments in the Port of Piraeus remains the flagship project of such bilateral cooperation. It is part of the group's growing shipping portfolio in Europe and China's increasing importance in shipping finance. Enlarging maritime connectivity for the Chinese merchant fleet seeks not only to increase trade flows,[15] but also to better control trade routes and international port access. COSCO is building global maritime supply chains in which Piraeus plays a central connectivity role. Establishing port infrastructure across Europe gives China leverage over maritime interconnectivity (Marantidou, 2018). Leasing constituted the initial investment option in Greece. One decade later, the financing profile of COSCO's investments is characterized by majority and minority shareholdings in numerous European ports (see Bastian, 2019a for more details).

In that respect, the financing arrangements for COSCO's master plan in Piraeus are significant. COSCO's investment includes the participation of EU loan financing. More specifically, the European Investment Bank (EIB) signed an agreement with OLP to finance parts of the master plan. The initial loan arrangement for the expansion and modernization of the port is set at €100 million and can increase by a further €40 million as project construction progresses. The EIB loan has a maturity of 20 years and is being guaranteed by the Export-Import Bank of China (China EXIM Bank). For the first time in Greece a major infrastructure investment initiative by a Chinese state-owned company includes the financing arm of the European Commission.

China's important role as an investor in Greece during the past decade has given it reputational capital that is paying dividends over time. The inclusion of the EIB in the financing architecture of COSCO's master plan is smart politics on the part of the Chinese. Despite the fact that COSCO can secure favourable financing terms from any of China's numerous state-owned policy banks, it opted to cooperate with an EU lending institution. The €140 million loan to COSCO via OLP is the largest funding agreement that the EIB has ever made available for a maritime project in Greece. By making the EIB a (lending) stakeholder in a major Chinese infrastructure project in Greece the EU now has skin in the game. But it can also be argued that the EIB's inclusion is a means to tamp down any EU opposition to China's expanding presence in Greece.

The financing arrangements for COSCO's master plan are also significant for another reason. Its execution facilitated the arrival of two Chinese state-owned policy banks in the Greek banking sector. After having secured part of the funds from the EIB, COSCO is structuring the additional financing needs with the assistance of two Chinese lenders. The Bank of China (Europe) opened a branch in Athens in mid-2019, while the Luxembourg-based subsidiary of Industrial and Commercial Bank of China (ICBC) has a representative office in Greece. It is also telling that the emerging financing architecture of COSCO's master plan includes the EIB and two Chinese lenders but does not (yet) include a domestic lending institution from Greece.

We can assume that the Chinese banks will not focus their business strategy on attracting deposits or providing consumer loans for Greek citizens. Rather, their primary focus will rest on infrastructure lending (e.g. for energy projects on the island of Crete) and COSCO's maritime financing needs. They can also be expected to cater to Chinese citizens that invest in the Golden Visa real estate programme. Furthermore, the Bank of China and ICBC offer their digital services to the growing number of Chinese tourists arriving in Athens on direct flights from Beijing and Shanghai. In a word, the entry of two Chinese banking behemoths into the Greek financial sector should be interpreted as a statement of strategic intent with a long-term investment horizon.

On the occasion of President Xi's visit to Athens in November 2019, both sides signed a total of 16 protocols and Memoranda of Understanding (MOUs) to expand bilateral cooperation. They include increasing, *inter alia*, Greek agricultural exports (e.g. saffron and kiwi fruit) to China. The establishment of a China Research Centre in Greece was agreed between the Aikaterini Laskaridis Foundation and the Chinese Academy of Social Sciences (CASS).[16] One of the most significant MOUs concerns joint ventures in the energy sector, e.g. the Attica-Crete electricity interconnector and the construction of a 50-MW solar power station on the island with technical assistance from the China Energy Engineering Group (CEEG). These initiatives emphasize the political will in Sino-Greek relations to diversify the agenda of investment cooperation across established and towards new sectors.

What started a decade ago as a leasing investment in the under-utilized Port of Piraeus has created remarkable pull factors in different sectors across Greece's political economy. The anchor investment in 2009 led to a dynamic of self-reinforcing developments that have deeply challenged and changed the FDI landscape in Greece one decade later. China is now firmly in play across the country as an investor with long-term objectives alongside more traditional countries such as Germany, France, Italy and the United States. Moreover, Beijing has established a level of reputational capital among Greek decision-makers in politics and across the corporate ecosystem that has enabled it to penetrate sectors that may once have been considered off-limits, e.g. in shipping finance, the banking sector and even agriculture.

Even during the COVID-19 pandemic, China remained active in Greece. In 2020 Beijing recalibrated its investment activities in Greece by also making medical protective equipment and pharmaceutical supplies available to hospitals across the country. But deal-making did not fall off the radar of Sino-Greek investment cooperation during the pandemic. As the examples of Alfa Agricultural Supplies SA and the FDL Group illustrate (see Table 9.1 above), Chinese acquisitions of companies in Greece—now expanding to the agricultural sector and in logistics—continued unabated during 2020. In 2021, COSCO Shipping was expected to exercise its right to acquire an additional 16% stake in OLP as stipulated in the sales contract from 2016.

Brussels reacts to China's footprint in Greece

The expanding nature of Sino-Greek cooperation has not escaped the notice of Greece's European partners, the Commission in Brussels and the US embassy in Athens. Both Beijing and Athens frame their bilateral investment engagement as a successful example of constructive cooperation between an EU member state and China. 'I think Greece is a good example of cooperation with China, and this could help other European countries consider having more Chinese investments.'[17] Such statements are not the mere rhetoric of diplomatic communiqués. But the government in Athens is acutely aware that it needs to build political trust in Brussels, Berlin, Paris and Washington for its evolving investment cooperation with China. At the same time the expanding nature of Sino-Greek investment engagement points to the limits of EU reach.

These efforts remain a work in progress. In June 2017, during the European Council summit, the then Greek Prime Minister Tsipras opposed a regulatory initiative of the Commission providing guidance to member states concerning FDI and the free movement of capital from non-EU countries. Greece was part of a coalition of EU member states that also included Finland, Sweden, the Netherlands, Portugal, Malta and the Czech Republic (Cerulus and Hanke Vela, 2017). Having profited considerably from Chinese direct investments—e.g. in Sweden the two largest carmakers (NEVS and Volvo) are owned by Chinese investors, in Portugal China invested in two major energy companies and in the Czech Republic it is in fact the largest shareholder in a football club (Slavia Prague)—this unlikely coalition of EU countries joined forces to water down the Commission's proposal.

This initial pushback did not deter the Commission. However, it changed focus. Since early 2019, EU member states and China have been confronted by a much more proactive European Commission. This new assertiveness first became apparent when the Brussels executive recalibrated its strategic outlook vis-à-vis China. In its March 2019 communication, the Commission labelled China '*simultaneously*, in different policy areas, a *cooperation partner* with whom the EU has closely aligned objectives, a *negotiating partner* with whom the EU needs to find a balance of interests, an *economic competitor* in the pursuit of technological leadership, and a *systemic rival* promoting alternative models of governance' (European Commission, 2019b, emphasis added). These multiple classifications are not a failure of conceptual clarity on the part of the Commission. They illustrate that from a European perspective China is indeed simultaneously a rival, competitor and a partner. Managing all three remains a challenge for the Brussels executive chiefly because EU member states place different emphasis on such classifications (Taylor, 2021). In Athens the Commission's characterization of China as a 'rival' is non-existent, while Berlin favours the portrayal of China as a trading partner.

To back up such rhetoric, the Commission adopted new regulations that established a framework for screening non-EU FDI (Regulation 2019/452). The regulation does not explicitly mention China. It entered into force in April 2019 and became fully applicable from mid-October 2020 onwards. The 27 EU member states, including the 12 EU countries that are part of the 17+1 Network, had to adapt their national investment legislation to reflect the Commission's new screening regulations.

While the EU regulation provides a framework, the right of each EU member state to decide whether or not to screen a particular non-EU FDI cannot be curtailed by the Commission. In other words, the foreign investment screening mechanism of the Commission represents policy guidance for EU member states that retain considerable leverage with regard to the adoption thereof into national legislation. Some member states such as Germany, France and Italy have proposed legislation that goes beyond the Commission's regulatory guidelines, while Greece, Portugal and Hungary focus on lighter versions of regulation vis-à-vis non-EU external investors.[18]

These different initiatives and regulatory interventions suggest that China's investments in EU countries are attracting increased scrutiny in Brussels and face institutional pushback in some EU member states. But China's presence cannot be reversed. The lesson learned is twofold:

- The demand for greater transparency is gaining currency. In September 2020, the European Court of Auditors published a report which argued that official information on Chinese direct investment is 'not timely [and is] fragmented and incomplete'. Chinese investments in European companies are 'a black hole for data' (*Wall Street Journal*, 2020).
- The new investment screening regulation of the Commission illustrates the determination of the Brussels executive to address the challenges

posed by non-EU external actors such as China, the Russian Federation, Turkey and some Gulf states. Where the Commission has regulatory leverage, it is—belatedly—addressing these challenges. However, the nature of these interventions is to adopt *defensive* policies. Necessary as they appear, they must confront obstacles from individual member states and expect that Beijing could retaliate vis-à-vis European companies doing business in China. In a word, it is 'a sober view of the limits to Europe's hard power' (Godement, 2020).

Conclusion

China's initial engagement in Greece in 2009 and its subsequent systematic expansion across economic sectors gave the political authorities in Athens an important opportunity to receive much-needed FDI at a time when scarcely any European or US companies were prepared to invest in the country. China's footprint in the Port of Piraeus reflected a statement of intent in a maritime infrastructure facility that was underutilized and lacked the financial means for comprehensive modernization. One decade later, the Port of Piraeus has changed beyond recognition and is on course to challenge Europe's leading peers in Rotterdam and Hamburg.

But the story of China's investments in Greece since 2009 cannot be written without addressing the responsibility of European policymakers. On the occasion of his visit to the China International Import Expo fair in November 2019 in Shanghai, the French President Emmanuel Macron argued that

> We [the EU] have led several countries to very tough reforms, fast, and forced privatizations without there being any European buyers … It is clear that we have put several countries in a situation to have only non-European buyers, that is to say, Chinese buyers.
>
> (*Teller Report*, 2019)

Macron's statement, made with hindsight, could not be any clearer. Not only does it reflect the treatment of Greece during its three macroeconomic adjustment programmes. It also illustrates how 'we' opened the door to non-EU external actors such as China to invest in Greece at cut-throat prices.

The actions and requirements of Greece's international creditors—particularly regarding the so-called prior actions in various privatization programmes—provided China with unique asset allocations at depressed price levels and simultaneously obliged policymakers in Athens to find willing investors from non-EU countries (Mathews, 2017). China made itself available as a long-term investor in the privatization of the Port of Piraeus and in the sale of a 24% equity stake in ADMIE. Establishing a major foothold in both the most important port (as a majority owner) and as the largest foreign shareholder in Greece's independent power transmission operator is a remarkable achievement that no European investor has managed to replicate during the past decade.

But make no mistake about causality and political co-responsibility. As some EU member states in 2020—in particular Germany and France—voiced diplomatically worded reservations about the level of Sino-Greek investment cooperation, they should not forget that enforcing fire sale privatizations by Greece in 2015 and 2016 succeeded in China expanding its footprint and enlarging its gateway to Europe via a bridgehead in southeastern Europe. The longer-term strategic significance and regional implications of these developments are gradually coming into view. But China is here to stay and remains a welcome investor in Greece.

Across the Atlantic, Beijing's engagement with Athens and Greece's openness to China is being viewed with a critical distance by the US Administration. Former Secretary of State Mike Pompeo made several visits to Athens in 2019 and 2020. His messages included references to China's expanding investment footprint in Greece as a strategic threat. The bilateral Mutual Defense Cooperation Agreement between Greece and the United States was upgraded in January 2020. Equally, the US embassy in Athens is encouraging American investment in two current privatization tenders, namely the ports in Alexandroupoli and in Kavala in northern Greece, respectively. The US Development Finance Corporation has identified both privatization projects as 'strategic priorities' (US Embassy and Consulate in Greece, 2020).[19]

It is obvious that the political support articulated by US representatives for American investments in Greek port infrastructure are a direct challenge to China's expanding foothold in the Port of Piraeus. With a time lag of a decade and under a significantly altered investment landscape in Greece the US Administration is starting to pull strings and attempt to nudge its partner in Athens towards greater distance from Beijing's investment profile. This renewed urgency by Washington risks creating a policy dilemma for Greece. It finds itself in the middle of a growing tug of war between Beijing and Washington. The US Administration is trying to put the brakes on burgeoning investment ties between Greece and China.

For its part, China continues to expand and diversify its engagement in Greece. The coming years will show if and how Athens can continue to cultivate investment ties with both the United States and China. In practice it remains a delicate balancing act to perform. Great power competition for high-value assets in strategic sectors such as maritime transport infrastructure and energy is already manifesting itself. What started in 2009 as an anchor investment is now a cluster of Chinese exposure across Greece's political economy. The configuration of countries and companies willing to commit capital to Greece has changed. Within a decade China has become an integral part of this foreign investment landscape. It is bound to stay and remain in play in Greece.

Notes

1 One such vocal and loss-plagued foreign investor is Prem Watsa. His Fairfax Group has committed considerable resources to the Greek financial sector (including the recapitalization of Eurobank in 2014), to the insurance asset management sector (Eurolife in 2015) and to the real estate sector (Grivalia Properties REIC in 2013). Born in India and based in Canada, Watsa is the chairman and chief executive officer of Fairfax Financial Holdings Ltd which he founded in 1985. Through its shareholding in Eurolife, Fairfax Financial also holds an 'important position' in Greek bonds (Watsa, 2019).

2 Greece and China have a so-called Comprehensive Strategic Partnership since 2006.

3 Official statistics about the total volume of Chinese FDI in Greece between 2009 and 2020 are surprisingly scarce in Athens. At the end of 2019, one source (Kathimerini, 2019) calculated that €7.5 billion of Chinese FDI had reached Greece. This contribution is closer to €10 billion when considering additional FDI in the course of 2020 (see Table 9.1) and the implementation of COSCO's master plan in the Port of Piraeus. It should also be noted that Chinese involvement in Greece includes cooperation agreements without publicly announced prices or published valuations. They thus evade scrutiny as Chinese FDI in Greece.

4 OBOR is the official Chinese abbreviation for its signature foreign economic policy project. Following its inception by President Xi Jinping in 2013, China's representatives used the term One Belt, One Road. The term Belt and Road Initiative (BRI) was introduced by Beijing in 2016. It is a linguistic adjustment to English. For our analysis we shall use the BRI terminology.

5 Based on mandatory investment benchmarks COSCO reserved the right to acquire a further 16% of OLP by 2021. The price for the 51% shareholding was €280.5 million. The additional 16% can be acquired for €88 million. In 2016, COSCO only had one competitor in the public tender, namely Maersk, an integrated Danish logistics and shipping company.

6 It remains to be seen if and when the fourth container terminal will be built. While the Greek government supports COSCO's intentions, there is opposition from municipal councils in Piraeus, trade unions representing metal workers in the port and from ship repair companies. This opposition has frozen parts of COSCO's master plan and as a result the total investment volume has been reduced by approximately €300 million.

7 TEU stands for twenty-foot equivalent unit, the standard measuring unit used for cargo capacity in container ships.

8 China's former ambassador to Greece, Zhang Qiyue, hailed the Sino-Greek engagement as exemplary, stating that 'even the pandemic cannot change the exchanges between our two sides' (Kathimerini, 2020).

9 In March 2020, the EU High Representative Josep Borrell explicitly criticized China for the way in which its 'politics of generosity' were being instrumentalized for geopolitical purposes in 'a global battle of narratives' (Borrell, 2020).

10 The number of investor citizenship or residence schemes has grown considerably in the EU during the past decade. In 2019, 20 out of 28 EU member states operated such schemes. Greece's programme requires the lowest level of minimum investment when compared to other EU member states. In Malta the level ranges between €275,000–€320,000, Cyprus stands at €300,000, Spain requires €500,000, Portugal demands €350,000, while in Latvia the limit is set at €250,000 plus a 5% tax for property purchased in Rīga, the capital city.

11 The European Commission is critically taking note of these residence programmes, not least regarding allegations of money laundering, fraud and tax

evasion (European Commission, 2019a). Public scrutiny is also increasing in Greece. There have been allegations that property transactions with Chinese nationals were administered through card terminals operated by Greek banks in violation of existing capital controls in China. In October 2020, the Cypriot government announced the temporary suspension of its residency programme for non-EU citizens due to corruption allegations against the Speaker of Parliament and an MP. Similarly, in October 2020 the European Commission launched legal action against Cyprus and Malta and urged both Mediterranean island states to stop their golden passport schemes. Bulgaria has also been warned by the Brussels executive about its investor citizenship scheme.

12 The Greek Golden Visa programme includes the issuance of residency permits to family members of the investor. In that respect, at total of 23.618 permits were issued by the Greek authorities (Ministry for Migration and Asylum) between mid-2013 and September 2020. The share of Chinese nationals accounted for 75.3 %, or 17.794 permits.

13 It has never been fully established how much Greek sovereign debt China held in 2010 prior to the announcement and what amounts it subsequently acquired in secondary capital markets. Beijing's move can rather be seen as lending (rhetorical) support to a struggling euro area country in which it had a material interest so that the Port of Piraeus investment would not find itself in rough waters. Five years later, in late March and early April 2015, China's treasury acquired two tranches of Greek T-bills each worth €100 million at public debt auctions in Athens. But the former Minister of Finance Yanis Varoufakis claims that China had initially promised to purchase T-bills totalling €1.5 billion (Varoufakis, 2017: 318–320).

14 The 17+1 Network (initially called the 16+1 Network or 16+1 Framework) was established in 2012. It is a cooperation network comprising China and 17 Central and Eastern European countries that was formed after the visit of Chinese Premier Wen Jiabao to Poland. The 17+1 Network includes 12 EU member states and five countries from the Western Balkans.

15 According to China's General Administration of Customs data, Sino-Greek trade volume reached €6.2 billion in 2018. However, the trade balance is heavily tilted in favour of China (Chun, 2019).

16 China also operates three Confucius Institutes in Greece: the Business Confucius Institute at the Athens University of Economics and Business; the Confucius Institute at Aristotle University of Thessaloniki; and the Confucius Institute at the University of Thessaly.

17 The quotation is from Adonis Georgiadis, Greek minister for development and investments, see Kathimerini (2019a).

18 In other policy fields the Commission is adding substance to its strategic outlook vis-à-vis China. In 2019, it adopted a new public procurement strategy which enables the EU to exclude companies from countries that have neither signed up to the WTO's International Procurement Agreement (IPA), nor concluded a bilateral treaty with the EU. A June 2020 White Paper of the Commission has been forwarded for consultation to member states which focuses on distortions created by foreign subsidies in the Single Market. The document seeks an extension of existing anti-subsidy rules to non-EU external investors.

19 The American investment fund Black Summit Financial is part of a consortium that includes US investors, Greek participants and a European port operator.

References

Bastian, J. (2015). *Defining a Growth Strategy for Greece: Wishful Thinking or a Realistic Prospect?* Bonn: Friedrich-Ebert Stiftung (Foundation).

Bastian, J. (2019a). Southeast European crossroads in China's Belt and Road Initiative. *Südosteuropa Mitteilungen*, 59(1), 38–51.

Bastian, J. (2019b). Sino-Greek engagement: Path to 'Win-Win Cooperation' is not always linear, *MacroPolis*, November 7. www.macropolis.gr/?i=portal.en.the-agora.8865.

Borrell, J. (2020). *The Coronavirus pandemic and the new world it is creating*, March 23. https://eeas.europa.eu/delegations/china_en/76401/EU%20HRVP%20Josep%20Borrell:%20The%20Coronavirus%20pandemic%20and%20the%20new%20world%20it%20is%20creating.

Cerulus, L., and Hanke Vela, J. (2017). Enter the Dragon, *Politico*, October 4. www.politico.eu/article/china-and-the-troika-portugal-foreign-investment-screening-take overs-europe/.

Chun, D. (2019). China-Greece cooperation can strengthen Sino-EU ties, *China Daily* November 12.

European Commission (2019a). *Investor Citizenship and Residence Schemes in the European Union*, January 23. https://ec.europa.eu/info/sites/info/files/com_2019_12_final_report.pdf.

European Commission (2019b). *Joint Communication [with the High Representative of the Union for Foreign Affairs and Security Policy] to the European Parliament, the European Council and the Council. EU-China: A Strategic Outlook*, March 12. JOIN (2019) 5 final. https://eur-lex.europa.eu/legal-content/EN/TXT/PDF/?uri=CELEX:52019JC0005.

Godement, F. (2020). *Europe's Pushback on China*, Institut Montaigne, Policy Paper, June. www.institutmontaigne.org/en/publications/europes-pushback-china.

Kathimerini (2019). Chinese investments worth 7.5 billion euros, November 3 (Greek edn).

Kathimerini (2019a). Cooperation with China an 'example for Euro peers', October 21 (English edn).

Kathimerini (2019b). Xi eyes deeper cooperation, November 11 (English edn).

Kathimerini (2020). Attica Region twinned with Sichuan Province in China, September 1 (English edn).

Maltezou, R. (2014). Greece seeks role as China's gateway to Europe. *Reuters Market News*, June 20. www.reuters.com/article/greece-china-assets-idUSL6N0P12Z020140 620.

Marantidou, V. (2018). Shipping finance: China's new tool in becoming a global maritime power. *China Brief*, 18(2), February 13.

Mathews, J.A. (2017). China's takeover of the Port of Piraeus in Greece: Blowback for Europe, *The Asia-Pacific Journal*, 15(13) July 1. https://apjjf.org/2017/13/Mathews.html.

Maundrill, B. (2020). Piraeus becomes top Mediterranean port. *Port Technology*, 21 (May). www.porttechnology.org/news/piraeus-becomes-top-mediterranean-port/.

Qiyue, Z. (2020). The single soul of empathy dwelling in our bodies. *Kathimerini*, March 23 (English edn).

Taylor, P. (2021). In defense of the EU-China investment deal, *Politico*, January 8. www.politico.eu/article/europe-at-large-eu-china-investment-deal/.

Teller Report (2019). China understands that Europe is organised, says Macron, November 6. www.tellerreport.com/news/2019-11-06—%22china-understands-tha t-europe-is-organized-%22-says-macron-.rkzSgYBesS.html.

Transparency International Hellas (2021). Siren or Trojan Horse? April. www.transpa rency.gr/wp-content/uploads/2021/04/GoldenVisas_FINAL-REPORT_2021.pdf.

US Embassy, and Consulate in Greece (2020). Ambassador Pyatt's remarks at Alex-androupoli Port, July 23.https://gr.usembassy.gov/ambassador-pyatts-remarks-at-a lexandroupoli-port/.

Varoufakis, Y. (2017). *Adults in the Room: My Battle with Europe's Deep Establish-ment*. London: The Bodley Head.

Watsa, P. (2019). Making Greece more investment-friendly, *Kathimerini*, 25, July (English edn). www.ekathimerini.com/242943/article/ekathimerini/business/prem -watsa-greece-must-become-more-investment-friendly.

Wall Street Journal (2020). Behind China's decade of European deals, state investors evade notice, September 30.

Xinhua (2019). Sino-Greek friendship hailed ahead of PRC founding anniversary, September 26.

Yongxin, Z. (2019). New energy in the friendship between China and Israel. *The Jerusalem Post*, November 17.

10 Reforming to stay in the Single Market

Product market reforms for an export-oriented economy

Michael Mitsopoulos

Introduction

Greece stood out from the 1980s until the beginning of the crisis as a country, society and economy in a number of ways. While its product market and labour market regulations were among the most stringent in the EU, or even the most stringent in certain dimensions or combinations of dimensions, after languishing during the 1980s and in spite of the build-up of public debt, from the mid-1990s onwards the country enjoyed a lengthy period of growth; indeed, a protracted 'growth episode' of the kind described by Rodrik (2007).

While this growth episode, in view of both the levels of regulation but also the overall institutional maturity and quality of governance and rule of law, seemed to defy perceived truths, there were numerous indications that the country was indeed heavily burdened by its widely documented weaknesses and deficiencies. For one thing, the period of rapid growth was paired with the emergence and entrenchment of the 'triple deficits' of the current account, public finances and wage competitiveness, pointed out in a most graphic way in the Governor's Annual Reports and intermediate reports published by the Bank of Greece during the years preceding the official onset of the Greek crisis (see e.g. Bank of Greece, 2008a, 2008b). At the same time the period of rapid growth could largely be explained by the cheap private and public credit ensured by the accession to Economic and Monetary Union, the continuing inflow of EU structural funds and the impact of the reforms and public works that were implemented, designed or at least initiated from 1990–1993 and rolled out during the following decade (Pelagidis and Mitsopoulos, 2009). But weak governance and the politico-economic equilibrium linked with a resistance to reform meant that this growth was increasingly paired with these salient macroeconomic imbalances.

While these were signs for any prudent economist that this period of strong growth ran a high risk of any sudden interruption leading to a significant decline in living standards, as documented for example by Anastasatos (2008), and there were also further signs that pointed towards the unsustainability of the observed growth episode. These included the relatively weak performance of the private sector job market, measured both by the

DOI: 10.4324/9780429202247-13

number of jobs and by the level of wages paid; the overall low employment-to-population ratio; the persistent inability of Greeks to form families as reflected by one of the lowest fertility rates in the ageing continent of Europe; the notable inability of young Greeks to enter the job market; a persistent brain drain of the most talented young; a very low participation in the job market of especially young women and mothers; poor environmental policy scores; poor quality of urban living, poor public education and health services and poor child support infrastructure, to name but a few of the key indicators taken from the Eurostat, Eurobarometer and OECD databases. As a matter of fact, it was almost impossible to square off the observed strong growth performance with these extremely poor scores that documented a broad and systematic inability of the economy to perform in a way that distributes wealth through jobs and that mobilizes strong growth to achieve inclusiveness and quality of life.

After three adjustment programmes spanning almost ten years and the often turbulent implementation thereof, it is difficult to assess what exactly has been achieved and what still needs to be done as part of a national reform agenda. A full documentation is missing, partly because of the often rapid turnover of governments during this period and the fact that the adjustment programmes did simply strike items off the list when they were considered to have been implemented, while a summary of achieved goals or of goals considered to have been achieved but that for some reason should be reconsidered was never published. This chapter will attempt an assessment of the key dimensions of the product market regulations, which, while not exhaustive, is still indicative of the progress made and of what still needs to be done in order to complete the job at hand.

The remainder of this chapter will first look at the legacy of product market reforms in Greece and the historic context of the reluctance to advance them. Subsequently it will be argued that this reluctance contributed to the shaping of key aspects of the Greek economy that in turn are linked with its low non-wage competitiveness. A brief documentation of the political economy challenges faced is followed by a closer examination of the state of play in the area of spatial planning, licensing and market regulation, network industry regulation, the application of the OECD Competition Assessment Toolkits and professional services regulation.

A brief overview of regulation in Greek product and labour markets

In this chapter the weak performance of product market reforms in the country will be cast as a focal point that can rationalize these contradictions. During the post-war period Greece started out as a poor country of the European periphery. While Greece did not differ significantly from those European countries that developed the attributes of a modern state and democracy during the early post-war years (Ziblatt, 2006), it had less of a tradition of strong governance and decentralization to build on (e.g. Veremis and Koliopoulos, 2014). At the same time, the centuries-old legacy of state intervention in the economy that was acceptable in the pre-war era, and during the war as a matter of fact, still ensured a tight regulatory grip of the state on the economy throughout most European countries. In that sense, state control of large parts of the economy and of many network industries, even if at the time they were not perceived as such, was not something that set Greece apart from its European peers. Even though many Greek infrastructure businesses were private at the time, ranging from rail, water to electricity to name but a few, a gradual process of state intervention could not be measured as a deviation from the practices observed in other European countries. The same could be said about the gradual regulation of various services and professions, a process that accelerated during the period of military rule and that was also widespread throughout Europe where it had deep roots in medieval economic realities. Even with the restoration of democracy, in 1974, the trend towards central planning and state intervention through regulation did not abate, despite the fact that the oil shocks rippled through tightly regulated economies in a way that demonstrated their inability to adapt to change.

The entry of Greece to the then European Community (EC) marks a turning point. Greece remained on a path of high state intervention at a time when most of the other EC member states, in the wake of the oil crisis, had started a determined move in exactly the opposite direction. While during the early 1980s Greece was among the countries with the most stringent product market regulations, which are the focus of this chapter, and labour market regulation (see Chapter 11 in this volume), by the time the Greek crisis started to broil it stood out alone among the other EU member states (Mitsopoulos, 2019b). In the meantime, the other EU countries went through a process of deregulation, leading to a deviation that amounted to the key contributor to the onset of the crisis and whose demise is a necessary, but not sufficient, condition to put the country on a path towards prosperity and social well-being.

A relatively brief episode of aggressive reforms (Pelagidis and Mitsopoulos, 2017) failed to reverse this reality, but sufficed to convey some key messages. First, Greece can reform, and when reforms are implemented, ultimately, they lead to growth spurts, albeit with a delay especially when their implementation coincides with an international crisis. This statement is consistent with OECD research (see Gal and Hijzen, 2016; Bouis et al., 2012), and with the conclusion of research on the timing of the impact of product and labour market reforms. Second, reforms can end the careers of the politicians that implement them, a lesson that was deeply rooted in the collective thinking of the political leadership after 1993 and well into the years of the three adjustment programmes. And as a final message, reforms once implemented can be reversed.

How regulatory weaknesses shaped the economy and society in the period leading up to the crisis

Over decades, the Greek business environment ended up tightly regulated (and thus unable to benefit from the application of the forces of competition network industries, e.g. Bourlès et al., 2010). It featured vague and haphazardly applied overregulation, which forms a breeding ground for corruption and at the same time creates high regulatory uncertainty, especially for whomever attempts to do things differently, and slow and at times unpredictable dispensing of justice. This situation made it almost impossible to introduce innovation along complex value chains, thus depriving the economy 'of the young' that according to Haltiwanger et al. (2013) ultimately drives job creation. In the meantime, other EU member countries benefited both upstream and downstream from the deregulation of key network industries, whose increased efficiency not only reduced prices but also facilitated a flexible incorporation of market needs, leading to the development of efficient and modern supply and value chains. In contrast, Greek producers of tradable goods, already burdened by their location on the periphery of Europe where these chains become thinner in any case, were hampered yet further by these inefficiencies.

Furthermore, the deficiencies in the way the market was regulated hit these same producers of tradable goods particularly hard, because of the nature of their businesses. Regulation usually has as a prime focus to ensure that the broad policy goals as well as the health and safety of consumers are respected. It also strives to ensure that activities and professions are licensed in a way that is compatible with the directions given by spatial planning and that these activities are performed according to appropriate technical and safety standards. In Greece the complexity and vagueness of its laws implied that activities that needed more specialized licensing or that combined many separate activities that in turn had to be licensed separately (which is usually the case for activities that have a larger footprint) were hampered by this situation. These activities, though, happen to be those activities that employ a more diverse array of professions, some of which also happen to be subject to special regulations. In other words, a manufacturing value chain has to pass a more stringent test versus the provision of services in all countries in the world owing to the simple fact that its direct impact on its surroundings is, in most cases, significantly higher. Furthermore, a manufacturing value chain brings together many different activities that are usually subject to separate health and safety regulations and that employ numerous technical professions that in most countries are subject to some certification process. Compare this to a hotel resort, for example, where the main licensing challenge usually stems from the proximity to a beach or some landmark. Thus, when some but not all the nodes of the aggregate licensing process are dysfunctional, legally performing such activities becomes very difficult. If in addition corruption and erratic auditing mechanisms are added to the equation, a major barrier to growth emerges.

Usually, such regulatory inefficiencies burden small companies particularly as their costs of complying with expensive regulations use a higher percentage of their financial resources. But if audits, for various reasons, target only larger companies, smaller companies can bypass the complex nexus of the dysfunctional regulatory framework and operate profitably, offering them a competitive advantage. But this comes at a high price, as this semi-legality exposes them to sudden increases in cost should they want to expand, thus marking the introduction of a significant barrier to growth. In addition, the inefficiencies of network industries and infrastructure that, when brought up to date and modernized, were geared towards transporting people rather than goods, again had a negative effect on larger manufacturing units, which need public policy-driven infrastructure in these dimensions in order to bolster their non-wage competitiveness.

Surely other factors also contributed towards cornering manufacturing in Greece, and it is noteworthy that they all contributed in the same direction, something that can be expected in a high-regulation, high-corruption, weak institutions environment (see, for example, Di Tella and MacCulloch (2009). For example, such factors were, and to some extent still are, the strong disincentives introduced by the social security system, the tax system (Mitsopoulos, 2019a), and the industrial relations framework (Mitsopoulos, 2019b.) against private sector employment, and in particular better paid salaried employment in the private sector. In contrast, (a) domestically, the self-employed were offered the opportunity as well as political and social acceptance to evade taxes and benefited from generous public sector employment tax and social security treatment, and (b) in competing EU countries, similar employment was treated more favourably (SEV Hellenic Federation of Enterprises, 2019).

With these facts at hand, the employment deficit stemming from larger companies and manufacturing companies, that both depend on better paid salaried labour, it can now be explained why the growth of the 2000s was unable to ensure a job-rich growth spurt that benefits the whole of society. A comparison with the share of employment in given sectors to population reveals sizeable gaps in employment in professions that support larger companies (from accounting and legal services to technical services), and that support the employees of these companies (such as health, education and social services for children and elderly, the uptake of women in the job market) (Mitsopoulos and Pelagidis, 2014). Thus, the footprint of the regulatory peculiarities of post-war Greece transcended the whole of society, but ultimately are linked with an employment deficit at the productive base of the economy.

As well as emphasizing the importance of streamlining the regulatory environment in Greece, and how it is related with the ability to ensure a vibrant revival of the job market, this analysis includes another key message. Greece does not suffer from 'too many small companies', which are often found in the tourism and retail sectors. The observed deficit in larger companies stems from the disincentives to grow, and although the country is missing relatively few of these companies, they are the ones which would be important for job numbers.

The political economy of reform during the adjustment programmes: reforms advanced and constrained

The adjustment programme initially had the support of many reform-minded Greeks, who for years had seen with desperation the squandering of many opportunities to apply reforms that are useful for all members of society. The reform programmes were conceived to focus on fiscal consolidation, through revenue increases and cost cutting, labour market and product market reforms, with this prioritization. Initially the fiscal adjustment targeted, in theory, a quite balanced mix of measures to increase revenues and cut expenditure. Unfortunately, the design of the adjustment programmes assumed, erroneously in retrospect as was clearly demonstrated, the willingness of the domestic political system to implement evenly such a plan.

Yet an acknowledgement of the fact that the political and economic forces at work that hindered reforms and supported the propagation of the given equilibrium that brought the country to the onset of the crisis would also influence the programme implementation, could have helped at this stage. Surely such an analysis would exceed the strict mandate of an economic adjustment programme and touch on the realities of the political procedures within a member state, a fact that explains why this dimension was not included in the calculation. It is not because it was neglected, but the structure of the EU did not facilitate an explicit and open incorporation of this dimension.

The unravelling of the Greek crisis was also influenced by a major factor that was not foreseen by policymakers, namely the rapid increase in uncertainty. Those affected were the companies that had import and export contracts, that depended on international collaborations, expected to receive payments from abroad or were expected to make payments abroad, and depended on trade finance. They happened to be export-oriented companies selling tradable goods, i.e. manufacturing companies. Such companies are generally larger in size and pay higher than average wages all year round; thus their employees constitute a large part of the upper-middle class group of taxpayers that were disproportionally affected by the adopted tax policies. It is thus no coincidence that during 2010–2015 manufacturing experienced the second largest percentage decline in employment among all the sectors, except construction, even though the initial adjustment programme explicitly championed a Greek recovery through export-led growth. At the same time, repeated tax increases burdened those who were already paying majority of taxes before the crisis.

On the positive side, in 2012 the deregulation of the private sector labour market produced wage decreases in the private sector rather than layoffs.

Following an initial forced fall of employment, the stabilization and recovery of employment numbers despite decreases in wages was the lesser of two evils and set the foundation for a path towards recovery.

At the same time, even if progress in cost rationalization and product market reforms lagged behind when compared to the speed at which the other developments unravelled, during the ten years of the adjustment programmes various governments advanced the reform agenda both with respect to product market reforms and cost rationalization. Progress was patchy, non-linear and relatively slow. But compared to other international reform episodes (see, for example, Koskei et al., 2015), it was noteworthy. Slowly a useful mass of reforms accumulated. Unfortunately, they could not demonstrate their growth-enhancing potential as the repercussions of the uncertainty reverberated.

Access to finance for the private sector had dried up by 2012. As the handling of a fiscal crisis by the domestic players and the lenders allowed it to morph first into a financial crisis and then into a textbook case of depression, any positive impact from reforms was more than cancelled out. Uncertainty fed into the system like a textbook increase of interest rates, whose impact is highlighted for example in Cacciatore et al. (2012). The legacy of this mishandling, which given the experiences of 1929 should not have occurred in the Western world, still reverberates today with the large stock of non-performing loans and a depleted corporate sector as a new crisis has emerged owing to the COVID-19 pandemic. Yet, despite this extensive groundwork, and a stoic advancement of reforms during all these years, key reforms did not reach a level at which the market could directly see the benefits. Of course, there were exceptions like the labour market and some professional services. But overall, significant steps were taken in the right direction but obstacles to the full roll-out of the reforms still remained, amounting to a rather unrewarding situation.

Business licensing, business parks and market supervision

First, it has to be noted that when the so-called troika first arrived in Greece in 2010, its members had little understanding of the depth and breadth of the problem. Gradually, they understood the problem and helped to outline the path reforms needed to take, even though progress was always slow because of the nature of these highly technical reforms, as well the fact that fiscal and labour market issues always dominated the agenda.

Licensing and supervision should be examined together, as in any legal system there needs to be some mechanism that sets the rules of where and how an activity can be established and then supervises the level of adherence to these rules. In Greece, a heavy bureaucratic procedure has traditionally preceded the issuing of any of three separate licenses required to build, establish premises and then operate a business. The system was fraught with contradictions. For example, if a bottle of milk on the shelves of a food store passed the expiry date, the food safety legislation would fine the company if that bottle of milk remained on the premises, even if it was stored separately from the other goods for sale, while the tax authorities would fine the company if this unsold bottle of milk was removed from the premises. Such details were heavily audited, often breeding petty corruption so that the auditor did not 'see' the bottle of milk, despite the fact that entire sectors of the market remained unaudited. At the same time companies could, in principle, legally be forced out of business owing to contradictions in the law such as the hypothetical bottle of milk. Another frequent problem stemmed from the need for companies to have numerous licenses, and this was particularly common in industry and manufacturing. For example, a license awarded for a more complicated industry, such as mining, may expire after ten years, in accordance with the law. The company therefore starts the renewal process three years before the expiry date as it knows how lengthy the process is, but the license is not issued before the ten-year period is up, thus leaving the company without a legal license.

These narratives may appear to have been taken out of Kafka's stories, but it was and in some cases still is the daily reality for numerous companies that make or move things in Greece. Reversing this situation is a monumental task, but it is also the most important non-tax reform for economic activity since the creation of the Greek state. Clarity in spatial planning is a prerequisite. Reasonable licensing according to EU guidelines is another. And a properly functioning auditing system is also needed to round off the reform proposition into a coherent and operable whole. The law-abiding businesses will not enjoy any benefits unless all these pillars somehow work efficiently. Progress on this long road of reforms can be unrewarding for politicians. Each step unnerves entangled interests in the administration and beyond and resistance to reform creates political costs to the reformer. The technical details and complications to get things right at each step can be mind-boggling. And each individual reform, one should recall, does not lead to measurable results at the end. In addition, the complexity of the whole exercise means it is easy to lose faith along the way.

During the period of the adjustment programmes there were numerous important milestones. The modernization of the antiquated regulations on how to audit companies and the health and safety regulations they have to comply with were prerequisites of the programme, as were numerous initiatives to facilitate business licensing. Especially from 2012 onwards, and throughout all the successive governments, this particular area of reform edged forward. Yet progress initially mostly benefited smaller providers of services and never reached a point during which especially complex manufacturing could face a more predictable and reasonable licensing procedure under most circumstances. For example, a €150 million pharma investment on the premises of a designated business park had to wait for almost two years in order to obtain an exemption of 1.5m from an excessively restrictive maximum limit on building height.

Still, the stage was set during this period so that in 2019 and 2020 a bold push forward brought within reach the objective of licensing most manufacturing companies that want to establish themselves in industrial parks or areas designated for industrial use through a simple notification process and according to standards set by the law. For more substantial businesses, this restriction to areas with designated use is helpful, as the legacy of loose spatial planning, coupled with the lack of clear policies to guide new businesses to designated areas with the proper planning, pushed businesses for decades to establish themselves in diverse areas that were then left without key infrastructure. Such infrastructure ranges from roads, rail and natural gas connections to key environmental impact management systems that are easier to install in business parks owing to significant economies of scale. Some issues, pertaining mainly to environmental licensing, archaeology, the designation of agricultural land and forestry remain but today, for the first time, easy business licensing for manufacturing appears within reach and for many cases it is already a reality.

On the other hand, towards the end of the adjustment programmes and after numerous legislative initiatives, the auditing mechanism came under an umbrella law (4512/2018) that designates a central planning and coordination of audits. For the first time, in principle, the new framework promises to eradicate duplications, gaps and inefficiencies in the supervision of market activities at all dimensions. Again, the road towards implementation is long and complex. Such a system of systematic and well targeted out of office audits on operating businesses instead of that in-office audit of paperwork before a business operates needs a widespread re-engineering of administrative structures, secondary legislation and rulebooks. Once again, continuous efforts have not yielded tangible results, but are slowly reaching the point that such results can become achievable. While this inching towards the set goal is not apparent to the operators in the market, the administration has been taking slow but steady steps to prepare the rulebooks, manuals and methods needed to take the fundamental step towards coordinated, systematic, targeted audits that can ensure a level playing field in a market with easy licensing.

As a result, today, given also the determined push made during 2019–2020 and building on all the groundwork of the previous years, for the first time in many decades Greece can advertise itself as 'open for business' in the sense that if an investor wants to proceed with the building of a business and its operations they can do so with predictable procedures in business parks and areas with the designated land use. Regarding the fact that these areas are still relatively limited, a bold programme to reform and complete spatial planning has set out after 2019 to complete the spatial planning in the largest part of the country.

It is time now to implement one more determined push to complete these important reforms. In particular, in areas with land use designated for manufacturing and supply chain activities, initiatives to do so should be advanced in the near future.

At this stage one has to also note that in Greece business parks were never advanced in a way that would make them an attractive choice to establish a business. To ensure the necessary investment and to guarantee attractive terms for the businesses that operate in these parks, certain reforms to use this tool strategically, to make it easier to establish them where demand is and where infrastructure can be placed and to make them more attractive to companies have to be advanced.

Finally, in order to ensure proper market supervision in these areas of facilitated business licensing for activities with a larger footprint, but also for the market overall to ensure a level playing field and the adherence to rules that protect the public interest, a number of key steps have to be taken in order to ensure the advancement of the implementation of the new umbrella law for market supervision.

OECD Competition Assessment Toolkits I, II, III

In Greece, during the adjustment programmes, there were three iterations of applying the OECD Competition Assessment Toolkit (CAT) (OECD, 2019) to 13 sectors of the economy that represent over one-third of the economy's total employment (SEV Hellenic Federation of Enterprises, 2020). During the first round the food, retail, building materials and tourism sectors were analysed, during the second round beverages, oil, textiles and apparel and equipment, and during the third round e-commerce, building, press and communication, wholesale trade and other selected sectors were scrutinized. In addition, over 2,300 applicable pieces of legislation and laws were examined to identify provisions that limit competition and, after assessing their significance and scope, over 150 of them were identified for revision. Over the years, many of these OECD recommendations have been adopted by successive Greek governments, although again not without backtracking and the occasional political upheaval as was the case for example with shop opening hours, the terms of operation of pharmacies and the sale of non-subscription pharmaceuticals outside pharmacies. In spite of the controversy over some of the reforms, overall the three rounds of the CAT exercise identified numerous outdated obstacles to doing business and helped to cut away a non-negligible amount of bureaucratic weed.

Yet the programme was faced with a number of major shortcomings. First, while once a sector was selected a solid methodology was applied, the selection of the individual sectors was not the result of any sound methodology but rather of political agreement. Therefore, the selection process largely steered clear of sectors which could prove problematic for the political system. Also, the scope of the exercise was on regulations that skewed the Greek playing field. It completely ignored issues that skewed the playing field against domestic producers in favour of importers. For example, inefficiencies in the energy market that increased the cost of energy for Greek producers to levels higher than the prices paid by other EU competitors were deemed beyond the scope of the exercise, even though they were a major contributor to the decline of the manufacturing sector during the adjustment programme years that aimed to lead Greece onto the path of an export-led recovery. In addition, taxation and other similar issues that played an even more important role in the needless destruction of the manufacturing sector were also deemed off limits. The argument was that there was a separate programme, again implemented under the adjustment programme, focusing on the reduction of the administrative burden.

However, this programme advanced less impressively than the OECD CAT exercise, meaning that the overall reduction of burdens that put Greek companies at a disadvantage lagged behind the reduction of barriers to competition, as also documented by the respective answers given by executives in the opinion survey of the World Economic Forum (Figure 10.1). In an environment in which on the one hand taxation and administrative practices increase costs and reduce non-wage competitiveness and on the other hand barriers to competition allow producers to pass these costs on to the consumer, domestic producers can survive. However, if the barriers to competition come down, while the burden of taxation and administrative costs remains higher than that faced by other EU producers, domestic producers cannot compete any more. This observation is not new. Many observers feared precisely such an impact when Greece joined the EC, and in retrospect one cannot say that they were wrong. They, in turn, could draw on earlier examples similar to

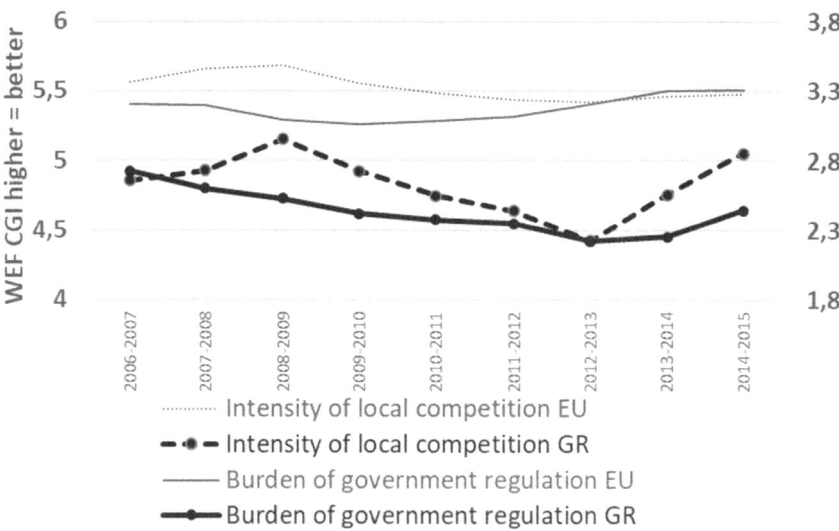

Figure 10.1 Domestic competition: WEF Global Competitiveness Index, series 'domestic competition' and 'burden of regulation'
Source: World Economic Forum executive opinion survey prior to the 2016 revision.

those described by Williamson (2011), who demonstrated how the specialization created by open trade led to the collapse of the manufacturing of tradable goods in developing countries, depriving them of the enrichment of the product space observed in developed countries. The *Atlas of Economic Complexity* (Hausmann et al., 2011) shows how the depletion of the product space can deprive an economy of growth potential, thus corroborating with hard facts the narrative of the historian. Lacking the complexity of the product space that will allow exponential improvements in an interconnected, knowledge-based economy, the prediction of convergence made by Solow (1956) will not always materialize, as suggested by Durlauf and Quah (1999).

Therefore, it would have been crucial to ensure that the two initiatives progress at least in parallel, and that preferably the reduction of costs and burdens should advance faster. Instead, the opposite happened, possibly as a result of the fact that the team in charge of the CAT had a clear methodology and was better organized to deal with the obstacles it wanted to identify, whereas the vast array of obstacles to doing business, were often very complex, required extensive regulatory and administrative re-engineering to rectify and, finally, only put Greek companies at a horizontal disadvantage. Still, it is noteworthy that the simple fact described before did not raise any concerns in Brussels, Washington or even Athens, as delays in the reduction of administrative costs and burdens continued apace. Neither is it easy to overlook the fact that the horizontal disadvantages posed by simple regulatory impediments, taxation, energy costs, and other network industries to domestic producers of tradable goods were so severely discounted in their importance for the survival of the domestic production base.

Network industries and professional services

Network industries are extremely important for the development of high value chains in modern economies. As these value chains become longer and more complex, materials and components are moved more often between companies and countries in order to achieve the specialized inputs that then will form a final product. Energy and communications are equally important to ensure the non-wage competitiveness of the producers of key components along these chains, especially as the digital age advances.

From 1975–1993 Greece was positioned among the EU countries with the highest level of regulation and state intervention in the economy, and this fact pairs with the rest of the description for the regulation of the economy presented so far. However, other countries recognized that stringent state regulation that stifles competition limits the ability of the economy to respond to shocks, such as the oil shocks, thereby propagating their negative effects. Thus, they started to aggressively deregulate these industries in tandem with EU legislation. At the time Greece resisted this trend until 1990–1993, when the index measured the deregulation of the communications market through the introduction of a mobile communications market with a competitive structure and the presence of non-state-owned service providers. Subsequently, from 1994–2009 Greece embarked on a downward trend imposed by EU law, but was clearly the laggard of Europe compared with the major EU member states. An unwillingness to really let the state grip on these industries go was surely a prime reason for these developments. While companies based in other EU countries ultimately enjoyed a competitive advantage from the better services provided at cheaper prices, Greek companies struggled with the high costs and in certain cases the poor service of haulage, energy and communications providers, a fact that put them at an ever-increasing disadvantage that contributed to the demise of many of them.

While many loose ends remain, and while in industries such as energy, road and rail haulage and port management infrastructure and pieces of legislation still need to be improved, the first steps for these improvements by now have largely been taken. The bulk of core legislative deregulation tracked by the OECD has been achieved during the adjustment programmes, as clearly documented by Figure 10.2.

Nevertheless, Greek companies did have to endure a long period of presence in a common market in which their goods competed directly on the shelves with other producers that benefited from these better network industry services. And this largely co-existed for the better part of a decade during the adjustment programmes that coincided with the exclusion of the Greek producers from the Single Market for financial services as a result of the uncertainty and political wrestling over the implementation of the agreed reforms and the ill-advised talk of Grexit (Mitsopoulos and Pelagidis, 2018).

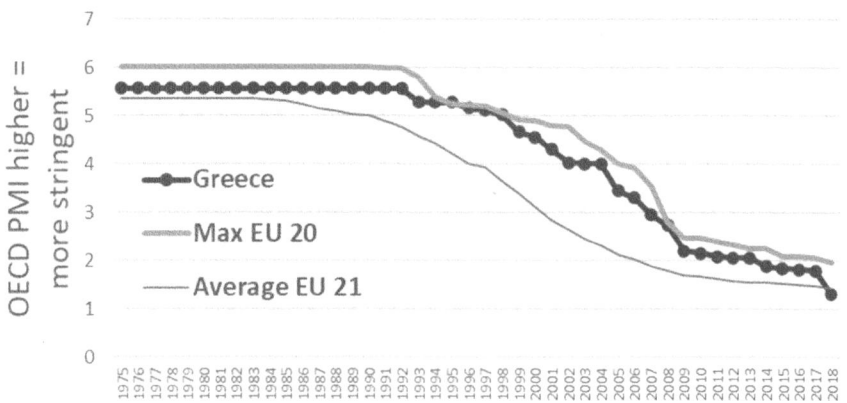

Figure 10.2 OECD, Product Market Regulation Network Sectors Indicator. 21 key EU countries, 1975–2018
Source: OECD.

However, in some areas improvements still need to be made.

- In the energy sector deregulation has to be advanced in a balanced way, which is an extremely technical and difficult task.
- Reform in freight haulage has to be completed, as it is key to the efficiency of supply chains.
- Infrastructure in communications and energy networks needs to be improved, along with a rationalization of regulations and taxes in the sectors and a proper planning of the requisite projects.

At the same time, the political upheaval during the implementation of the adjustment programmes was greatly influenced by the reluctance to advance reforms that aimed to deregulate professional services, and the insistence of the so-called troika to pursue these structural reforms. According to the OECD, in 2018 the regulation of these services, with the exception of the traditionally competitive real estate agent market, was still above the EU average. While the regulation of these services does not seem to be critical to the revival of the Greek product space, which is mostly dependent on progress in the areas of network industries, licensing, spatial planning and the taxation of labour, the regulation of professional services is important for the development of the market for supporting services. It is equally important for the creation of job opportunities in these markets for the youth that should grow when competitiveness prevails.

The completion of the reforms listed in the previous three sections is key to the recovery of the country. An important message emerging from the handling of the adjustment periods was that a delay in the advancement of reforms that improve the non-wage competitiveness of the Greek economy in the face of a need to ensure the unwinding of macroeconomic imbalances (e. g. wage competitiveness and current account deficits), will ensure that the pressures of adjustment will be disproportionally pushed on the part that can yield, namely the labour market. This takes the form of wage or employment reductions and, thus, ultimately inflicts the adjustment costs on society. The advancement of these reforms is thus necessary to insulate society from the need for adjustments during future downturns and to ensure that it can reap the benefits of growth during upturns.

In addition, by providing opportunities for business growth, these reforms can ensure that the representation of larger companies in the Greek business ecosystem will become more balanced through the growth of existing companies and a diverse increase in employment through the growth of these companies as well as from supporting services. This is the constructive way to rectify the imbalances and deficits observed today in the corporate sector and job market, rather than the decline of smaller companies, a development that would have unnecessary and harmful consequences for both the economy and the bulk of society.

Conclusion and a vision for the future

While progress in product market reforms has been slow when compared to the speed at which other developments unfolded during the ten years of the adjustment programmes, a significant number of reforms had been made by the end of these programmes. Building on these reforms, determined progress in key areas after the exit from the adjustment programmes means that reasonable terms of business licensing are an attainable goal for Greek businesses for the first time in decades. At the same time, progress has been made in implementing reforms in key network industries. Taken together, the impact of these developments may lay the foundations for a revival of the Greek production base and the employment that is associated with it. But beyond the advancement of the policies documented earlier, a key policy dimension that should be now a policy priority is the development of the country's *internal capacity* to design and implement policies that ensure inclusive growth aligned with the aims for a greener economy.

Interestingly, while the adjustment programmes had provisions for the advancement of an improved regulation agenda, the legislative initiatives implemented during these programmes were explicitly exempt from the application of such an agenda. As a result, the programme years were not used to build policy drafting and implementation capacity in the administration and the political system, a matter of particular disappointment to Greek politicians, as shown by Featherstone and Papadimitriou (2015). The problem has been previously documented by Spanou (2020) in view of the practices of international lender organizations that have the leverage to offer financial support, while the application of the OECD CAT demonstrated that the development of a domestic capacity to perform such exercises would be beneficial. However, it is noteworthy that a recent law (4622/2019) reiterated and completed provisions regarding the improved regulation agenda, while in the meantime detailed guidelines have been issued by the competent administrative office, as designated by the law, spelling out the details of impact assessment and consultation processes. At the same time a visible effort to improve coordination at the government level is ongoing, even though an organic interconnection with the European Semester is still nascent. Since these efforts are taking place after the completion of the adjustment programmes, it is obvious that ultimately the full implementation of useful reforms and policies that ensure inclusive and balanced growth remain the prerogative of the national government.

References

Anastasatos, T. (2008). The deterioration of the Greek current account balance: Causes, implications and adjustment scenarios. *Economy and Markets* 3(6), Division of Economic Research and Forecasts, EFG Eurobank.

Bank of Greece (2008a). *Monetary Policy 2007–2008, February.* Athens: Bank of Greece.

Bank of Greece (2008b). *Monetary Policy Intermediate Report, October*. Athens: Bank of Greece.

Bouis, R., Causai, O., Demmoui, L., Duvali R., Zdzienicka, D. (2012). *The Short-Term Effects of Structural Reforms: An Empirical Analysis*, OECD Economics Department Working Papers, No. 949. Paris: OECD Publishing. https://doi.org/10.1787/5k9csvk4d56d-en.

Bourlès, R., Cette, G., Lopez, J., Mairesse, J., Nicoletti, G. (2010). *Do Product Market Regulations in Upstream Sectors Curb Productivity Growth?: Panel Data Evidence for OECD Countries*. OECD Economics Department Working Papers, No. 791. Paris: OECD Publishing. https://doi.org/10.1787/5kmbm6s9kbkf-en.

Cacciatore, M., Duval, R., and Fiori, G. (2012). *Short-Term Gain or Pain? A DSGE Model-Based Analysis of the Short-Term Effects of Structural Reforms in Labour and Product Markets*, OECD Economics Department Working Papers, No. 948. Paris: OECD Publishing. https://doi.org/10.1787/5k9csvkkr3xn-en.

Di Tella, R., and MacCulloch, R. (2009). Why doesn't capitalism flow to poor countries? *Brookings Papers on Economic Activity*, Economic Studies Program, 40(1), 285–332.

Durlauf, S., and Quah, D. (1999). The new empirics of economic growth. In J.B. Taylor, and M. Woodford (Eds.), *Handbook of Macroeconomics,* vol. 1A (pp. 235–308). Elsevier.

Featherstone, K., and Papadimitriou, D. (2015). *Prime Ministers in Greece: The Paradox of Power*. Oxford: Oxford University Press. doi:10.1093/acprof:oso/9780198717171.001.0001.

Gal, P., and Hijzen, A. (2016). *The Short-Term Impact of Product Market Reforms: A Cross-Country Firm-Level Analysis*, OECD Economics Department Working Papers, No. 1311. Paris: OECD Publishing. https://doi.org/10.1787/18151973.

Haltiwanger J., Jarmin, R., and Miranda, J. (2013). Who creates jobs? Small versus large versus young. *The Review of Economics and Statistics*, 95(2), 347–361. doi:10.3386/w16300.

Hausmann, R., Hidalgo, C.A., Bustos, S., Coscia, M., Chung, S., Jimenez, J., Simoes, A., Yıldırım, M. (2011). *The Atlas of Economic Complexity: Mapping Paths to Prosperity*. Cambridge, MA: Puritan Press.

Koskei, I., Wanner, I., Bitetti, R., Barbiero, O. (2015). *The 2013 Update of the OECD's Database on Product Market Regulation: Policy Insights for OECD and Non-OECD Countries*, OECD Economics Department Working Papers, No. 1200. Paris: OECD Publishing. doi:10.1787/5js3f5d3n2vl-en.

Mitsopoulos, M. (2019a). Overtaxation of private sector salaried employment as a key impediment to the recovery of Greece. In D. Thomakos, and K. Nikolopoulos (Eds.), *Taxation in Crisis: Tax Policy and the Quest for Economic Growth* (pp. 289–336). Cham: Palgrave Macmillan. https://doi.org/10.1007/978-3-319-65310-5_12.

Mitsopoulos, M. (2019b). Industry and unions: The relationship with labour. In A. Kefalas (Ed.), *Aspects of Industrialization 1945–2010: A Story* (pp. 149–198). Athens: Sideris (in Greek).

Mitsopoulos, M., and Pelagidis, T. (2014). *Greece: From Exit to Recovery?*Washington, DC: Brookings Institution Press.

Mitsopoulos, M., and Pelagidis, T. (2018). The lessons Quebec offers to Greece and Europe. *Managerial and Decision Economics*, 39(8), 846–853. https://doi.org/10.1002/mde.2967.

Organisation for Economic Co-operation and Development (OECD) (2019). *Competition Assessment Toolkit*, vols I, II, III. http://www.oecd.org/competition/assessment-toolkit.htm.

Pelagidis, T., and Mitsopoulos, M. (2009). Vikings in Greece: Kleptocratic interest groups in a closed, rent-seeking economy. *Cato Journal*, 29(3), 399–416.

Pelagidis, T., and Mitsopoulos, M. (2017). *Who's to Blame for Greece? How Austerity and Populism are Destroying a Country with High Potential*. Cham: Palgrave Macmillan.

Rodrik, D. (2007). *One Economics, Many Recipes: Globalization, Institutions, and Economic Growth*. Princeton University Press.

SEV Hellenic Federation of Enterprises (2019). *All-Encompassing Super Taxation in Greece. Can We Still Hope for Growth?* June (in Greek). www.sev.org.gr/uploads/documents/Overtaxation_2019_F2.pdf.

SEV Hellenic Federation of Enterprises (2020). *Healthy Competition, Stronger Economy: Taking Advantage of the Legacy of the OECD Toolkit*. Special Report 51, February 4 (in Greek). www.sev.org.gr/Uploads/Documents/52659/2020-02-04_SR_Toolkit_FINAL.pdf.

Solow, R. (1956). A contribution to the theory of economic growth. *Quarterly Journal of Economics*, 70(1), 65–94. doi:10.2307/1884513.

Spanou, C. (2020). External influence on structural reform: Did policy conditionality strengthen reform capacity in Greece? *Public Policy and Administration*, 35(2), 135–157. https://doi.org/10.1177%2F0952076718772008.

Veremis, T., and Koliopoulos, S. (2014). *Modern Greece: A History since 1821*. Athens: Patakis (in Greek).

Williamson, J. (2011). *Trade and Poverty: When the Third World Fell Behind*. Cambridge, MA: MIT Press.

Ziblatt, D. (2006). How did Europe democratize? *World Politics*, 58(2), 311–338. doi:10.1353/wp.2006.0028.

11 The divergent Greek labour market

Christos A. Ioannou

Introduction

Greece exited three consecutive adjustment programmes (in 2010–2012, 2012–2014, 2015–2018) aiming to keep the country in the euro area by rebalancing public finances, restoring competitiveness, and by implementing reforms across the board, including of the labour market and industrial relations. Regular accounts of labour market developments and reforms, either of the programme and post-programme surveillance (European Commission, 2020a), or of the annual overview of employment developments in the European Union (European Commission, 2020b) provide data that lead to the question: have the labour market reforms that were introduced in 2010–2018 met expectations?

Reviews that probe beyond mere descriptive analysis stress a recurring need for further reforms. According to the Organisation for Economic Co-operation and Development, 'large and long-standing gaps remain relative to other OECD countries in terms of the number and inclusiveness of jobs, the quality of jobs and prospects for skill development' (Bulman, 2020). Surprisingly, the International Labour Organization has continued to produce frequent technical assistance reports and policy recommendations for Greece, rather unusual for a euro area member state (see, for example, ILO 2014).

This chapter analyses the Greek labour market's (under)performance during the adjustment period. One decade before and one decade after the 2010 debt crisis, Greece's employment rate in 2000 and 2019 were almost the same (61.9% in 2000 compared to 61.2% in 2019). Unemployment in 2019 (17.3%) was much higher than the 2000 level (11.4%), despite its improvement since its peak of 27.5% in 2013. Greece's gross domestic product (GDP) in 2000 and 2019, measured in constant 2015 prices, was similar. In this context, the chapter discusses the structural deficiencies to this adjustment that were left untouched by the private labour market reforms in 2010–2018; these proved to be suspensions of 'bad habits' and rigidities, which in many cases expired at the end of the adjustment programme(s).

There are multiple factors that explain why Greece's potential output and actual employment rate had fallen since the 2009–2010 crisis and remained

DOI: 10.4324/9780429202247-14

rather stagnant, even though there was some improvement in the relationship between GDP and employment in 2013–2019. All relate to the one core factor: that, after buttressing in 2000–2009, the fundamental structural asymmetry that refers to the division of economic activities and resources in the internationally tradable (T) and non-tradable (N) sectors, Greece does not have enough of the high growth, tradable sectors necessary to boost the economy and the employment rate. The adjustment programmes did not prioritize this reallocation of resources. Policy priority was given, de jure and de facto, to the inflated N sector in the Greek economy by supporting its core, the protected public sector. The policy mix for balancing public finances, the taxation mechanism, the wage formation system, the lack of education reform (i.e. the labour supply), have not facilitated the support and transfer of resources to the tradable growth sectors. Labour market regulation and institutions have been stuck in an anachronistic model of a closed and (no longer) protected (but still less open) economy. They have not turned towards the basic prerequisites of a competitive, small and open economy belonging to a common currency area. That, apart from active and stability-oriented fiscal and monetary policies, requires the productive and exporting industries to lead the growth process, to set the standard for wage settlement and leadership, for the flexible regulation of the labour market, and the education and skills policy to support endogenous growth and innovation.

Laggard or divergent?

After ten years of adjustment, and prior to the new economic crisis caused by the outbreak of the coronavirus (COVID-19) pandemic, the Greek labour market has been underperforming. From the beginning of the previous economic crisis, in 2008–2009, to the current pandemic-induced economic crisis that started in 2020, the Greek economy has been underperforming too. By all basic criteria, e.g. GDP growth, GDP per capita, employment rate, employment growth, Greece appears to be a laggard but, in fact, it is an outlier, and is diverging unlike the other EU and euro area member states.

In terms of GDP growth (in 2015 constant prices) Greece suffered the largest loss in 2008–2013: GDP declined by a startling 26.6%, compared to an average of –0.6% in the EU and of –1.9% in the euro area. During the EU recovery period (2013–2019) Greece recorded the lowest growth with a total of 4.6%, compared to 12.8% in the EU and 11.6% in the euro area. In terms of GDP per capita on a purchasing-power parity (PPP) basis the Greek record is no better. Greece is again at the bottom of the list, with a decrease of 21.8% in 2008–2013, compared to gains of 2.7% in the EU and 1.1% in the euro area. Greece recorded the lowest gains in 2013–2019 with 10.1% in GDP per capita in PPP, compared to gains of 19.3% in the EU and 17.8% in the euro area.

The recovery in euro area GDP since the second quarter of 2013 was accompanied by higher than expected employment growth (ECB, 2016). The strong labour market dynamics continued and, despite the considerable heterogeneity observed across different euro area countries, the aggregate euro area and its member states recovered their pre-crisis employment levels and rates (ECB, 2019). The employment rates and their trajectories again positioned Greece at the bottom of the EU and the euro area list. It is not only that in 2019 Greece had the lowest employment rate in the EU-28, at a notable 61.2%, far below the EU (73.9%) and the euro area (72.7%) averages. The member states' trajectories are also very different. In the EU, all the other member states recovered their 2008 employment rates rather early after the crisis in the decade. In 2019 employment rates reached higher levels, compared to 2008, but with one notable exception: Greece. The employment rate in Greece stood at 66.3% in 2008; however, at that time, it was not the lowest in the EU-28. Member states that had lower employment rates than Greece in 2008 displayed fast catch-up trajectories during the period 2008–2019, e.g. Malta (up from 59.2% in 2008 to 76.8% in 2019), Hungary (up from 61.5% to 75.3%) and Poland (up from 65% to 73%). That left Greece at the bottom of the league, and well below its 2008 level of employment rate. Italy, which recorded the second lowest employment rate (63.5%) compared to Greece (61.2%) in 2019, had also improved slightly from its 2008 level of 62.9%. Greece, in terms of its employment rate, is not simply a laggard, it is a diverging outlier.

In terms of employment growth, following the 2008 global financial crisis, Greece suffered in 2008–2013 the far highest rate of job losses in the EU (–23.1% compared to –3% in the EU and –3.7% in the euro area). In 2013–2019 it displayed an above-average rate of job creation of 10.6%, well above the EU (7%) and the euro area (6.8%) average. This contributed to an increase in the employment rate from its historic low of 52.9% in 2013 to 61.2% in 2019. The combination of above-average job creation and below-average GDP growth in 2013–2019 indicates a structural change in Greece's GDP, namely the employment relationship that has probably been caused by the cost adjustment and labour market reforms of the period. But these changes did not prevent Greece from lagging behind EU and euro area averages in term of GDP growth and employment rates.

The Greek economy had been subject to a huge shock, and indeed its labour market had been subject to a huge shock during the Great Recession. That in the Greek case compares only to the Great Depression. Despite the adjustments and improvements both the economy and the labour market entered the new shock of the COVID-19 pandemic-induced crisis without having fully recovered from the previous crisis. Being a laggard is one challenge. Being a diverging outlier is a rather different one. The rest of this chapter aims to explain the structural sources of divergence and its association with the lack of effective and lasting labour market reforms.

The fundamental asymmetry

In historic comparative terms the Greek economy suffered not one, but two lost decades. Its employment rate in 2019, of 61.2%, is similar to its employment rate in 2000 (61.9%). In 2015 constant prices the Greek GDP in 2019 (€183.6 billion) is close to its GDP in 2000 (€181.7 billion). This regression calls into question both the 2000–2009 trajectory of the country and the 2010–2019 decade-long (and still incomplete) adjustment process. What are the reasons that caused Greece in 2019 to fall back to its 2000 GDP levels in real terms, and to its 2000 employment rate levels, given, or despite, impressive progress with fiscal rebalancing and the reforms implemented during three adjustment programmes?

In my view, the intensity, breadth and characteristics of the regression in GDP and employment rates during the Greek crisis are symptoms of the fundamental structural asymmetry in the Greek economy that was exacerbated during the first decade of Greece's participation in the euro area and that to a large extent persisted during the three successive adjustment programmes in 2010–2018. The fundamental structural asymmetry refers to the division of economic activities in the T and N sectors. Economic growth emanates from the T sector, where 'real' average productivity rises intertemporally. Therefore, it is this sector that should lie at the centre of interest of all those framing and implementing economic policy for competitiveness, growth and welfare. However, external competitiveness is not only related to the export sector, or to the T sector. The N sector is important for trade balance adjustments. The relationship between real exchange rates and the trade balance depends on the relative price of non-tradable to tradable goods and services (including the relative wages between the two sectors).

In the light of this division, the crisis of the Greek economy could be interpreted as the result of the asymmetrical growth of the two sectors in a currency regime of fixed exchange rates and a concurrent situation of continuous excessive demand present in the economy. Or (in a different articulation) it could be interpreted as the result of the collapse of the N sector after an unhealthy enlargement during the first period of volcanic nominal growth of GDP (2001–2009), generated by the massive entry of monetary means from abroad through lending and debt, that was followed by a second period (2009–2013) of violent contraction of the same sector. The motivational force in both periods was fiscal and monetary policy that was over-active in the first period and, unavoidably, contractionary in the second, due to Greece's debt default (Ioannou and Ioannou, 2017: 66).

While in other euro area countries the divergences were caused by financial developments, i.e. private credit growth, in Greece they were driven mainly by public deficits. The boost in domestic demand led to current account deficits and to changes in the relative prices and wages of the N and T sectors that caused an appreciation of the real effective exchange rate. Productive capacities were reallocated from the T sector towards the N sector (construction, retail trade, public employment and other domestic sectors) and trade deficits soared. The reverse reallocation of resources from the N sector to the T sector has been very slow and incomplete, leading to the divergence in GDP and in the employment rate compared to the EU and the euro area, and to regression to its 2000 levels.

The allocation of countries' resources across sectors determines growth paths. The composition of GDP in 2019 in terms of the T and N sectors indicates that the share of the T sector started recovering from its historic low of 21% in 2009–2011, to 24% in 2019, which is similar to the T sector's share of GDP in 2003–2005. The trend was negative from 2000 (26%) until 2011 (21%). Gradual recovery started in 2012. The composition of the T sector itself also matters regarding potential levels of activity and growth dynamics. The division within the T sector between what we call the 'Baumol' sector (Tb) which includes manufacturing and ICT and the 'Dutch disease' sector (Td) which includes tourism, transport, shipping, and the extractive industries is important. In the Tb sector the productive process benefits from continuous technological progress and innovation, the accumulation of capital and economies of scale while improvements in productivity lead to economic growth across the board. The share of the Tb sector in gross value added declined from 13.7% in 2000 to a historic low of 11.3% in 2009. In 2019 it was almost stagnant at 11.9%. The share of Td in gross value added declined from 15.0% in 2000, bottomed at 11.9% in 2009, and peaked again at 16.0% in 2019. The share of T (Tb + Td) in gross value added in 2019 (27.8%) recovered from its historic low level in 2009 (23.2%) but remained lower than its 2000 level (28.8%). The composition of Greece's GDP that has scarcely changed in the past decade lies behind the very weak economic growth and the lack of dynamism in job creation. T is the locomotive for growth and Tb is the engine that drives it. Relative prices (and wages) matter in this (re)allocation of resources.

Wage formation buttressing the fundamental asymmetry

Restoring price and cost competitiveness was a key priority in the adjustment programme(s). The unit labour cost-based relative effective exchange rate (ULC-REER[1]) is an appropriate measure for identifying the reasons behind the loss of cost-related competitiveness in Greece (ILO, 2014: 52–53). During Greece's first decade in the euro area, real wage growth consistently outpaced productivity gains, in part reflecting spillovers from excessive public deficits and public debt, and wage (and pension) increases. Driven largely by wage developments in the N sector (ibid.: 54), collective bargaining partners in the wage setting process systematically trailed the excessive national inflation rate, with the illusion that being a euro area member implied the right to convergence of pay to the same level as that of the most developed eurozone member economies, regardless of national and sectoral productivity and competitiveness performance.

Competitiveness, as measured by the REER between a country and its trading partners, is roughly identical to the ratio of relative prices between the T and N sectors in the country. The preservation of competitiveness requires the ratio of unit labour costs (wages to productivity) to remain stable between the two sectors. Wage increases in the N sector, which are not related to or driven by productivity, when imposed on the T sector cause a loss in competitiveness, given that prices in the T sector are determined by international markets. The distortion in the relative prices in the T and N sectors due to macroeconomic demand policies lead again to deterioration in the competitiveness of the T sector, which begins to shrink. This is what happened in Greece during the period 2000–2009. Until 2009, following N sector-driven excessive wage increases, the REER for the whole economy increased incrementally and competitiveness deteriorated. The adjustment measures between 2010 and 2015 led REER to decrease steadily before spiking again in 2016. From 2013 onwards, the REER recovered the losses accumulated since 2003, indicating a restoration of the international competitiveness of the Greek economy (SEV, 2019b).

Overvaluation and real appreciation implied the need for devaluation, which in conditions of common currency could only take the form of internal devaluation. The systematically eroding productive and export capacity, i.e. the build-up of the fundamental asymmetry between the T and the N sectors, on the one hand, and the product complexity mix on the other (Abdon et al., 2010; Felipe and Kumar, 2011), according to which Greek products and exports were increasingly competing not with Germany, Ireland, France, Italy or Spain, but with the product baskets of Bulgaria, Romania, Portugal, India or China, called for emergency cost adjustments. Wage setting reforms were part of the three successive adjustment programmes. In the private sector pay determination through collective bargaining has been subjected to changes towards more decentralized collective bargaining. Minimum wage setting was taken away from the national social partners and became a government responsibility. A one-off 22% reduction in the minimum wage in 2012 created room for labour cost adjustments (Ioannou, 2012). Adjustments in wage levels and wage relativities between the T and the private N sectors followed (Ioannou, 2019a). The public sector wage premium survived the crisis (Ioannou, 2019b).

The significant wage cost correction was the main way to shift from a sharp decrease in employment in 2010-2012, to stabilization in 2013 and, subsequently, to a slow but steady increase from 2014, albeit with low growth rates. The absence of effective reforms to promote (prior to the crisis) and to re-establish (after the crisis) the economy's non-wage competitiveness (open competitive product and service markets, lower energy costs for industry, successive increases in taxation despite the fiscal derailment being mainly driven by the expenditure side) that transferred an unequal burden of correction and adjustment to wages and minimum wages in the private sector (SEV, 2019a), have not facilitated the transfer of resources to the T growth sectors and have therefore caused the Greek labour market to stagnate and diverge.

Reforms or suspension of bad habits?

The pre-crisis wage setting system was based on a multi-level bargaining structure. The national general collective agreement (EGSSE) set the national minimum wage and the ceiling for further top-ups, and provided for higher percentage pay rises at the lower levels of the bargaining structure, i.e at the sectoral, occupational or company level. The core of the bargaining structure consisted of more than 150 occupational collective agreements (occupations and specialties across sectors), more than 40 sectoral collective agreements and an average of more than 250 company-level collective agreements. The settlement of more than 50% of occupational and sectoral collective agreements depended heavily on unilateral recourse by the labour side to compulsory arbitration awards. Their coverage (i.e. the number of employees and companies that are subject to the pay provisions of the collective agreements) was based on the systematic abuse of the extension mechanism applied by the Ministry of Labour. Typically, this required a 51% representation of the signatory parties, but the extension of collective agreements and of compulsory arbitration awards was implemented without any check on the validity of the representation of the parties involved.

This produced a mechanism of leap-frogging in the wage formation process from level to level, through compulsory arbitration and through the extension mechanism, ending up in a first wave domino effect in wage formation. At the same time, a second wave domino effect was the continuous and incremental seniority-based entitlements incorporated in sectoral and occupational collective agreements and compulsory arbitration awards. In 1976–2012 clauses regarding automatic wage increases based on seniority in the labour market and on actual jobs expanded across the board in all sectoral and occupational collective agreements and compulsory arbitration awards. These caused Greece to display the strongest seniority impact in wage formation in the EU, being at the extreme end with the highest continuous and strong seniority multiplier of 1 to 2.4 (Eurofound, 2019) compared to 1.1 in Sweden, 1.5 in Belgium, 1.9 in the EU-28 and 2.2 in Portugal.

In order to deactivate the domino mechanisms of increasing the cost of labour, without this being sustained by a corresponding increase in productivity, and to create scope for wage flexibility and adjustments, the 2010–2018 programmes suspended, in piecemeal fashion, some of these malfunctions. The ministerial right to extend the coverage of sectoral and occupational collective agreements to all firms was suspended from 2011 until the end of the third programme (20 August 2018). For the same period, the favourability clause was suspended so that company-level agreements could take precedence over sectoral agreements, to facilitate company-level wage adjustments. Automatic pay increases due to seniority were frozen in 2012, until the unemployment rate returns to 10%. Compulsory arbitration was reformed in February of the same year by making arbitration voluntary until September 2014. The right to unilateral recourse to compulsory arbitration was reinstated following a decision by the Council of State (no. 2307/2014).

Compulsory arbitration survival indicates that institutional elements of divergence from EU and international labour standards persist. Compulsory arbitration has been a cornerstone of the wage formation system in Greece for decades and was the reason for the ILO's systematic supervision of the application of Convention no. 98 (the Right to Organize and Collective Bargaining Convention, 1949) as Greece has been failing to implement it.[2] The 2010–2018 reforms did not lead to a collective bargaining system complying with ILO and revised European Social Charter standards, which also provides (in Article 6 on free collective bargaining) that compulsory arbitration is not compatible with free collective bargaining.

During the period when some of these malfunctions were suspended collective bargaining agreements were concluded and renewed in fewer sectors and occupations compared to the pre-crisis period. Renewal was possible only when the social partners were ready to adjust to the new economic and labour market conditions (e.g. the tourism sector, tobacco industry, cement industry, confectionery industry, banking) and had some representativeness. Trade unions, and employers' associations to a certain extent, had been significantly weakened by their past abuse of compulsory arbitration for obtaining collective agreements by parties lacking representativeness and their past abuse of the extension mechanism without checks for representativeness.

Trade unions, some employers' associations and most politicians still believed that the pre-crisis institutional and economic setting for wage formation, in operation prior to the 2009–2018 crisis, was the appropriate one by right, and simply waited for it to be reinstated. Unions and most political parties, if not all, have been fixated on returning to the glorious past, of the Greece's first decade in the euro area. Their beliefs and understandings have not facilitated the need to realize the structural aspects of the crisis, the importance of the fundamental asymmetry between the T and N sectors in the Greek economy, and of competitiveness, the need for structural reforms, while at the same time other EU and euro area economies were progressing even further towards GDP recovery, competitiveness, job creation and labour market flexibility.

Pay relativities and resource allocation

In the variety of wage setting models in the euro area, based on the type of private-public (or T-N) sector links, the Greek wage setting mechanism in operation during the first decade (2000–2009) in the euro area has been the exact opposite of that required in conditions of being member in a currency union: i.e. the T sector, or the export sector, being in the wage leadership in the wage formation process. This is linked to the next decade-long crisis (2010–2018). This pattern is rather old, but operated in a more protected economy with, indeed, a national currency. Public sector wage leadership has been dominant since the ending of the civil war in 1949. For decades, there was no interest in any wage policy that was supportive of the productive sector in general, or of the T and export sectors. Wage leadership from the public sector utilities, and from the core public sector, dominated from the 1970s, when wage policy in the private sector was explicitly linked to whether the public sector was to receive pay increases. Since joining the EC in 1981, and indeed following the country's membership of the euro area in 2002, private sector pay and especially pay in the (diminishing) T and export sectors was subject to market pressures and restrictions of the open economy, resulting into systematic labour market and growth model distortions (Ioannou, 2016). Irrational policies also ignored the implications of rising tax wedges for labour in the T sector.

In December 2010, during the first stages of the economic adjustment in Greece, total employment amounted to 4.3 million, of which 2.7 million were in salaried and wage employment. One million public sector employees had their collective agreements frozen and annulled in March 2010. From 2011 onwards their wage setting was removed from the jurisdiction of collective bargaining (Ioannou, 2016).

In the euro area, pay relativities between public and private wages (as described by the public-private pay gap) are accounted for by the degree of exposure to international competition, and by the size of the public sector labour force and its composition (i.e. the intensity in the provision of pure public goods), while labour market institutions play a very limited role. These pay gaps narrowed significantly during the 2008–2012 financial crisis not because of structural factors (i.e. linked to national state traditions) but because of the widespread process of fiscal consolidation (Campos et al., 2015). Since 2009 there has been major fiscal consolidation in Greece as well as a radical reform of public sector wage setting. Despite institutional changes in public sector wage setting and the unprecedented fiscal consolidation, public-private pay relativities have not changed.

Table 11.1 General government expenditure as a % of GDP

	Greece 2009	*EU-28 2009*	*Greece 2019*	*EU-28 2019*	*EU-27 2019*
Compensation of employees	13,1	11,0	11,9	10,0	10,1
Pensions	14,3	12,6	15,7	n.a.	12,8
Social benefits other than social transfers in kind	17,5	16,4	18,9	15,7	16,2
Social transfers in kind	3,1	4,8	2,3	4,8	5,3
Intermediate consumption	6,7	6,3	4,6	5,9	5,5
Gross capital formation	5,1	3,7	2,5	3,0	3,0
Interest	5,0	2,6	3,0	1,6	1,5
Capital transfers, subsidies, other current transfers	3,3	5,0	4,1	4,5	4,6
Total	54,1	50,2	47,5	45,8	46,7
Surplus/deficit	−15,1	−6,6	1,5	−0,8	−0,5

Source: Eurostat, government revenue, expenditure and main aggregates, https://appsso.eurostat. ec.europa.eu/nui/show.do?dataset=gov_10a_main&lang=en. Expenditure on pensions, https://ec. europa.eu/eurostat/databrowser/view/spr_exp_pens/default/table?lang=en.

For fiscal adjustment and consolidation one key policy objective was to bring the share of public sector wages closer to the EU average. This is a useful benchmark given the cross-country heterogeneity in the evolution and the composition of the public wage bill and the variation in public employ- ment and wages across countries in the EU and the euro area (Pérez et al., 2016). The rather slow adjustment of the public wage bill in Greece as a share of GDP (Table 11.1) from 13.1% in 2009 (EU-28 11%) to 11.9% in 2019 (EU-28 10%), is due to the combined variations in wages and in the public employment level changes. Public sector employment was not the main means for fiscal and labour market adjustment during the crisis. Public sector employment (Table 11.2) was relatively less affected in the adjustment period 2010–2012 and later in 2013–2014, compared to the T sector and the N private sector (Np). During the third adjustment programme (2015–2018)

Table 11.2 Percentage of total employment by sector, 2000–2018

Year	Tradable (T)	Non-tradable excluding public sector (Np)	Public sector (P)
2000	40,21	38,73	21,07
2001	39,17	39,73	21,10
2002	38,48	40,13	21,39
2003	37,48	41,21	21,31
2004	34,23	42,88	22,90
2005	34,21	43,76	22,02
2006	33,61	44,05	22,34
2007	33,31	44,38	22,31
2008	32,55	45,32	22,13
2009	32,71	45,32	21,97
2010	32,66	45,14	22,20
2011	32,35	45,00	22,65
2012	32,73	44,46	22,81
2013	33,34	43,55	23,11
2014	33,98	43,84	22,18
2015	34,07	44,47	21,46
2016	34,33	44,29	21,38
2017	34,08	44,58	21,33
2018	34,28	44,38	21,34

Sources: ELSTAT, Eurostat, Census of ministries.

Note: The statistical classification of economic activities in the European Community, abbre- viated as NACE, is the classification of economic activities in the EU; the term NACE is derived from the French Nomenclature statistique des activités économiques dans la Communauté eur- opéenne. 2000–2007 NACE T = Codes 1–36, 55, 61, 62, 72,73. 2008–2016 NACE Rev.2, T = Codes.

wage increases were released for certain groups in public sector. Employment cuts were abandoned and restrictions on hiring were relaxed. Public sector employment expansion has recovered since 2015.[3] Despite the decade-long crisis and the successive fiscal adjustment programmes, the share of public sector employment in total employment in Greece has remained (Table 11.2) above the level of 21% in 2018, much closer to its historical average for the period since joining the euro area.[4]

Although in many cases 'public sector wage setting is the first and most accessible policy domain from which governments glean resources in hard times' (Di Carlo, 2018: 51), and this has been the case in many EU member states during the latest crisis (for national cases see Bach and Bordogna, 2016), in Greece that was not the first option. It was easier to change/raise taxation even when, during the adjustment programmes, that was needed to meet fiscal objectives. The first option was increasing taxation and over-taxation (Ioannou, 2019b).

Public sector crowding out tradable growth sectors

The allocation of resources across all sectors of the economy (T and N, private and public, Tb and Td), between investment and consumption (and ultimately between generations), is shaped by how the institutions and interest groups of the real world affect the way in which policy is formulated and impacts the economy.

The general government balance since 2016 indicates that Greece made significant progress with fiscal consolidation. Fiscal imbalances had come mainly from the public expenditure side (Giannitsis and Zografakis, 2015: 16; Ioannou, 2016: 50–53). Public finances adjustment aiming to reach a primary balance by closing a gap of more than 10% of GDP was attempted mainly by raising taxes; this was achieved during the third adjustment programme. Greek expenditure on the compensation of public sector employees and, indeed, on pensions has been persistently above the EU average (15.7% in 2019, compared to 14.3% in 2009 versus EU-27 12.7% in 2019 from EU-28 12.8% in 2009) despite the need for major fiscal adjustment. This persistent divergence above the EU average denotes a tenacious structural imbalance (Table 11.1).

On the expenditure side, the fiscal instruments used were the cuts in public investment (that directly affects growth dynamics) and cuts in operational costs for producing and delivering public goods and services. These were policy options, instead of a reduction in the wage bill (by reducing the public-private pay gap and controlling the public employment share and its expansion).

With regards to the taxing wages performance, the tax wedge in Greece has become high and very progressive. The tax wedge for the average single worker increased by 2.1 percentage points from 38.7% to 40.8% between 2000 and 2019. During the same period the average tax wedge across the

OECD decreased by 1.4 percentage points from 37.4% to 36.0%. Greece (of the ageing demographics) had the second highest tax wedge in the OECD for an average married worker with two children at 37.8% in 2019, much higher than the OECD average of 26.4%. Greece occupied the fourth highest position in 2018 (OECD, 2020a). In terms of taxing wages for net incomes between €20,000 and €40,000 it has edged closer to the EU top. .

This takes us to the divergent growth regime of Greece as a member of the EU and the euro area. This policy mix is not supportive of GDP and employment growth. It remains an open question whether it has an inclusive or an extractive function (Ioannou, 2019b). Aggressive taxation that mainly affects productive work in the T sector creates, by imposing high and progressive tax wedges, a barrier to growth, a barrier to rebalancing the fundamental asymmetry between the T and N sectors in the Greek economy (and another push factor that has resulted in the 'brain drain' that has affected Greece and the Tb sector over the past decade). The political economy of public sector operations in its broader context, in the division between T and N, is critical. Other member states returned to the growth path and remained competitive even with high taxes. Furthermore, they succeeded in this by having a 'retributive' function of their high taxes, and without being dominated by a public sector wage system whereby public sector pay was the leader in wage formation and in pay relativities, as has been case in Greece for decades. They succeeded though either by being in a model where the public sector wage setting has been a function of export-sector interests, or by being in wage restraint for institutional reasons (Di Carlo, 2018).

The Greek public sector and public administration have been also subject to extensive, intensive and ambitious reform requirements outlined in the corresponding Memoranda of Understanding that revealed an 'institution-building' perspective on a 'big bang' scale (Spanou, 2019; see also Chapter 8 in this volume). Despite reforms the Greek general government services remained more labour intensive across the board with many indications of lower productivity, misallocation of public expenditure and labour, no scope for tax alleviation of productive labour. Public goods and services to be produced and to be delivered require public sector employees to get paid for their services, but also require other types of expenditures, intermediate goods to finance the operation of the public services and the provision of public goods, investment and social transfers. Seen from this perspective the structure of public sector expenditure (see Table 11.1), compared to the EU-28 average, appears rather biased towards public sector pay (and pensions).

Disaggregating public sector (general government) expenditure by function and by type of expenditure (Table 11.3) suggests that the prima facie bias of expenditure towards public sector pay is not only related to its vertical composition and distribution to major categories (i.e. pensions, wages, investment, social protection, interest, etc.). It is also present in the composition of the operating expenditure of the ten major functions or purposes of the general government sector, which lies at the core of the N sector. In

Table 11.3 Compensation of employees as a % share of general government operating expenditure, Greece vs the EU-28, 2017

	Greece	*EU-28*
Total	72,0	63,1
General public services	58,1	61,3
Defence	80,5	59,8
Public order and safety	94,1	75,1
• Police	93,9	82,5
• Fire protection	93,7	71,0
• Justice	98,5	64,5
• Prisons	90,9	65,8
Economic affairs	49,3	42,4
Environmental protection	48,8	27,4
Housing and community amenities	27,1	45,8
Health	58,4	60,7
Recreation, culture and religion	64,3	39,8
Education	92,3	79,9
• Pre-primary and primary education	98,5	83,7
• Secondary education	99,9	84,3
• Tertiary education	72,0	73,0
• Social protection	54,3	60,5
• Sickness and disability	51,3	61,6
• Old age	62,2	62,6
• Survivors	61,6	48,7
• Family and children	34,6	66,1
• Unemployment	61,7	51,3

Source: Eurostat, General government expenditure by function (COFOG). https://appsso.euro stat.ec.europa.eu/nui/show.do?dataset=gov_10a_exp&lang=en.

Note: Compensation of employees/compensation of employee and intermediate consumption.

Greece, the general government sectors allocate relatively more resources to the compensation of employees and less to intermediate consumption to produce and deliver, by the combination of these two inputs, of public goods and services. This is systematic in six out of the ten major functions and purposes of central government operations. The bias towards compensation of employees, compared to the EU-28 average, is systematically present in most of the ten major functions and in the main sub-functions too.[5]

The ability of the sovereign employer to pay public sector employees depends on taxation and therefore requires taxes to be paid by the rest of the population, in exchange for public goods and services. Public sector employees are hired, and enjoy a special employment status, with the objective to provide public services and goods. Therefore, public sector employment and wage setting should be viewed from the broader political economy context. In Greece, the combination of rising and high taxation for public sector expenditure has meant that retributive public goods and services are not being delivered, and this implies that additional pressure is being placed on the other sectors of the economy: the T and the Np sectors. The misallocation of resources has been crowding out the economic growth sectors, thereby acting as an impediment to growth.

Education and skills mismatches hindering T sector growth

Demand for labour has been distorted by the misallocation of resources, and by the distortion of relative prices/wages, so that at the same time labour supply suffers. Another factor that does not facilitate the growth of the T sector is simply that the unemployed lack the knowledge and qualifications to work in those economic sectors capable of expanding the economy. This is also related to the underperformance of the public sector education and skills formation system, as well as of the skills formation policy. As in most labour markets, in Greece the demand for labour and skills has been changing. The changes have accelerated during the three adjustment programmes as a result of technology and innovation, climate change, globalization, demographic change and of new forms of work organization. Before, during and after the adjustment programmes, the supply of labour and skills, which is shaped by early and lifelong education and training systems, has not adjusted to those changes, thus creating skills mismatches in the divergent labour market.

The OECD's Programme for International Student Assessment (PISA) measures 15-year-olds' ability to use their reading, mathematics and science knowledge and skills to meet real-life challenges. Greece's performance in the seven rounds of the PISA survey has been below the OECD average and has deteriorated further since 2009. The share of low performers in the Greek education system has been increasing. This is alarming as the findings refer to successive cohorts of 15-year-old students. OECD's Programme for the International Assessment of Adult Competencies (PIAAC) indicates that in Greece the mean proficiency score of 16–65-year-olds in literacy and numeracy is significantly below the average of the OECD countries participating in the survey. Indeed, tertiary-educated adults in Greece have relatively low proficiency in literacy, numeracy and problem solving in technology-rich environments (OECD, 2015).

In 2020, Greece ranked 30th in the European Skills Index, 26th on its skills development pillar, 27th on the skills activation pillar and 31st on the skills matching pillar (ESI, 2020). According to the OECD (2019a) dashboard for Priorities of Adult Learning (PAL), in comparison to the adult learning systems of other member states along the dimensions of coverage, inclusiveness, alignment with skills demand, Greece belongs to countries facing skill challenges which they are not prepared to address. At the same time Greece has the highest proportion of over-skilled employees among all the OECD member states participating in the OECDS's Survey of Adult Skills, and a very low intensity of skills use in the workplace (OECD, 2019b). As a result, the country has a poor track record of meeting the needs of both employed and unemployed workers and employers. The skills development system is not linked to the labour market needs.

A recent survey (SEV, 2019c) at the core of the T (and Tb) sectors that involved 831 firms from six sectoral ecosystems, namely the agro-food chain, pharma (health and medicine), digital economy (information and communication technologies), metal industry and building materials, supply chain (logistics in transport, and energy) showed that 35.6% of businesses in the productive sector of the economy are having difficulty filling vacancies because of the lack of skilled labour. The percentage is higher in export-oriented (45.9%) and large companies (44.7%). Such companies are active in more competitive markets, have higher demands of their human resources in terms of qualifications and skills, and apply stricter methods of staff selection. This mismatch was observed during a period when the rate of unemployment was in the range of 17%–18%. In 2019, the participation rate of adults aged 25–64 years in education and training was 4%, while the average rate in EU member states was 11%. The critical components of an efficient labour market policy are missing, such as continuously monitoring demand and supply for jobs and skills, and skills intelligence, monitoring and evaluation of education and training programme results. In most cases, the funds allocated for training and lifelong learning through the European Social Fund have been mainly used as a substitute for the low coverage of the unemployment benefit system. It is noteworthy that services that should be provided by the public sector have been the skilling, upskilling, reskilling and matching of labour supply to labour demand. Instead, the education system has been rather inward-looking and this has contributed to the divergent labour market. Thus, this hinders the flow from education to work, the transfer of resources to the T growth sector, and innovation. To explain the unemployment rate, which jumped from 7.8% in 2008 to 27.5% in 2013, before falling to 17.3% in 2019, but remained well above 11% in 2000 (with comparable real GDP), and the low employment rate, we need to understand the operation of the fundamental asymmetry in the Greek economy and the need for a new reallocation of resources from the N sector to the T sector, for relative prices, and public policies (including education and labour market regulation) that facilitate this process.

Notes

1 The REER is one of the indicators that was introduced in 2011, in the context of the EU Macroeconomic Imbalance Procedure (MIP), to signal a possible external imbalance.

2 In June 2018, the Committee on the Application of Standards (CAS) urged the government to 'ensure that unilateral recourse to compulsory arbitration as a way to avoid free and voluntary collective bargaining is employed only in very limited circumstances'. The Committee of Experts on the Application of Conventions and Recommendations (CEACR) in the 2019 report stated that with regard to Greece and concerning Convention no. 98: 'The Committee recalls that compulsory arbitration in the case that the parties have not reached agreement is generally contrary to the principles of collective bargaining'.
3 It accelerated further in the first semester of 2019 probably related to the political-electoral cycle, as European elections were scheduled for May 2019 and the national parliamentary elections for September (early election took place in July).
4 The public sector employees as a share of the population aged 15 years and above amounts to a share slightly lower that the eurozone average, at approximately 9% in 2018.
5 In sectors where it appears slightly lower than the EU average, such as in the health services, the compensation of employees' share can be underestimated because of the notorious overspending in intermediate goods that has been the subject of successive reforms aiming to curb the supplier-induced demand. In the case of housing and community amenities the gap between Greece and the EU-28 average is due to the weakness and marginal role of such functions in the Greek general government structure.

References

Abdon, A., Bacate, M., Felipe, J., Kumar, U. (2010). *Product Complexity and Economic Development*, Working Paper, No. 616. Annandale-on-Hudson, NY: Levy Economics Institute of Bard College.

Bach, S., and Bordogna, L. (Eds.) (2016). *Public Service Management and Employment Relations in Europe: Emerging from the Crisis?*London: Routledge.

Bulman, T. (2020). *Rejuvenating Greece's Labour Market to Generate More and Higher-Quality Jobs*. OECD Economics Department Working Papers, No. 1622. https://dx.doi.org/10.1787/8ea5033a-en.

Campos, M. M., Depalo, D., Papapetrou, E., Pérez, J.J., Ramos, R. (2015). *Understanding the Public Sector Pay Gap*. Working Paper, No. 1539. Madrid: Banco de España.

Di Carlo, D. (2018). *Does Pattern Bargaining Explain Wage Restraint in the German Public Sector*. Discussion Paper 18/3. Cologne: Max Planck Institute for the Study of Societies. www.mpifg.de/pu/mpifg_dp/2018/dp18-3.pdf.

Eurofound (2019). *Seniority-Based Entitlements: Extent, Policy Debates and Research*. Luxembourg: Publications Office of the European Union.

European Central Bank (ECB) (2016). The employment-GDP relationship since the crisis. *ECB Economic Bulletin*, 6.

European Central Bank (ECB) (2019). Employment growth and GDP in the euro area. *ECB Economic Bulletin*, 2. www.ecb.europa.eu/pub/economic-bulletin/focus/2019/html/ecb.ebbox201902_03~29ccc5ebf4.en.html.

European Commission (2020a). Enhanced Surveillance Report: Greece. *European Economy Institutional Paper*, 137, November.

European Commission (2020b). *Proposal for a Joint Employment Report 2021*, November 18. https://ec.europa.eu/social/main.jsp?langId=en&catId=101&furtherNews=yes&newsId=9834.

European Skills Index (ESI) (2020). *European Skills Index Technical Report*, CEDEFOP. www.cedefop.europa.eu/en/events-and-projects/projects/european-skills-index-esi.

Felipe, J., and Kumar, U. (2011). *Unit Labor Costs in the Eurozone*, Working Paper, No. 651. Annandale-on-Hudson, NY: Levy Economics Institute of Bard College.

Giannitsis, T., and Zografakis, S. (2015). *Greece: Solidarity and Adjustment in Times of Crisis*, Study 38, March. Düsseldorf: Macroeconomic Policy Institute, Hans-Böckler-Foundation.

International Labour Organization (ILO) (2014). *Productive Jobs for Greece*. Geneva: ILO.

Ioannou, C. (2012). Recasting Greek Industrial Relations: Internal Devaluation in Light of the Economic Crisis and European Integration. *The International Journal of Comparative Labour Law and Industrial Relations*, 28(2), 199–222, Spring.

Ioannou, C. (2016). Public sector employment relations in Greece: Adjustment and reforms. In S. Bach, and L. Bordogna (Eds), *Public Service Management and Employment Relations in Europe: Emerging from the Crisis?* (pp. 29–56). London: Routledge.

Ioannou, C. (2019a). Collective bargaining decentralisation and wage adjustment for internal devaluation. In H. Voskeritsian, P. Kapotas, and C. Niforou (Eds.), *Greek Employment Relations in Crisis: Problems, Challenges and Prospects* (pp. 31–58). London: Routledge.

Ioannou, C. (2019b). *Public Sector Wage Setting as Janus: Is There an Extractive Side?* Paper presented at the Max Planck Institute for the Study of Societies Conference, 'The Political Economy of Public Sector Wage Setting in Europe', Cologne, September 16–18.

Ioannou, D., and Ioannou, C. (2017). The fundamental asymmetry in the economy of Greece. *Greek Economic Outlook*, 33: 62–70.

Organisation for Economic Co-operation and Development (OECD) (2015). Adult Skills *Survey of Adult Skills, PIAAC*. Paris: OECD Publishing. https://gpseduca tion.oecd.org/CountryProfile?primaryCountry=GRC&treshold=10&topic=AS.

Organisation for Economic Co-operation and Development (OECD) (2019a). *Skills Matter: Additional Results from the Survey of Adult Skills*, OECD Skills Studies. Paris: OECD Publishing.

Organisation for Economic Co-operation and Development(OECD) (2019b). *OECD Skills Strategy 2019: Greece*. Paris: OECD Publishing.

Organisation for Economic Co-operation and Development(OECD) (2020). *Taxing Wages 2020*. Paris: OECD Publishing.

Pérez, J.J., Aouriri, M., Campos, M.M., Celov, D., Depalo, D., Papapetrou, E., Pesliakaitė, J., Ramos, R., Rodríguez-Vives, M. (2016). *The Fiscal and Macroeconomic Effects of Government Wages and Employment Reform*. Occasional Paper Series, 176. Frankfurt am Main: European Central Bank.

SEV (Hellenic Federation of Enterprises) (2019a). *Prerequisites for Restarting Social Dialogue and Increasing Income in the Future*. SEV Special Report, January 10. Athens: SEV.

SEV (Hellenic Federation of Enterprises) (2019b). *Wages, Productivity and Competitiveness*. SEV Special Report, March 15. Athens: SEV.

SEV (Hellenic Federation of Enterprises) (2019c). *Lack of Education and Skills an Obstacle to Productive Transformation and Modern Competitive Production*. SEV Special Report, July 3, Athens: SEV (in Greek).

Spanou, C. (Ed.) (2019). *Reforms in Public Administration under the Crisis: Executive Summary*. Athens: Papazisis. www.eliamep.gr/wp-content/uploads/2019/02/Reform s-In-Public-Administration_translation.pdf.

12 Challenges and opportunities in a post-pandemic Greece

Jens Bastian

Introduction

It is a challenge to write the concluding chapter of this volume with a view towards a post-pandemic Greece. The challenge is made more difficult when one undertakes to argue a case for more or less optimistic scenarios for Greece in 2021. Greece had an over-supply of *anni horribili* during the turbulent period 2010–2018. The memories of these experiences, namely soaring unemployment, corporate bankruptcies, private household loan defaults and a troika of external actors demanding vigorous policy changes, still linger in the minds of Greek citizens.

A decade later a new external challenge arrived in Greece in the form of a pandemic. Many hoped that the *annus horribilis* that the coronavirus (COVID-19) pandemic constituted for Greeks and EU citizens alike would be replaced by needles delivering vaccines into the arms of willing individuals in 2021.[1] A metaphorical shot in the arm to recover from the economic trauma of the pandemic was equally in high demand. To what degree supply would actually be able to meet this recovery demand in 2021 and beyond remained to be seen. The economic rebound can be expected to be uneven across sectors, uncertain in terms of its fiscal sustainability and subject to vigorous public scrutiny regarding its distributional outcomes. Against this background an uneven recovery carries the risk of widening pre-existing fault lines within Greece.

The experience of reaching the other side of the bridge is all too fresh in the memories of Greek policymakers and citizens alike. The lessons learned during the three macroeconomic adjustment programmes that were implemented from 2010–2018 may also have contributed to a resilience among members of Greek society and the political economy that could assist in once again 'getting to the other side' in 2021. This previous crisis experience may also help to explain why there was virtually no public backlash against repeated lockdown measures, numerous travel restrictions and strict 'stay at home' orders in 2020 and early 2021. While there were some notable exceptions, e.g. the manner in which representatives of the Greek Orthodox Church challenged the government's lockdown measures, public opinion

DOI: 10.4324/9780429202247-15

expressed in polling data suggests a wide societal adherence towards anti-COVID-19 measures (Bouloutza, 2020).

The COVID-19 shock

COVID-19 came as an external shock to the Greek economy. Its arrival and spread through the population in subsequent waves and mutations derailed an economic recovery that had been slowly taking root across sectors since 2017. The economic consequences of the pandemic stalled employment growth which had started to stagnate and then to decline as of mid-2020 (Traa and Bastian, 2021b). According to Organisation for Economic Co-operation and Development (OECD) calculations, Greece's economy contracted by 10% in 2020 and was projected to gradually recover in 2021 (OECD, 2020). Meanwhile, in its intermediary monetary policy report of December 2020, the Bank of Greece confirmed that it expected an economic contraction of the same magnitude. Its baseline scenario provided for a 4.2% rebound in 2021. However, this outlook was likely to be constrained by a number of factors. As the Bank argued,

> A further escalation of the pandemic, accompanied by an extended duration of restrictions on economic and social activity could have a stronger and more persistent impact on the real economy, in particular on the services sector, most notably tourism. In addition, an increase in non-performing loans as a result of the recession would divert resources from productive investment.
>
> (Bank of Greece, 2020: 4)

The devastating impact of the COVID-19 pandemic on employment prospects, private companies' balance sheets, disposable household income and sectors such as tourism, shipping, restaurants, culture, hotels and retail defined Greece's recovery prospects in 2021 and beyond. Numerous government support measures sought to soften the impact of the pandemic on companies and citizens alike. The range of domestic assistance measures included (i) special purpose compensation for employees whose contracts had been suspended; (ii) social security contributions covered by the state; (iii) the suspension of tax obligations for companies and private households; (iv) a reduction in rent payments; (v) eight phases of cheap state loan programmes; and (vi) extraordinary expenditure required by the ministries of national defence, health and citizens' protection.

The total monthly cost of these measures for the state was estimated at €2 billion during the first half of 2021 (Hatzinikolaou, 2021). But these domestic measures were not unlimited. Their impact on the budget deficit was part of an emerging debate when such horizontal assistance needed to be more targeted or gradually phased out. Some programmes were scheduled to expire as lockdowns were suspended. Other measures were curtailed in terms of the volume of assistance provided and their duration. Similarly to other European capital cities, in 2021 Athens was starting to hear the siren calls of fiscal hawks who sang the praises of returning to a 'new normal' of fiscal rectitude that again endorsed budget discipline and enforced EU state aid rules.

The measures and programmes were costly in terms of accrued levels of public debt and the commitment of political capital. The longer the pandemic lasted and the more likely the risk of a third or indeed a fourth wave throughout Europe in 2021, the more policymakers in Athens would be challenged to maintain or even extend the support network. Against this background, the EU's Recovery and Resilience Facility (RRF) would have been welcome even sooner in Greece, together with urgently needed anti-COVID-19 vaccines. But it took months to start administering vaccines into the arms of willing citizens and for EU funds to be disbursed in Greece, and even longer for them to show any of their hoped for impact.

Getting to the other side

Reaching the other side of the bridge critically will depend on a variety of continuous support measures from external European institutions. Chiefly among them are the EU and the European Central Bank (ECB). In March 2020, the ECB launched the Pandemic Emergency Purchase Programme (PEPP). The volume was initially set at €750 billion and subsequently increased by €600 billion in June and by a further €500 billion in December. The new total of €1,850 billion represented the single largest temporary asset purchase programme of private and public sector securities which the ECB has ever introduced. The non-standard monetary policy measure was scheduled to run until the end of March 2022. Because the ECB issued a waiver of eligibility requirements for securities issued by the Greek government the PEPP included unprecedented purchases of sovereign debt issued by Greece. Moreover, their eligibility as collateral in euro system refinancing operations provided Greek banks with a major source of cheap liquidity during the pandemic.

Moreover, the ECB's Single Supervisory Mechanism (SSM) gave commercial banks additional regulatory flexibility. Since March 2020, lenders across the euro area had been allowed to operate below the level of capital defined by the Pillar 2 Guidance (P2G), the capital conservation buffer (CCB) and the liquidity coverage ratio (LCR). The relaxation of these capital buffer instruments was linked to an expectation 'not to increase dividend distributions or variable remuneration' for the duration of the measures. Finally, due to the pandemic, the European Banking Authority (EBA) postponed the 2020 EU-wide stress testing process for commercial banks (ECB, 2020).

The European Commission supplemented the ECB's unprecedented pandemic crisis intervention with the temporary suspension of fiscal rules in the Stability and Growth Pact (SGP). The activation of the so-called escape clause was the first time that the Commission had resorted to this instrument since the creation of the SGP in 1997. The largest (by financing volume) intervention of the Commission included a new €90.3 billion job support programme (known by its acronym SURE[2]) for member states affected by the COVID-19 crisis. In addition, the Commission relaxed EU state aid regulations for member states regarding state guarantees for bank lending. It also introduced regulations permitting member states to provide conditional financial assistance in equity or hybrid capital instruments to businesses directly impacted by the pandemic.

The manner in which European institutions confronted the COVID-19 pandemic and its economic consequences illustrates some striking differences from their crisis management a decade earlier. Unlike in 2010–2012, the 'whatever it takes' moment in Europe took weeks rather than years to arrive, as it did during the sovereign debt crisis. After some initial hesitations, the ECB reactivated and then massively expanded its quantitative easing programme, albeit under a new name, using different justifications and for the first time it included Greece. The toolbox of policy instruments underscored its hitherto unprecedented financial volume and range of combinations including credit facilities, loan guarantees, targeted financial interventions and relaxation of EU and ECB-specific regulations (Bastian, 2020).

Against this background an unprecedented fiscal and monetary architecture took shape across Europe as a result of the pandemic. During the sovereign debt crisis in 2010–2012 various EU member states constantly argued for rules-based policymaking. In 2021, the mantra of compliance with existing monetary rules and fiscal conditionality was (temporarily) suspended. The devotion to technocratic obligations was radically overwhelmed by waves of the COVID-19 pandemic across Europe. The Dutch academic Luuk van Middelaar calls such a development as moving from 'a system based purely on the politics of rules to a system that can also engage in the politics of events' (van Middelaar, 2019).[3]

The policy responses to the COVID-19 pandemic by national governments in Berlin, Paris, Rome, Madrid and Athens signified the 'biggest paradigmatic shift in economic policy that Europe has witnessed since the 1980s' (Featherstone, 2020). The manner in which these policy interventions were undertaken has been justified as a matter of urgency and by asserting national sovereignty to do so. However, it has to be emphasized that many of these interventions came at the expense of parliamentary debate, let alone voting by members of parliament on these measures.

The most striking example of a coordinated European policy response to the pandemic is the December 2020 agreement between the European Council and the European Parliament on the Recovery and Resilience Facility (RRF). The €672.5 billion facility (in 2018 prices) is the heartbeat of the EU's Next Generation EU (NGEU) €750 billion recovery instrument agreed by EU leaders in July 2020. Although they focus on economic recovery from the pandemic, both facilities have earmarked at least 37% of each plan's allocation to support the green transition and at least 20% is budgeted for digital transformation. The RRF is being financed by the direct issuance of securities by the EU. While avoiding the characterization as 'pandemic bonds' or 'corona bonds', the EU's new financial engineering instrument has unprecedented volumes and leverage capacity, and henceforward will make Brussels a key player in sovereign debt markets. To what degree such EU bonds can become a permanent credit facility will very much depend on the political will of countries such as Germany, the Netherlands, Austria and other northern members of the currency bloc.[4]

In addition, in mid-December 2020, with consent of the European Parliament, the Council adopted the EU's multiannual financial framework (MFF) for the period 2021–2027. The MFF budget provides for a total of €1,074.3 billion for the EU-27 in 2018 prices, including the integration of the European Development Fund. Together with the NGEU it will allow the EU to provide an unprecedented €1.8 trillion of funding over the next seven years to support economic recovery from the COVID-19 pandemic. The extended negotiations about apportioning the resources and rule of law conditionality included the threat of a veto by the governments of Hungary and Poland. The unprecedented threat objected to tying disbursements to democratic standards. Budapest and Warsaw argued that the so-called conditionality clause made them targets for potential funding cuts.

Domestic political and policy challenges

From the RRF Greece expects to receive €32 billion in EU funding, €19.4 billion of which was to be provided in the form of grants. As Greece's Alternate Minister of Finance, Theodoros Skylakakis, stated at a virtual event in November 2020 to present Greece's plan for using these European funds, 'the amounts are so large that with correct use they can change the course of the country' (Tugwell, 2020). The Bank of Greece predicts that the multi-year funding resources will increase gross domestic product (GDP) by 2.3% per year on average during the period 2021–2026.

Greece's track record regarding absorption capacity of EU funding instruments improved over the course of the past MFF (2014–2020). In the ranking of 28 EU member states at the end of 2019 (this being before Brexit) Greece received total payments amounting to €9,266 billion (2014–2019). That amount corresponded to an absorption rate of 42.8% at the end of 2019, putting Greece in 11th position (tied with Hungary; see European Court of Auditors, 2020: 84). One year later, Greece's ranking improved to sixth place out of the EU's 28 member states (at that point still including the UK). Greece's absorption rate of community funding in 2020 reached 62% and total expenditure of €11.6 billion. This was the highest amount of annual funding Greece absorbed from the 2014–2020 MFF. In particular, funding absorption increased via the European Regional Development Fund (ERDF) and the European Social Fund (ESF, see *Kathimerini*, 2021b).

The Greek government intends to absorb the RRF funds by covering an investment gap that had already been endemic to the performance of the domestic economy prior to the onset of the debt crisis in 2010. Large-scale infrastructure investments include the interconnection of Greek islands and a massive programme to boost energy efficiency for the residential, commercial and public sectors. The proposals were partly the result of the Pissarides Report which was published in November 2020, shortly after the Greek government submitted its national plan for the RRF to the European Commission (Macropolis, 2020).[5] The Pissarides committee's recommendations outlined the longer-term direction of the Greek economy, while the government's vision focused on the immediate administrative and project-related requirements of the RFF. Both programmes share key benchmarks, e.g.

- advocating structural reforms to make the Greek economy more efficient by modernizing public administration (e.g. in contract adjudication);
- improving public-private sector collaboration when designing, executing and accounting for EU-funded projects.

The urgency of submitting proposals for the RRF gave the government a timely opportunity to include some of Pissarides' recommendations in its own plan. It remains to be seen what practical challenges and political opportunity costs will ensue during the complex implementation process of the RFF. Equally, some of the more politically charged reforms proposed by the Pissarides Report (e.g. in taxation, pensions and education reform) are likely to meet organized opposition inside and outside the Greek parliament.

Despite the optimism resulting from the availability of an unprecedented combination of loan and grant facilities, it is reasonable to caution that rapid success of the NGEU programme is not guaranteed, neither in Greece nor in other countries eagerly awaiting disbursements which were only expected to start from mid-2021 onwards. What some observers have labelled 'soft money' while calling for 'hard standards' in order to avoid 'state capture and pork-barrel politics' (Pisani-Ferry, 2020) is a major allocation and execution challenge at the national level. Moreover, the European Commission, the European Court of Auditors and the bloc's anti-fraud office (commonly known as OLAF) will have their work cut out for years to oversee that national spending programmes adhere to concurrent effectiveness and transparency tests. As the controversies with Budapest and Warsaw illustrated regarding rule of law conditionality tied to the EU's 2021–2027 MFF budget and the NGEU facility we can expect that enforcement capacity will be challenged.[6]

The European Commission issued guidance to member states on the implementation of the RFF in October 2020. The staff working document defines in detail the funding conditions for loans and grants and links these to reforms 'in areas such as quality of public institutions and services, as well as the business environment, education or social protection' (European

Commission, 2020a). For a country like Greece, with its recent experience of three macroeconomic adjustment programmes and lingering frustration about intrusive 'troika conditionality', such wording can easily become a sensitive political issue. Any notion of having yet again to abide 'by diktats of faceless Brussels bureaucrats' (Pisani-Ferry, 2020) will not go down well either in the Greek parliament or among members of civil society.[7]

Is a new policy mix emerging?

Possibly one of the lasting consequences of the economic impact of the COVID-19 pandemic will be the recalibration of governments' attitudes to public (health) spending and accumulated debt levels. Fresh waves of external demands for austerity would risk a major popular backlash, not only in Greece. Any calls for turning pandemic-related deficits and accumulated debt into fiscal rectitude reminiscent of the troika policies between 2010 and 2018 could trigger a revolt among citizens and voters. The scars from these experiences still run deep among many members of Greek civil society.

The unprecedented stimulus programmes of 2020–2021 adopted by the Greek government and supplemented by EU and ECB measures were mostly able to hold popular frustrations during the COVID-19 pandemic in check. One of the lessons learned from Greece's twin sovereign debt and economic crises during the past turbulent decade includes the acknowledgement that the timing and depth of any fiscal tightening is essential. So is the political and social acceptance of any such measures. Cheerleading austerity policies in Greece in a post-pandemic economic environment will be a hard sell and its advocates should be aware of the tone in which they are communicated. Given the experience of three macroeconomic adjustment programmes in Greece an outsize focus on short-term numerical fiscal targets, primary budget surpluses and public debt levels is a political non-starter.

During the period 2020–2021 the pandemic, its subsequent fiscal measures and monetary programmes deferred cornerstones of economic compliance requirements in EU treaties and euro area fiscal benchmarks. This suspension also gave rise to a vibrant debate about the theoretical underpinning of these treaties and benchmarks. Suspension of the debt limit of 60% of GDP, massive subsidy support for a variety of economic sectors, and zero to negative interest rates for the foreseeable future as a result of various ECB bond buying initiatives were deemed necessary emergency measures by policymakers across Europe. Their cumulative effect can also be seen in recalibrating the economic orthodoxy that underpinned previous calls for fiscal rectitude. In an unprecedented display of institutional unity, the ECB, the European Commission, the OECD and the International Monetary Fund (IMF) all recommended that governments continue stimulus spending throughout 2021 until output returns to pre-COVID-19 levels (Taylor, 2021). In short, the pandemic has forced policymakers and regulators to adjust to the 'new normal'.

Not only in Athens will this fundamental policy shift and conceptual recalibration impact on the interplay between governments, central banks and international capital markets in defining the mix of measures required in the post-pandemic environment. If various countries have to implement a start-and-stop recovery with intermittent lockdowns, then the road to reaching the other side of the bridge will only become more arduous. As the chief economist of the OECD argued, the distributional impacts of fiscal and monetary policies for the recovery are unequal in terms of targeted beneficiaries. '[Monetary policy] has distributional impacts and it's not meant to. Fiscal policy has a distributional effect and is meant to have a distributional effect—and it's implemented by people who are democratically elected and are directly accountable' (*Financial Times*, 2021).

Imponderables

The discussion about new conceptual policy frameworks triggered by the COVID-19 pandemic is facing the reality of various imponderables on the ground. This reality adds fuel to the emerging debates. But it also highlights additional challenges. Some of these uncertainties are affecting all EU member states, while others are more specific to Greece since they include legacies of the past crisis and its management.

- A certain degree of legal drama and fiscal uncertainty in 2021 rested in forthcoming decisions of the Greek Council of State regarding cases of pensioners claiming retroactive dues from curtailed holiday bonuses and auxiliary pensions. A similar review process was taking place at the State Audit Council concerning pensions in the public sector. Any decision by either Council had considerable fiscal implications for the Ministry of Finance. They could add up to €2.5 billion.
- To what degree could the economic consequences of the COVID-19 pandemic hinder export growth in 2021? Export growth during the past three years has been a major driver of the recovery process in Greece. The closure of borders during the first half of 2020 and in the repeated lockdowns adversely affect a cornerstone of the Single Market, trade and mobility of products, services and employees.
- The fall in nominal GDP in 2020 will affect the public debt ratio of every country. The fiscal support measures provided by the Greek government are a contributing factor, but are not the main reason for rising debt-to-GDP levels. However, this dynamic may fuel new discussions about debt sustainability risks and trigger demands for (fiscal) adjustment measures to counter the upward trend.

While on a declining trajectory in 2019–2020, the large stock of non-performing loans (NPLs) on Greek banks' balance sheets remains a major policy challenge for decision-makers. The measures adopted, e.g. the new asset protection scheme Hercules, are being implemented, albeit with delays. A 'bad bank' architecture is being negotiated between the ministry of finance and the central bank in Athens. A new generation of NPLs is being registered as a result of rising insolvencies among companies and private households' difficulties in servicing existing credit obligations, e.g. residential and retail mortgages.

In 2020, Greek banks deferred repayments on €30 billion worth of loans to assist borrowers with the financial consequences of the COVID-19 pandemic. According to the Hellenic Banking Association, lenders granted payment deferrals to approximately 400,000 citizens and businesses between January and November 2020.[8] However, given the experience with deferred credit obligations in Greece during the past decade, there are legitimate concerns that some of these outstanding loan repayments will become impaired when the grace period ends, thus increasing the stock of NPLs on banks' balance sheets.

In 2021, every country was being challenged to revisit medium- to longer-term debt sustainability targets. Debt commissions and debt-brake instruments as they exist among euro area countries will have to justify their rationale and sustainability targets. While Greece's public debt is increasing, the higher debt-to-GDP ratios should not be the primary indicator for analysis and policy responses. Greece's debt servicing profile is structured in a manner so that the pandemic-related increase appears manageable. Significant progress has been achieved by the Greek Public Debt Management Agency (PDMA) in terms of interest rates, the conversion of floating-rate loans into fixed rates, extending the weighted average maturity of loans and various other liability management exercises.[9] Moreover, as was illustrated during 2020, the Greek sovereign can access international bond markets with record-low yields for its debt and investors' interest is oversubscribed. This is a key difference to the turbulence experienced a decade earlier when seeking—and being refused—access to capital markets.

Fiscal resiliency constitutes a major policy challenge in the post-pandemic environment. Adopting a fiscal framework that reflects the medium-term uncertainties affecting the budgets of euro area members will be a matter of considerable domestic debate and inter-European controversies in the post-pandemic era. The fiscal flexibility afforded to euro area members during the pandemic are extensive and justified. But they were only achieved after considerable argument among countries that risked re-energizing existing fault lines. In the near future these cleavages can easily re-emerge when fiscal resiliency meets calls for fiscal rectitude.

The pandemic exacerbated some of the structural challenges that Greece was already facing prior to the outbreak of COVID-19. Key among these are two factors, one short-term and the other long-term, that will define that direction and pace of a post-pandemic economic recovery. The first concerns access to and the cost of credit for Greek companies, in particular regarding the backbone of the domestic economy, namely small and medium-sized enterprises (SMEs). To illustrate, in November 2020 the average floating interest rate for a business loan up needing €250,000 stood at 5.99% (compared to 5.53% in the previous month). This increase in the cost of bank lending to SMEs that are the key constituency to demand such credit volumes was neither an outlier during 2020 nor in the previous years.

But in comparison to other euro area peers in southern Europe, Greece is an outlier. In Italy the same amount of credit was available at an interest rate of 2.32%, in Spain the level was 1.6%, while Portugal reached 2.80% and Cyprus 3.42%, respectively (*Kathimerini*, 2021a). This increase in the cost of microfinancing is taking place against the background of unprecedented access to liquidity and *negative* interest rates for Greek commercial banks when refinancing themselves in Frankfurt with ECB lending facilities.[10] Without a sustainable lending recovery supported by Greek lenders towards SMEs the hopes for a post-pandemic economic upturn risk being delayed or even disappointment for many businesses.[11] An uneven (lending) recovery can easily turn into the inequality of recovery.

The other structural challenge to be addressed is characterized by its long-term impact. They key word here is *demographics*, i.e. the gradual reduction in the country's population.[12] Economic confidence, or the lack thereof, is one of the fundamental factors influencing medium- to long-term population dynamics in a country. Over the course of the past decade, Greece's population has been shrinking at alarming rates. Once a fringe issue in contemporary politics, demographic trends, projections and their consequences for the Greek economy, the labour market as well as social security systems have gradually moved to the centre of public policy debates.[13]

In its April 2020 version of EU population projections (based on 2019 data), Eurostat (2020) estimated that the Greek population peaked in 2011 at 11.1 million people and stood at 10.7 million in 2019. During the rest of this century Eurostat is projecting that the population will gradually decline to 9.5 million in 2050 and to approximately 8.1 million people by 2100. In this baseline projection, Greece is expected to become smaller in population during the lifetime of the current young generation who still have their working careers ahead of them.

Net migration turned positive only once during the past decade. This was the case in 2016 when large inflows of refugees, mainly from Syria, Iraq and Afghanistan arrived in the country (starting in mid-2015), albeit without the intention of staying there (Macropolis, 2019).[14] The past decade was also characterized by outward migration of educated Greeks seeking better labour market prospects elsewhere. Between 2008 and 2015, more than 427,000 Greeks emigrated, in particular young professionals seeking their fortunes in Germany, the UK and new destinations such as the United Arab Emirates, India and Brazil (Lazaretou, 2016). Reversing the brain drain phenomenon of the past decade into brain gain and encouraging members of the Greek diaspora towards return migration will require sustained policy reforms and rolling out the welcome mat for Greeks who successfully sought work abroad.[15]

Conclusion

Undoubtedly, the COVID-19 crisis will continue to affect the lives of citizens in the years to come. Health policy and health economics will equally dominate the agendas of domestic and European policymaking in 2021 and beyond. We are still learning how a resurgent virus mutates and how vaccines have to adapt accordingly. We are also learning how a pandemic affects sectors of the economy and constituencies of the labour market disproportionately. We have to distinguish between job losses specifically due to the virus, which are concentrated in sectors such as restaurants, hotels and travel, against job losses resulting more broadly from the economic downturn in Greece. It will remain challenging to identify the underlying signs of economic momentum in the country. To what degree things could hold together in 2021 and beyond is anyone's guess. Until the arrival of a sustainable reopening of economic activity and social life the resilience of Greek businesses and the patience of private households would be severely tested.

The economic impact of the COVID-19 pandemic has reawakened painful memories of the last crisis in Greece. But unlike its predecessor, the COVID-19 challenge can be mitigated to remain a transitory shock. Unlike the one which emerged in 2009, it is not (yet) a structural crisis. Today's policy responses must focus on avoiding precisely such an adverse development. As difficult as it is for citizens and businesses to get through this pandemic, Greece has every chance to reach the other side of the bridge. To what degree this favourable outcome could be achieved in 2021 remains to be seen. It does not only depend on decisions and developments originating in Athens.

The debate over how to reconstruct Greece's economy after the pandemic is intensifying. The massive economic recovery funding earmarked for Greece from European institutions is a unique opportunity. The government's economic revival plan combined with the reform proposals of the Pissarides commission provide a challenging roadmap. But building new bridges and highways, important in their own right, will not suffice. Investments in higher education, a root-and-branch re-evaluation of health care spending and catching-up expenditure to address the consequences of climate change in Greece are as necessary as they are politically charged policy issues.

For any post-pandemic economy in the euro area, the process of recovering from an annual decline of GDP by 10% (year-on-year) is arduous and fraught with obstacles. But in contrast to the previous crisis, Greece in 2021 neither lacked access to international capital markets nor liquidity from sovereign debt issuance. Moreover, it can leverage unprecedented volumes of EU funding in the coming years and has the stability of single-party government until the next scheduled general elections in mid-2023.

The crisis experience of Greek society during the turbulent decade from 2010–2018 can be an enabling factor in addressing the challenges and opportunities that lie ahead. Equally, Greece's reputational capital abroad has changed markedly, in particular in Berlin, Brussels and Washington. It can leverage this capital and is in a position to build policy coalitions at the European and international level that were hardly available a decade before.

Notes

1 At May 24, 2021, five months after the commencement of the rollout of the Covid-19 vaccination programme across the EU on December 27, 2020, more than 3.2 million people—or 30.71% of the Greek population—had received at least one dose. That share put Greece below the EU average (34.64%). Over 1.8 million citizens (17.20%) in Greece had received two jabs. The EU average for fully vaccinated citizens stood at 14.50%. For more details see Our World in Data (2021).
2 The temporary instrument stands for Support to Mitigate Unemployment Risks in an Emergency (SURE). The loans from the EU to affected member states seek to address sudden increases in public expenditure for the preservation of employment. Up until December 2020, Greece had received €2 billion from the SURE programme. For the duration of the programme Greece is eligible to receive a total of €2.7 billion (European Commission, 2020b).
3 Van Middelaar is the former speechwriter for Herman Van Rompuy, the first full-time president of the European Council, in post from 2010 to 2014.
4 The German Minister of Finance, Olaf Scholz, argued in October 2020 that the RRF may not be a fiscal union yet, but it is a decisive step towards it. 'We are moving towards fiscal union, a major step forward in the financial capacity and sovereignty of the EU' (Reuters, 2020).
5 The co-recipient of the 2010 Nobel Prize for Economic Sciences, Sir Christopher Pissarides (London School of Economics), chaired the expert committee appointed by the Greek government in 2019.
6 The December 2020 compromise achieved at the EU Council requires that a direct causal link between rule-of-law breaches and negative consequences for the EU's financial interests must be identified. The legal redress process until sanctions are imposed could take years to resolve.
7 In Italy the debate over Brussels-monitored reform conditionality contributed to the collapse of the governing coalition of Prime Minister Giuseppe Conte in early 2021. He was repeatedly criticized by the leader of the junior coalition member (Italia Viva) and the former Prime Minister Matteo Renzi about the manner in which the government planned to disburse the €209 billion available from the RFF (see Renzi, 2020). In February 2021, the former President of the ECB, Mario Draghi, became prime minister of Italy.
8 The reduction of NPLs on Greek banks' balance sheets over the past four years has made considerable progress. In March 2016 they had reached a peak of €106 billion and declined by €59 billion in late 2020. But the banks' overall NPL ratio of 36% at the end of September 2020 remained far above the eurozone average of 2.9% (ekathimerini.com, 2021).
9 The maturity extensions for Greece's €204-billion bailout loans are with the EFSF and the ESM. The maturity profile of Greek debt due to its European official creditors has repeatedly been extended since 2016. This includes a ten-year pro-longation (from 2023–2033) of the grace period Greece has been granted before paying principal and interest on its EFSF loans. Furthermore, a liability man-agement exercise in November 2017 by Greece's PDMA included a €30 billion debt swap. Finally, a decision taken by the Eurogroup of ministers of finance in June 2018 increased the weighted average maturity of EFSF loans that Greece

received between 2011 and 2013 from 32.5 years to 42 years. As a result of these different adjustments—and it is not inconceivable that more could follow in the future—Greece's debt profile now has a clear servicing roadmap all the way up to 2060. For more details of this remarkable—but often underestimated—Greek success story see Risk.net (2018).

10 In late September 2020, Greek banks had access to €40 billion of various ECB liquidity facilities at negative interest rates reaching to –0.50% (*Kathimerini*, 2021a).

11 The Hellenic Development Bank (HDB, established by legislation in early 2019) is becoming a major new lender to enterprises, in particular SMEs, in Greece. In 2020, the HDB channelled liquidity totalling €8.6 billion to the corporate sector. During the pandemic the HDB distributed loans through the COVID-19 Guarantee Fund. For more details on the HDB see Bastian (2021).

12 The following paragraphs on demographics draw on a joint article by Traa and Bastian (2021a) published on the website of Macropolis.

13 The domestic debate about demographic developments and their likely impact is being addressed by the Bank of Greece (Lazaretou, 2016), the independent Greek think tank DiaNEOsis (2019) and the February 2019 report from the Hellenic Parliamentary Committee on Demographics (2019). In particular, the latter report played a key role in underwriting the public debate with quantifiable scenarios.

14 The number of refugees arriving in Greece has dropped considerably since 2016. But the challenges to provide adequate housing, schooling and health care are as pressing today as they were five years ago. The new dimension that Greece, and by extension the EU, have to confront is the manner in which Greece's neighbour Turkey is prepared to instrumentalize the refugee issue, e.g. by threatening to open borders on the Evros river as it did in March 2020. The repeated provocations by President Erdoğan have changed the role of Greece in, and its cooperation with, the EU.

15 Nurturing opportunities for the Greek diaspora have been a recurring public policy issue during the past decade. The ongoing Greek Diaspora Project by the South East European Studies programme at Oxford University (SEESOX), St Antony's College, focuses on Greeks migrating to EU countries and the potential to lure them back home.

References

Bank of Greece (2020). *Interim Report on Monetary Policy 2020*, December 14. Athens: Bank of Greece.

Bastian, J. (2020). Massive but divisive: Crisis management and EU responses to Covid-19. *ELIAMEP Policy Brief*, No. 111 (April).

Bastian, J. (2021). The rise, fall, and return of promotional banking in Greece. In D. Mertens, M. Thiemann, and P. Volberding (Eds.), *The Reinvention of Development Banking in the European Union: Industrial Policy in the Single Market and the Emergence of a Field*. Oxford: Oxford University Press.

Bouloutza, P. (2020). Study finds Greeks responded well to lockdown despite uncertainty. *Kathimerini*, May 5 (in English).

DiaNEOosis (2019). *The Low Fertility Rate in Greece: Demographic Crisis and Family Policies*. Athens: DiaNEOosis (in Greek).

eKathimerini (2021). Bank loans subject to COVID-19 repayment relief hit $37 billion last year, January 5. www.ekathimerini.com/260909/article/ekathimerini/business/bank-loans-subject-to-covid-19-repayment-relief-hit-37-billion-last-year.

European Central Bank (ECB) (2020). ECB Banking Supervision Provides Temporary Capital and Operational Relief in Reaction to Coronavirus, March 12. Frankfurt am Main: European Central Bank. www.bankingsupervision.europa.eu/press/p r/date/2020/html/ssm.pr200312~43351ac3ac.en.html.

European Commission (2020a). Guidance to member states: Recovery and resilience plans. Commission Staff Working Document, September 17, SWD(2020) 205 final. Luxembourg: European Commission.

European Commission (2020b). *Support to Mitigate Unemployment Risks in an Emergency (SURE)*, December 1. https://ec.europa.eu/info/business-econom y-euro/economic-and-fiscal-policy-coordination/financial-assistance-eu/funding-me chanisms-and-facilities/sure_en.

European Court of Auditors (2020). *Annual Reports for the Financial Year 2019*. Luxembourg: European Court of Auditors.

Eurostat (2020). *Population (Demography, Migration and Projections)*, April. http s://appsso.eurostat.ec.europa.eu/nui/show.do?dataset=proj_19np&lang=en.

Featherstone, K. (2020). Coronavirus kills off neoliberalism. *Kathimerini*, April 3 (in English).

Financial Times (2021). OECD warns governments to rethink constraints on public spending. Interview with OECD chief economist Laurence Boone, January 4. www. ft.com/content/7c721361-37a4-4a44-9117-6043afee0f6b.

Hatzinikolaou, P. (2021). Targeted handouts from April. *Kathimerini*, February 20–21 (in English).

Hellenic Parliamentary Committee on Demographics (2019). *Special Report on Demographic Projections for Greece*. Athens: Hellenic Parliamentary Committee on Demographics.

Kathimerini (2021a). Lending costs for Greek businesses increase. *Kathimerini*, January 8 (in Greek).

Kathimerini (2021b). *Greece among top six in 2020 for European Union fund absorption*. *Kathimerini*, January 9 (in English).

Lazaretou, S. (2016). The Greek brain drain: The new pattern of Greek emigration during the recent crisis. *Economic Bulletin: Bank of Greece*, 43, July, 31–54. www.ba nkofgreece.gr/Publications/econbull201607.pdf.

Macropolis (2019). *Population Projections Show Demographic Problem Set to Worsen in Coming Decades*, January 7. www.macropolis.gr/?i=portal.en.society.7935.

Macropolis (2020). *RRF Proposals and Pissarides Report Chart Direction of Travel for Post-Pandemic Greece*. November 24. www.macropolis.gr/?i=portal.en.greek-p olitics.10193.

Organisation for Economic Co-operation and Development (OECD) (2020). *OECD Economic Surveys: Greece. Overview*, July. Paris: OECD Publishing.

Our World in Data (2021). *Share of people who received at least one dose of COVID-19 vaccine*, May 10.https://ourworldindata.org/covid-vaccinations.

Pisani-Ferry, J. (2020). The EU that can't say no. *Project Syndicate*, December 29. www. project-syndicate.org/commentary/european-union-recovery-package-risks-by-jean-pisa ni-ferry-2020-12.

Taylor, P. (2021). Two options for Europe's coronavirus economy: Bad or a lot worse. *Politico*, January 1. www.politico.eu/article/europe-2021-coronavirus-economy-ba d-or-worse/.

Renzi, M. (2020). Le condizioni di Renzi a Conte 'Svolta o crisi'. *La Repubblica*, December 17.

Reuters (2020). EU moving towards fiscal union with pandemic recovery plan: German FinMin, October 12. www.reuters.com/article/us-eu-economy-germany-idUSKBN26X13H.

Risk.net (2018). Sovereign risk manager of the year: Greece Public Debt Management Agency, November 27. www.risk.net/awards/6162181/sovereign-risk-manager-of-the-year-greeces-public-debt-management-agency.

Traa, B., and Bastian, J. (2021a). Structural considerations for a prosperous Greece. *Macropolis*, January 4. www.macropolis.gr/?i=portal.en.the-agora.10438.

Traa, B., and Bastian, J. (2021b). Labour market developments in Greece during Covid-19. *Macropolis*, March 3. www.macropolis.gr/?i=portal.en.the-agora.10708.

Tugwell, P. (2020). EU crisis funding could 'change the course' of Greece, government says. November 25. www.bloomberg.com/news/articles/2020-11-25/greece-sees-potential-change-in-course-from-eu-crisis-funding.

Van Middelaar, L. (2019). *Alarums and Excursions: Improvising Politics on the European Stage*. Newcastle upon Tyne: Agenda Publishing. https://doi.org/10.2307/j.ctvnjbf19.

Index

Page numbers in *italics* and **bold** indicate Figures and Tables, respectively.